Praise for *Modern Poetry and the Idea of Language*

"The readings of Mallarmé, Flaubert, Joyce, and Beckett, are incisive. . . . At all points they demonstrate the appropriateness of Bruns's critical approach to these authors."—*Quarterly Journal of Speech*

"The real value of this work is in its demonstration of how fundamentally our ideas about literature are ideas about language and go back to assumptions about the nature of being and reality."—*Modern Philology*

"*Modern Poetry* draws on many theorists and poets, is filled with striking and illuminating quotations . . . and is both pleasant and interesting to read." —*Review of Metaphysics*

"Bruns has brought together an extensive literature of philosophical, literary, and linguistic thought on the nature of language in poetry."—*Journal of Aesthetics and Art Criticism*

"Bruns offers a new perspective on literary language."—*Journal of English and Germanic Philology*

"A really necessary book in that it provides an excellent scholarly overview of a subject that is nowadays constantly tossed about in a pretentious but amateurish fashion."—*Comparative Literature*

Other Books by Gerald L. Bruns

Heidegger's Estrangements:
Language, Truth, and Poetry in the Later Writings

Hermeneutics Ancient and Modern

Inventions: Writing, Textuality, and Understanding in Literary History

Maurice Blanchot: The Refusal of Philosophy

Tragic Thoughts at the End of Philosophy:
Language, Literature, and Ethical Theory

Modern Poetry and the Idea of Language

A Critical and Historical Study

GERALD L. BRUNS

Preface by the author

Dalkey Archive Press

Originally published by Yale University Press 1974
Copyright © 1974 by Yale University Press
Preface copyright © 2001 by Gerald L. Bruns

First paperback edition, 2001

Library of Congress Cataloging-in-Publication Data:

Bruns, Gerald L.
  Modern poetry and the idea of language / by Gerald L. Bruns.– 1st Dalkey Archive ed.
     p.   cm.
  Originally published; New Haven : Yale University Press, 1974.
  Includes bibliographical references and index.
  ISBN 1-56478-269-7
    1. Language and languages–Philosophy. 2. Poetics. I. Title.

P107 .B78 2001
401–dc21

                                        2001028040

Partially funded by a grant from the Illinois Arts Council, a state agency.

Dalkey Archive Press
www.dalkeyarchive.com

Printed on permanent/durable acid-free paper and bound in the United States of America.

In writing this book, I have had earnest respect
to three special points: truth of religion, honesty
in living, right order in learning. In which three
ways, I pray God my poor children may diligently
walk; for whose sake, as nature moved, and reason
required, and necessity also somewhat compelled,
I was the willinger to take these pains.

Roger Ascham, *The Scholemaster*

Preface to new edition

The bulk of *Modern Poetry and the Idea of Language*–all but the introduction and conclusion–was written between 1964 and 1968, whereupon it acquired the usual coffee stains and frayed edges before finding a reader. Basically the book was, or is, an attempt to investigate a family of topics suggested by (among other things) Mallarmé's thesis that a poem is made of words but not of any of the things we use words to produce: meanings, concepts, propositions about the world, narratives, expressions of feeling, and so on. Poetry is not a form of mediation. It is, to put it plainly, not a species of discourse at all but occupies the hither side of speech where language remains thick and, except at grievous cost, impermeable like skin or a tongue. It is no wonder that most people experience poetry as a failure of meaning, but this failure is not a deprivation. Poetry bears witness to the resistance of language–and, in the bargain, to the irreducibility of all that exists– to consciousness, intentionality, or the workings of a logical subject exercising conceptual control over whatever is presented to it. In Francis Ponge's words, poetry "sides with things" against our appetite for turning them into objects. So there is an intimacy of poetry and things that cannot be captured by philosophical experience.

My thought was that the ancient story of Orpheus, whose power of song could summon things into being, testified to this intimacy. The materiality of language, whether of voice or of writing, is not dead weight but is "magical" in something like the sense in which Walter Benjamin uses this term when he tries to invoke a language that is very different from the system for framing representations that we find in logic, linguistics, and various philosophies of language. In "Language as Such and the Language of Man" (1916), Benjamin says that there is a language of things as well as of names, a "language as such" in which things are created and a "language of man" in which this creation is brought to completion by the naming of things, where naming is not so much predication as a kind of "voicing" or "translation of the mute into the sonic."[1] Benjamin's idea is that "language of man" is a prelapsarian language in which there is an echo of a metaphysical unity of words and things. Emphatically this is *not* a language made of signs—it is only in "the bourgeois view of language . . . that the word has an accidental relation to its object, that it is a sign for things (or knowledge of them) agreed by some convention. Language never gives *mere* signs" (p. 69). Signs belong to a restricted economy of balanced accounts and contracted agreements. Signs came into existence after the Fall when the language of man proliferated into multiple and heterogeneous tongues, in none of which can any name give us the thing itself. *Brot* and *pain* give us different ways of saying "bread" but bread itself remains speechless. Fallen language is "prattle" or "talk" *(Geschwätz, Gerede)*. Only by translating from one language to another and from each into all can we begin to intimate that "pure language" in which words and things share the same ontology and which therefore allows things themselves to speak. In "The Task of the Translator" (1921), Benjamin writes: "Whereas in the various tongues that ultimate essence, the pure language, is tied only to linguistic elements and their changes, in linguistic creations it is weighted with a heavy, alien meaning. To relieve it of this, to turn the symbolizing into the symbolized itself, to regain pure language fully formed from the flux, is the tremendous and only capacity of translation. In this pure language—which no longer means or expresses anything but is, an expressionless and creative Word, that which is meant in all languages—all information, all sense, and all intention finally encounter a stratum in which they are destined to be extinguished" (SW1, p. 261). The idea is that meanings, not words, get in the way of things.

How to imagine a language purified of meanings? As Benjamin suggests when he cites Mallarmé in "The Task of the Translator" (SW1, p. 259) this is exactly the language Mallarmé tried to bring to earth by means of poetry, which is not a language of signs to be exchanged in the marketplace of communicative action but one in which things are restored to their purity precisely by absenting them from predication. "Je dis: une fleur! Et, hors de l'oubli où ma voix relégue aucun contour, en tant que quelque chose d'autre que les calices sus, musicalement se lève, idée même et suave, l'absente de tous bouquets."[2] As Maurice Blanchot glosses this famous line, the task of poetry is to redeem the singularity of things from their subsumption into categories or transformation into fungible concepts.[3] This redemption is the achievement of literary modernism, or what Benjamin, in his essay on the Surrealists, calls "the magical experiments with words . . . the passionate phonetic and transformational games that have run through the whole literature of the avant-garde . . . whether it is called Futurism, Dadism, or Surrealism."[4] But for Benjamin the literature of the avant-garde is only a late chapter in a vast unwritten "history of esoteric poetry," which is a history that is inaccessible and doubtless unimaginable to academic scholars: "For written as it demands to be written—that is, not as a collection to which particular 'specialists' all contribute 'what is most worth knowing' from their fields, but as the deeply grounded composition of an individual who, from inner compulsion, portrays less a historical evolution than a constantly renewed, primal upsurge of esoteric poetry—written in such a way, it would be one of those scholarly confessions that find their place in every century" (SW2, 2.212).

The thesis of *Modern Poetry and the Idea of Language* is that (in absolute contrast to philosophy) it is in the nature of poetry to materialize language, to thicken or condense it, and that if this is so poetry has always been modern, the once and future "upsurge" of the *ainigma* or "dark saying." The difficulty is in finding the poetic and conceptual resources that might support or, at least, clarify such a thesis. These resources are in much greater supply now than they were forty years ago, the more so since the only thing I knew about poetry in those days is what I had learned in school. *Modern Poetry and the Idea of Language* is self-evidently the kind of book Walter Benjamin learned how *not* to write, the work of a schoolman rather than, say, a collector. My book was published in 1974 (thanks to my colleague at Iowa, the late Sherman Paul, who pressed the book on his reluctant friends). In this same year Jerome Rothenberg published his anthology, *The Revolution of the Word: A New Gathering of American Avant-Garde Poetry, 1914-1945,* which gives a very different picture of what counts as poetry from the one that appears in my book. Here is a distinctly, although not exclusively, American tradition of "esoteric poetry," in contrast to my decidedly Europeanist or, anyhow, Comparative-Literature selection, which concludes (as every history of poetry seemed to in those days) with Wallace Stevens, arguably the greatest French poet ever to write in English. Rothenberg's anthology gives us a "deschooled" tradition of "magical experiments with words" that starts with Walter Arensberg and ends with Louis Zukofsky, with revealing selections from Gertrude Stein, Kenneth Fearing, Charles Olson, Jackson Mac Low, George Oppen, and Charles Reznikoff—poets whom academic critics have hardly begun studying even now. *The Revolution of the Word* includes "The Aquarium Keeper," a piece published in 1916 (the year of Benjamin's "Language as Such") by Bob Brown, whom to this day no one in school knows anything about. It begins:

> I chew tobacco moistly
> And keep the aquarium.
> My gold fish are goopy eyed
> And droopy;
> The lady ones wear bridal veils
> And float about the drawing room
> Languorously toying with their
> Gorgeous Japanese fans
> (That stupid folks call fins)
> Closing and opening them dreamily

Like soft-eyed Spanish senoritas;
Flirting with me,
Flashing filmy handkerchiefs of crepe
And lace before my fascinated eyes.
Pruning their weeping willow tails
For my praise.[5]

If you ask, What is revolutionary or avant-garde about these words, which sound and look so much like plain speech?, the answer will almost certainly have to borrow William Carlos Williams's statement that "A poem can be made of anything," on the theory that poetry is more likely to be a product of listening to the words in one's social environment than an expression of a fine imagination. Not for nothing the *genius loci* of Rothenberg's volume is Marcel Duchamp, the Aristotle of Readymades, for whom the question of art is determined by the situations in which things turn up rather than by the nature or identity of the things themselves. The principle of inclusion governing *The Revolution of the Word* is the basic principle of avant-garde theory, namely that anything goes, even if not everything is possible at every moment. So in order to experience anything as art or poetry one has to feel at home in very local and contingent situations, say transient art-worlds and floating poetic communities. It is less than obvious that the university study of literature provides necessarily much less sufficient conditions for this sort of habitation.[6] The best student of poetry under optimal conditions (a Marjorie Perloff or a Steve Fredman) is most likely to resemble an anthropologist with an impressive history of field work, one who has learned how to listen to the languages circulating in the air he or she breathes.

As if poetry were not the work of a speaking subject gifted beyond the rest of us with linguistic competence, but were rather the work of the world, much the way John Cage thought music a constant if clandestine companion that people had been trained not to notice. The domain of listening is a region that has been and is still being explored by poets like Charles Bernstein, Steve McCaffery, Lyn Hejinian, Ron Silliman, Susan Howe, and others for whom poetry is made of language, although not the pure or purified language that Mallarmé and Wallace Stevens desired but the material language of everyday life–one needs a poetic ear to hear the poetry in prattle.[7] Steve McCaffery seems to me to take things to the edge by arguing that, before everything else, but excluding nothing, poetry is made of the sounds a human voice makes as it circulates through language, not necessarily guided by syntax. Poetry here becomes less a work than a limit-experience that can no longer be framed within a text but requires something like a theatrical space of the sort that Antonin Artaud envisioned in his "theater of cruelty," in which words are corporealized rather than dramatized, and, raised to level of the shout or the scream, aimed directly at the audience rather than handed back and forth among actors.[8] Imagine poetry as something that exposes us to the violence of language. There is a link here between poetry and anarchy that is worth close study.

GERALD L. BRUNS
2001

---

1   *Selected Writings, Volume 1: 1913-26,* ed. Marcus Bullock and Michael W. Jennings (Cambridge, Mass.: Harvard University Press, 1996), pp. 68-70. Subsequently cited as SW1.

2   Mallarmé, "Crise de vers," *Œuvres complètes,* ed. Henri Mondor et G. Jean-Aubrey (Paris: Gallimard, 1945), p. 368.

3   "Literature and the Right to Death" (1947-48), *The Work of Fire,* trans. Charlotte Mandell (Stanford: Stanford University Press, 1995), pp. 327-29. See below, pp. 199-202.

4   *Selected Writings, Volume 2: 1927-1934,* ed. Michael W. Jennings, Howard Eiland, and Gary Smith (Cambridge, Mass.: Harvard University Press, 1999), p. 212.

5   (New York: Seabury Press, 1974), p. 10.

6   I try to develop this line of thinking in "'The Accomplishment of

Habitation': Danto, Cavell, and the Argument of American Poetry," in *Tragic Thoughts at the End of Philosophy: Language, Literature, and Ethical Theory* (Evanston: Nortwestern University Press, 1999), pp. 133-64.

7   See *Close Listening: Poetry and the Performed Word,* ed. Charles Bernstein (New York: Oxford University Press, 1998), esp. Steve McCaffery's contribution, "Voice in Extremis," pp. 162-77.

8   See McCaffery, "Lyric's Larynx," in *North of Intention: Critical Writings, 1973-1986* (New York: ROOF Books, 1986), pp. 178-84; and Artaud's "Letters on Language," *The Theatre and Its Double,* trans. Mary Caroline Richards (New York: Grove Press, 1958), pp. 105-21.

Contents

Acknowledgments

I am grateful to Professors Merle Brown, Stavros Deligiorgis, John Grant, David Hayman, James Kincaid, Sherman Paul, Robert Scholes, and Thomas Whitaker, who have read parts or all of this book, and whose comments, suggestions, and (not the least) encouragement made it possible for me to bring my project to completion. My special thanks to Sherman Paul for his considerable help and many kindnesses, and to James Kincaid, whose delight in unrestrained absurdity kept me working during a difficult period. My thanks also to the University Research Council and the Graduate College of the University of Iowa for grants which provided me with time to finish the writing of this book and funds to defray the cost of preparing a typescript.

Portions of this book, in versions now revised and expanded, have appeared in the following periodicals: "Rhetoric, Grammar, and the Conception of Language as a Substantial Medium," in *College English,* 31 (1969–70), 241–262, reprinted by permission of the National Council of Teachers of English; "Mallarmé: The Transcendence of Language and the Aesthetics of the Book," in *The Journal of Typographic Research,* 3 (1969), 219–240, reprinted by permission of the Cleveland Museum of Art; "The Storyteller and the Problem of Language in Samuel Beckett's Fiction," in *Modern Language Quarterly,* 30 (1969), 265–281, reprinted by permission of the editor; "Silent Orpheus: Annihilating Words and Literary Language," in *College English,* 31 (1969–70), 821–827, reprinted by permission of the National Council of Teachers of English; "Poetry as Reality: The Orpheus Myth and Its Modern Counterparts," in *Journal of English Literary History*, 37 (1970), 263–286, reprinted by permission of The Johns Hopkins University Press.

G.L.B.

Introduction: Toward a Dialectic of Orphic and Hermetic Poetries

The purpose of this book is to inquire, by diverse means, into two broadly antithetical conceptions of poetic or literary language: the idea of the "pure expressiveness" of literary speech, in which a writer's use of language deviates sufficiently from the structures of ordinary discourse to displace or arrest the function of signification; and the idea of poetic speech as the ground of all signification—as an expressive movement which "objectifies" a world for man (according to the Kantian model) or which establishes the world within the horizon of human knowing and so makes signification possible. We can call the first idea "hermetic," because the direction of the poet's activity is toward the literary work as such, that is, the work as a self-contained linguistic structure (the ideal or absolute form of which would be Flaubert's imaginary "book about nothing, a book dependent on nothing external, which would be held together by the strength of its style, just as the earth, suspended in the void, depends on nothing external for its support; a book which would have almost no subject, or at least in which the subject would be almost invisible").[1] We can call the second idea "Orphic," after Orpheus, the primordial singer whose sphere of activity is governed by a mythical or ideal unity of word and being, and whose power extends therefore beyond the formation of a work toward the creation of the world.

As we shall see, these two ideas may be played off against one another in interesting ways, but the initial point to mark is that both assert the primacy of language. The one seeks to establish the transcendence of language in the face of a universe of meaning by transforming language from a medium for thought or feeling into a power of pure formation, in which words take on value as realities in their own right and not simply as signifiers in a structure of meaning:

> Plus silencieux que le silence
> (À peine un chant)
> Les mots font des cercles immenses
> Dans le néant.[2]

Silent words that articulate not meanings but immense circles in the void—purely formal structures, whose intelligibility, like the intelligibility of music, is entirely of an intransitive order: these are words in which language itself speaks and so offers itself as an object for experience. In ordinary discourse, Heidegger says, "at whatever time and in whatever way we speak a language, language itself never has the floor. Any number of things are given voice in speaking, above all what we are speaking about: a set of facts, an occurrence, a question, a matter of concern. Only because in everyday speaking language does *not* bring itself to language but holds back, are we able simply to go ahead and speak a language, and so to deal with something and negotiate something by speaking." [3] But in poetry, even in poetry which does not close itself off to all but its own medium, language finds a form of discourse in which it need not hold itself back but can speak on its own behalf. "Language is pure being," writes Max Picard, "that is, it is more than the sum total of all the things which it mediates and effects. It is something that exists on its own, beyond all immediate purpose and effect." [4] Or, again, "Language is more real than the reality by which it is confronted" [5]—and in poetry this transcendent reality, this being of language, can be heard and felt.

The language of Orpheus, by contrast, seeks its transcendence not in isolation but in relation to the world of natural things:

> Ein Wort, ein Satz—: aus Chiffren steigen
> erkanntes Leben, jäher Sinn,
> die Sonne steht, die Sphären schweigen
> und alles ballt sich zu ihm hin.
>
> Ein Wort—ein Glanz, ein Flug, ein Feuer,
> ein Flammenwurf, ein Sternenstrich—
> und wieder Dunkel, ungeheuer,
> im leeren Raum um Welt und Ich.[6]

Here, in a poem by Gottfried Benn, the word is said to traverse the void, not to execute a purely formal maneuver, but to form the ground of the world, and not the world only but "Welt und Ich": the becoming of man's world, that is to say, is predicated upon the movement of the word. For Heidegger, who uses Benn's poem to epitomize his own thinking about language, this means that the reality of language is revealed as a power or activity—what Wilhelm von Humboldt called an *energeia*—which "first brings that given thing, as the being that is, into this 'is'; . . . the word is what holds the thing there and relates it and so to speak provides its maintenance with which to be a thing." [7] The world is brought into being and upheld there by the energy of words, and this primitive energy of language defines for Heidegger the original function of the poetic utterance. It is by means of poetry that the world finds itself present before man. Indeed, the world is by this means able to speak to man, and this speech of the world, its appearance before man by means of words, is the Orphic poem. "Poetry is the original language," writes Mikel Dufrenne, "language considered as true. . . . This language is true because it carries a meaning that cannot be said otherwise; it is the world itself that speaks." [8]

The concern of this book, then, is with two extremes of speech—the speech of language and the speech of the world. One could with considerable profit situate these two conceptions in a purely theoretical context and so elaborate an "aes-

thetics" of language or even a theory of poetry for which these
two ideas would provide the defining boundaries. But what
is truly fascinating and important about these ideas of poetic
speech is their historical meaning, which is to say the diverse
and complicated ways in which they have been adumbrated
and articulated in literary history. The only way to take into
account this historical meaning, and thus to suggest how far
these ideas have dominated poetry and poetics from antiquity
to our own day, is to ground all inquiry upon a sequence of
topics that, so far from forming the several parts of an argu-
ment or the several stages of a theory, are provided by history
itself—and this is what I have tried to do.

Accordingly, Part One of this book takes up two broad his-
torical areas, which we might call, for purely descriptive pur-
poses, "classical" and "romantic." The purpose here will be to
discover those conceptions of language which seem to charac-
terize these areas. Thus the first chapter examines the ten-
dency among ancient, medieval, and Renaissance rhetoricians
and grammarians to think of language as a substance, an ob-
ject of parts and extension, and particularly the tendency to
think of style in terms of spatial and visual analogies—anal-
ogies which, as it happens, are bound up with the problems
of meaning that, from the very beginnings of philosophy, the
literary use of language was said to pose. The second chapter,
by contrast, takes up those poets and thinkers of the eighteenth
and early nineteenth centuries who approached language from
the standpoint of such concepts as function, process, and activ-
ity, that is, in terms of the dynamics of speech or the dynamics
of thought and feeling. Here our concern will be with the
word conceived not as an object but as a presence, in the crea-
tion of which the poet is able to restore that primitive identity
of word and world that the classical tradition of linguistic
thought had brought progressively under attack.

Chapter 1 sets the theme for Part Two of this book; chapter
2 sets the theme for Part Three. The dominant idea in Part Two
is that of literature considered as "a problematics of language"
—a phrase coined by the French critic Roland Barthes as part

of his argument that "modern poetry . . . destroys the spontaneously functional nature of language, and leaves standing only its lexical basis." [9] This is a radical statement of a traditional formalist idea of literary language, and in chapter 3 the development of this idea is traced through the writings of the Russian and French Formalist poets and thinkers, as well as the writings of certain figures in the Prague School of Linguistics. It is here that we will encounter, in an explicitly formulated version, the idea that the theme of poetry, and indeed the reason for its being, is not the world, not a universe of meaning, but language itself, which takes possession of literature and through it seeks to articulate its own transcendence. This idea opens the way to the sequence of critical analyses which follow, whose purpose is to establish the function or (at least) the status of language in a number of modern literary texts: the poetry of Mallarmé, and the fiction of Flaubert, Joyce, and Samuel Beckett. In each case attention will be paid to the special nature of these texts and to the special problems of language which they pose: Mallarmé's efforts to find typographical substitutes for syntax, the opposition between language and narrative in Flaubert and Joyce, and the relation between the use of language and linguistic skepticism in the fiction of Samuel Beckett.

Part Three sets Orphic speech over and against the hermetic uses of language studied in Part Two. Here the theme is that of the relation of poetry to the being of the world ("being" is understood here in Heidegger's sense of being as "presence"). It is at this point that this book confronts two questions that have regulated it from the beginning: (1) Does not the idea of the "pure expressiveness" of literary speech reflect a desire on the part of the poet to be free of the world—to oppose poetry and reality by establishing the poem as a closed or hermetic form that is suspended, as Flaubert's "book about nothing" is suspended, "like the earth in the void"? And (2) do we not have in the idea which finds poetry to be the condition of the world's possibility an opposite impulse: namely, the desire to overcome all opposition between poetry and reality by regarding poetry as an integral and essential part of man's world—"Part of the res itself," as Wallace Stevens puts it, "and not about it"? [10] Chapter 7 engages this first question by taking up the idea of literary language and the several ways in which a number of writers have related it to the concept of negativity, and particularly to Hegel's conception of speech as an act which has power to annihilate the world. Such a notion implies something like a negative unity of word and being, an inversion of the Orpheus myth, which for its part is predicated upon the power of the word to call up the world into the presence of man. Chapter 8 confronts the second question by examining modern variations on this Orphic myth of poetry, that is, the idea that it is only upon the ground of the poetic word that the world can take on meaning and reality.

What is interesting, however, is how these positive and negative conceptions of the unity of word and being seem to be related. In "Le Poète et le mythe," for example, Pierre Emmanuel writes:

> The poet, as a matter of instinct, abolishes the object and returns the thing to its silence, which is the ancient respiration of all things. He thus re-establishes in the world an innocence and a nothingness: innocence, because the world recovers itself as it was before speech, and nothingness, because speech (if only temporarily) is excluded from it. Doing this, the poet destroys with astonishing boldness the trench which separates man from the world. Insofar as he is a man, he cannot invert the sense of time; and from the contradiction between the original act, the *sole* act which he has just accomplished in returning matter to its primordial waters, and its guilty, limited, historically overwhelming nature, there is born the proud nostalgia for pure nothingness, the will to be the creating God, who holds the Word ready to cast it upon the waters.[11]

This passage presents us with a curious dialectic: the poet, by what is evidently a negative act of speech or indeed an act of destruction, splits off the word from the object and thereby returns the object to the void whence it came; he does so,

moreover, in order that he might return to the moment be-
fore speech, which becomes in this instance the moment be-
fore time—the moment of "pure nothingness" which preceded
the original creation of the world. For the poet's intention is
to speak that original word of God by which the world first
came into being. In one of his "Adagia," Wallace Stevens
states the matter as follows: "The mind that in heaven created
the earth and the mind that on earth created heaven were,
as it happened, one." [12] The poet's concern, in this context, is
thus not with a language of signs but with what Heidegger
calls "the language of being," which is, we may say, the lan-
guage of Orpheus. "The word must be the thing it repre-
sents," Steven says, "otherwise it is a symbol. It is a question of
identity." [13] For it is by virtue of the identity of word and
being that the poet is able once more to play his Orphic
role, according to which the world itself becomes a kind of
ultimate poem, within whose harmonious contours man dis-
covers his true dwelling-place.

PART ONE

*The Idea of Language from a
Literary Point of View*

1

Rhetoric, Grammar, and the Conception of Language as a Substantial Medium

In an essay entitled " 'Spirit' and 'Life' in Contemporary Philosophy," Ernst Cassirer makes the point that our understanding of language is governed in large part by what we imagine it to be. Applying his favorite distinction between substance and function, Cassirer writes:

> Language is misjudged if it is taken in some way or other as a thinglike being, as a substantial medium which interposes itself between man and the reality surrounding him. However one were then to define this medium more precisely, it always appears nevertheless—while wanting to be the *connecting link* between two worlds—as the barrier which separates the one from the other. However clear and however pure a medium we may then see in language, it always remains true that this crystal-clear medium is also crystal-hard—that however transparent it may be for the expression of ideas, it still is never wholly penetrable. Its transparency does not remove its impenetrability.

Skepticism toward language, from this point of view, is likely to be a "self-created difficulty," what Cassirer calls the unfortunate and unnecessary consequence of "an inadequate metaphorical description" of language.[1] Instead of taking language to be a kind of thing-in-itself, Cassirer says, we should approach it in terms of its function, which broadly conceived is that of signification. For language does not exist except in the form of an activity; it exists as a force or process, and not simply as a system of discrete signs to be applied as if they were so many tools.

Cassirer's complaint against the "inadequate metaphorical description" of language raises questions that are full of interest, particularly as these questions touch upon the problem of literary language, which is to say the problem of meaning that from the beginning has formed a central theme in man's inquiries into the nature and function of poetry. We can begin to engage some of these questions by asking first whence the notion of language as a "thinglike being" comes. We do know, for example, that Pope's lines

> *Words* are like *Leaves;* and where they most abound,
> Much *Fruit* of *Sense* beneath is rarely found [2]

reflect a view of language widely held during the Enlightenment. Cassirer, for his part, was probably thinking of Berkeley, whose conviction it was that "we need only draw the curtain of words to behold the fairest tree of knowledge, whose fruit is excellent, and within the reach of our hand." [3] We may say that Berkeley's metaphor grows out of the Baconian critique of language, according to which language, though ideally a system of notations which mirrors a world of phenomena, tends to enclose man in a purely verbal universe. For it is ever the habit of words to multiply without the warrant of experience, to enforce generalities where there are only particulars, in short to propose to the mind of man that realities exist when none, upon investigation, can be found.

What is important to notice about Cassirer's complaint, however, is the suggestion that Berkeley's metaphor, far from growing out of the critique, actually serves to generate it. What is suggested is that such metaphors for language as are to be found in Pope and Berkeley have antecedents in ways of thinking about language that are much older than any empiricist inquiry into human understanding. Bacon's depreciation of words, after all, is as much a response to the study of rhetoric and grammar and to the value traditionally attributed to amplified discourse as it is to the arcane terminology of the philosophers. Indeed, as I intend to show in this chapter, in rhetoric and grammar we have two quite ancient traditions in which language is conceived explicitly as a "thinglike being," or (what amounts to the same thing) in which analogies with objects in space are used to explain what language is and what it does.

Let me clarify briefly the issues with which we shall shortly be involved. In the first place, it is to be noticed that Cassirer's distinction between substance and function provides the ground for a distinction between the logical and the poetic approach to language. For does not the poet, almost as a matter of nature, regard language not only in its functional but in its material character, as something to be shaped? It is certainly true, as Cassirer says, that "when the physical sound, distinguished as such only by pitch and intensity and quality, is formed into a word, it becomes an expression of the finest intellectual and emotional distinctions. What it immediately is, is thrust into the background by what it accomplishes with its mediation, by what it 'means.' " [4] But has it not always been the business of the poet to retard this process by which language effaces itself, that is, to deflect meaning in order to keep language resonating in the foreground? The poet Valéry, for example, has also observed that "in practical or abstract uses of language, the form—that is the physical, the concrete part, the very act of speech—does not last; it does not outlive understanding." [5] But in poetry "language is no longer a transitive act, an expedient. On the contrary, it has its own value, which must remain intact in spite of the operations of the intellect on the given propositions. Poetic language must preserve itself, through itself, and remain the same, not to be altered by the act of intelligence that finds or gives it a meaning." [6] Valéry offers us here, as we shall see in a later chapter, an identifiably modern view of poetic language; but attention to sound and form in language, if not indeed the explicit subordination of meaning to the form by which meaning is ordinarily articulated, is by no means a uniquely modern phenomenon. For Valéry may be said to have reproduced, however much in modern terms, a view of language that forms a central part of traditional rhetorical theory and which reveals itself in a use of language aimed at giving representation not to a subject matter but to those "deviant forms" of language which make up the body of stylistic study.[7] The traditional rhetorician was, like Valéry, preoccupied with the sounds and shapes of language, and accordingly it was his inclination to conceive language not merely as a "transitive act" but as an object whose reality it was the purpose of his calling to underscore.

Secondly, there is to be considered what is commonly called the "metalinguistic" approach to language, according to which language is regarded as an object for analysis. The problem here centers upon ways of describing the structure of language. Modern structural and transformational linguists have tried to think of language in terms of such concepts as process, system, and function.[8] Against the view that language is a set of isolatable units, they have argued that it is a whole superior to its parts—a whole upon the activity of which the parts depend for their significance. In this modern linguists are historically almost unique. The nineteenth-century linguistic tradition had almost uniformly approached language from the standpoint of the isolated word conceived as a physical or psychical entity— an item in a mechanical system or a natural object possessed of its own life cycle or a psychic unit within a larger bundle of psychic units called images and ideas.[9] Similarly, the older grammatical tradition took for its object not spoken but written (and, most often, literary) language, and as a consequence tended to regard human speech as a wholly spatial and visual affair, the utilization of a phenomenon of quantity and extension. As we shall see, so far from being an isolated, academic image of language, such a view has direct ties with the suspicion, widespread among logicians and moralists, that language is a mirror which offers not only a distorted picture of the world but is in fact inclined to shadow the world with fictions of its own making.

To begin our inquiry into the rhetorical concept of language, we may take the opposition between Cassirer and Valéry as a kind of model which reflects in theoretical fashion the historic controversy between the ancient philosophers and rhetoricians, as well as the later, less sharply defined debate between Renaissance humanism and scholasticism. The terms of this conflict, as it touches upon language (for there are moral questions involved here as well), can be marked out with some precision in the difference between two Greek words, *logos* and *epos*. Both words have to do with human speech, but they represent the reality of human speech understood from different points of view. In *logos* human speech is seen in its orientation toward thought; in *epos* the orientation is toward song. Now the point to mark is that *epos* acknowledges the world of sound, and as it does so it attests to the substantial character of language. The logician, for his part, is apt to dismiss the sounds of words, remarking only perhaps that it was Cratylus who believed that between name and thing, sound and meaning, there existed a natural or necessary relationship. The *Cratylus* of Plato suggests that Plato himself at one time inclined toward this view; but later in his career, as he concerned himself more and more with the problem of knowledge, Plato sought to remove language from sound. During the discussion of knowledge in the *Theaetetus*, for example, Socrates pauses momentarily to explain that the act of thinking is

> the conversation [logos] which the soul holds with herself in considering of anything. . . . The soul when thinking appears to me to be just talking—asking questions of herself and answering them, affirming and denying. And when she has arrived at a decision . . . this is called her opinion. I say, then, that to form an opinion is to speak, and opinion is a word spoken,—I mean, to oneself and in silence, not aloud to another.[10]

Here language is regarded not as a substance but as an activity which moves the soul toward definition. In a curious way, this passage takes us some distance not only from the *Cratylus* but from the world of Socrates—that is, the Socrates, for example, of the *Apology*. For in the world of silent discourse we transcend the personal encounter, as though to move toward a more pure act of knowing. Just so, as Plato explains in the *Seventh Epistle,* the pursuit of definition—the pursuit in which so much of Socrates seems consumed—is but a prelude to authentic knowledge: "For every real being there are three things that are necessary if knowledge of it is to be acquired: first, the name; second, the definition; third, the image; knowledge comes fourth, and in fifth place we must put the object itself, the knowable and truly real being." [11] In this hierarchy language constitutes a preliminary exercise which must engage the soul before the encounter with "the knowable and truly real being" is possible. But true knowledge (*epistêmê*) resides "in our minds, not in words or bodily shapes" (342c). Moreover, Plato goes on to say, whoever would return to the world of words after he has attained knowledge of what is real, cannot have understood the significance of his journey: "no sensible man will venture to express his deepest thoughts in words, especially in a form which is unchangeable" (343a).

For Plato, then, knowledge belongs to the world of silence: it is an unmediated vision, with which language can finally have nothing to do. By thus removing language from the world of sound, and in turn knowledge from human speech, Plato moved against the very spirit of ancient Greek culture. For the traditional moral and practical wisdom of the Greeks, as Eric Havelock has shown, had from the beginning been enclosed in sound—had been preserved and transmitted through the *epos,* that is, the rhythmic formulations of the epic singers.[12] Even such Pre-Socratics as Heraclitus, who instituted the *Logos* over and against the *epos* of the poets, were, in Havelock's phrase, essentially "oral thinkers." [13] By the time of Socrates the function of preserving and transmitting the wisdom of the culture had passed to the Sophists, who maintained the basic oral, indeed the basic rhythmic character of Greek culture through the teaching of rhetoric. Eloquent speech, the Sophists insisted, was the way to wisdom and thus to power.[14]

One of the most important and famous of the Sophists was Gorgias, who delighted in arguing, if we are to believe Sextus Empiricus, "firstly, that nothing exists; secondly, that even if anything exists, it is inapprehensible by man; thirdly, that even if anything is apprehensible, yet of a surety it is inexpressible and incommunicable to one's neighbor." [15] It is hard to imagine a statement that would call the efficacy of language more perfectly into doubt than this one. Gorgias, as Plato was later to do, dissociates language and knowledge, but he does so from precisely the opposite point of view. For, as Sextus explains, Gorgias insisted radically upon the physical nature of language: "the means by which we indicate [that is, communicate] is speech, and speech is not the real and existent things; therefore, we do not indicate to our neighbor the existent things but [only] speech, which is other than existing realities." [16] Language, being one thing, cannot be another; it cannot communicate anything but itself. We speak, and in doing so we utter words purely and simply. That meanings are attributed to certain words, Gorgias well knew, but such meanings can only be of an arbitrary and problematical character. Beyond the problem of linguistic meaning, however, there is the one obvious and fundamental fact of human speech: it entails the creation of sound, and it is in sound that for Gorgias language has its value. For when it is said that "we do not indicate to our neighbor the existent things but [only] speech," what is meant is that the proper function of language is not representation but incantation: language does not mean, it is, and being what it is, it generates certain effects: "The inspired incantations of words," Gorgias says in the *Helen*, "can induce pleasure and avert grief; for the power of incantations, uniting with the feeling in the soul, soothes and persuades and transports by means of wizardry." [17] So language is efficacious after all, but in a magical or psychological rather than logical sense. Accordingly, Gorgias adds that in order to discover the true and indeed only value of language, we need simply observe such phenomena as the "legal contests, in which a speech can sway and persuade a crowd, by the skill of its composition, not by the truth of its statements."

Implicit in the *Helen*, of course, are those moral issues which Plato elucidated in his attacks upon rhetoric. To be

sure, from the *Helen,* as well as from Plato's *Gorgias,* we get a
one-sided view of Gorgias—the rhetorician figured not as an
educator but as dealer in words, who finds power not in the
wisdom of reason but in the magic of sound. Yet this is the
view which possesses historical significance, for it is in this
image of Gorgias that we find, in its purest and most striking
form, the rhetorical concept of language. Language, being
sound, appears as a malleable substance capable of being
shaped into an infinity of forms: it is the orator's clay, the
material in which the power of his art is to be realized. Now
it is this view of language which is inherent in virtually all
rhetorical treatises and implicit in those utterances which are
executed according to rhetorical models. That the orator's art
is a purely stylistic one, of course, is a thesis which few stu-
dents of rhetoric, after Plato's powerful critique, would ex-
plicitly defend—thus Aristotle sought to redeem rhetoric by
defining it in terms of the enthymeme, that is, as a mode of
thought. One has only to read Cicero's *Orator,* however, to
discover what was to be the central theme of rhetorical study
throughout the Middle Ages and into the Renaissance: that
it is in what the orator does to language, not in what he says
or in what he knows, that his special character is to be found.
"We must turn now to the task of portraying the perfect
orator and the highest eloquence," Cicero writes in a famous
passage. "The very word 'eloquent' shows that he excels be-
cause of this one quality, that is, in the use of language, and
that all other qualities are overshadowed by this." [18] Such ef-
forts as Quintilian's, to make of rhetoric not only a study of
deviant linguistic forms—the figures of style—but a distinct
form of knowledge, were never really able to displace this
view.

The point is that the very concept of style, which alone is
the property of rhetorical theory, implies the conception of
language as a substantial medium, that is, as an object set
over and against a subject matter. Indeed, the earliest instance
of rhetorical theory suggests that this is so. In Book III of the

Iliad, Antenor tells us that when Menelaus and Odysseus "began to weave the web of speech and counsel" at a conference between Trojans and Greeks, "Menelaus in truth spoke fluently, with a few words, but very clearly, seeing he was not a man of lengthy speech nor of rambling." Odysseus, for his part, seemed at first like "a man of no understanding. . . . But whenso he uttered his great voice from his chest, and words were like snowflakes on a winter's day, then could no mortal vie with Odysseus." [19] Distinguished here are what were to be called the plain and the grand styles, but what is important to notice is the metaphorical description which Homer gives to language: Odysseus's words are like so many objects —"snowflakes on a winter's day." What this spatial and visual simile suggests is that Odysseus's speech is not, to borrow Valéry's words, "a transitive act, an expedient." In contrast to Menelaus—and indeed to all other mortals—Odysseus transforms his speech from an utterance into something very like an object, precisely because language is for him more than a medium. It is a material to be shaped—a material whose opacity serves to arrest the attention of the audience, compelling it to contemplate the speech itself, thus in due course to mark how the speaker is set apart from ordinary men and so to give special credence to what he says.

Homer's simile is the more worthy of attention because, unlike the grammarian (to whom, as we shall see, spatial and visual analogies came quite naturally), Homer is describing spoken, not written language. Spoken words, as Walter Ong has so often argued, belong to the world of time and presence, not to the world of objects in space.[20] Nevertheless, Homer prefigures here (as elsewhere) such writers as Dionysus of Halicarnassus, in whose treatise *On Literary Composition* (ca. 20–10 B.C.) words are considered from the standpoint of their stylistic effects rather than in terms of meaning. In the austere style, Dionysus says,

> words should be like columns firmly planted and placed in strong positions, so that each word should be seen on every side, and

that the parts should be at appreciable distances from one an-
other, being separated by perceptible intervals. It does not in the
least shrink from using frequently harsh sound-clashings which jar
on the ear; like blocks of building stone that are laid together
unworked, blocks that are not square and smooth, but preserve
their natural roughness and irregularity. It is prone for the most
part to expansion by means of great spacious words.[21]

The smooth (or florid) style, by contrast, "requires words to
come sweeping along on top of one another, each supported
by that which follows, like the onflow of a never-resting stream.
. . . From this point of view the style resembles finely woven
stuffs, or pictures in which the lights melt insensibly into the
shadows." [22] Dionysus is preeminently the grammarian, for
whom words are physical particles to be arranged (by means of
a "stylus") within a spatial field. Accordingly, his concept of
style is largely a matter of how words stand (and move) in rela-
tion to one another within this field. He gives only passing
attention to the figures of rhetoric—the schemes and tropes
and figures of thought with which the orator is chiefly con-
cerned. Yet we should observe that in traditional rhetorical
theory the same recourse to spatial and visual analogies is
taken to describe the rhetorical figures and how they function.
Deviant linguistic forms are regarded as the "colors," "lights,"
"flowers," "ornaments," and "clothes" which adorn the
speaker's subject. And what a speaker may hope to achieve by
these devices is nowhere more vividly explained than by
Henry Peacham in *The Garden of Eloquence* (1577; 1593), a
manual devoted entirely to the classification and description
of the rhetorical figures:

> By figures he may make his speech as cleare as the noone day: or
> contrarywyse, as it were with cloudes and foggy mistes, he may
> couer it with darknesse: he may stirre up stormes, & troublesome
> tempestes, or contrariwyse, cause and procure, a quiet and sylent
> calmnesse, he may set forth any matter with a goodly perspecuitie,
> and paynt out any person, deede, or thing, so cunninglye with
> these couloures, that it shall seeme rather a lyuely Image paynted
> in tables, then a reporte expressed with the tongue.[23]

That a speaker's subject should "seeme rather a lyuely Image paynted in tables, then a reporte expressed with the tongue," concerns one function of the rhetorical figures: the subject is not merely embroidered but transformed, as in Horace's *ut pictura poesis,* so as to exist no longer in an oral–aural sphere but in the visual field of imagination. But the point is that the utterance itself assumes in this process a substantial character: it does not simply mediate between the subject and a world of images but, moving as it does along a continuum between "foggy mistes" and "perspecuitie," is conceived to occupy a ground of its own between the subject (or the speaker) and the audience. Thus what characterizes the figures is their capacity to "distance" the subject, that is, to control the accessibility of the subject. For they serve, Peacham says, as a means of "tournying from the common manner and custom of wryting and speaking" (p. B. j.), thus to create an unconventional form of discourse that tends to displace the attention of the audience from the subject to the language itself.

We shall deal with this question of "displacement" at greater length in chapter 3 and again in chapter 5. For now, let us consider the problem which the creation of an unconventional (or specifically literary) form of discourse was understood to pose. It is a problem as old as Pindar,[24] if not older, and underlies the ancient controversy between Asianism and Atticism, the Renaissance dispute concerning Ciceronianism, and the enduring tradition of literary cultism that extends from Lycophron's *Alexandra* (third century B.C.) through the Baroque or Mannerist poetry of seventeenth-century Spain to our own day. It is the problem of art's ability (or even compulsion) to obscure or distort its content—a problem that is intimately bound up with the Sophist's question of whether language is at all commensurate with those things it is said to convey. The figures of rhetoric, that is, raise the old issue of *apate,* or deception, precisely as they appear to accentuate the distance or disproportion between words and things, and again precisely as they increase or becloud the distance between an audience and the subject or meaning of an utterance.

George Puttenham spoke directly to this problem in his *Arte of English Poesie* (1589):

> As figures be the instruments of ornament in euery language, so be they also in sorte abuses or rather trespasses in speach, because they passe the ordinary limits of common vtterance, and be oc-cupied of a purpose to deceiue the ear and also the minde, draw-ing it from plainnesse and simplicitie to a certain doublenesse, whereby our talke is the more guileful & abusing.[25]

Puttenham's conception, in this critique of the rhetorical figures, seems to be that the "common vtterance" is tied, if not by nature at least by convention, to reality. The problem of figurative speech is that, by exceeding "the ordinary limits of common vtterance," it breaks this tie, thus to establish a world of words that deceives the mind by drawing it away from the truth with which it ought rightly to be concerned. Puttenham's purpose here was doubtless not to forbid the use of figures and so prevent poets from being poetic; it was rather to save the poets, by urging upon them a classic re-straint, from the ancient charge of duplicity. The poet must simply avoid those "heresies of language," whereby his speech so far deviates from the forms of common discourse as to be-come an array of words without "conueyance and efficacy" (p. 155).

Puttenham offers a frankly ethical solution to the problem of the figures, but there was available to him another equally commonplace solution: namely, the argument that poetry, and indeed all human speech, is deceptive only on the surface, for if speech, and particularly poetic speech, is deceptive, it is so in order to preserve and reinforce its truth. "Sub verborum tegmine vera latent," wrote John of Salisbury in the *Entheti-cus de dogmate philosophorum* (ca. 1159): beneath the veil of words truths lie hidden.[26] This notion takes us back to the mystery cults and the paradoxes of Heraclitus; it was already a commonplace among the Stoics, who used it to defend the piety of Homer, and by its means St. Augustine explained away scriptural obscurities. Defenders of poetry delighted in arguing, as did Bernardino Daniello in *Poetica* (1536), that "there is not one of [Plato's] Dialogues . . . in which he does not express his concepts under a fabulous veil and mystery (in the form which poets alone are accustomed to create) but with the brightest and most resplendent flames of words, and with the grandest numbers." [27] What is to be noticed, however, is that the image of the "veil of words" seeks to deal with the problem of deceptive speech by making discourse a substance of extension and depth, of outer and inner spheres—as in the familiar husk and kernel of the allegorical tradition.

That is to say, by this image language is conceived to be more than a medium, something which only reluctantly effaces itself before the "act of intelligence" that seeks a meaning. Indeed, to the extent that words are said to conceal (and, ultimately, to be separable from) their meanings, they may in turn be said to possess an independent existence. In one of the dialogues in Bartolomeo Maranta's *Lucullianae questiones* (1564), precisely this point is made: "Words produce speech, things themselves the sententia. Without speech, that is, without words, sententia cannot exist: but words can exist without sententia." [28] Words in this view seem less a part of the act of speech than things in their own right. To be sure, no one doubted that words serve a mediating function: those who took recourse to the "veil of words" understood, as Rosamond Tuve once vigorously argued, that the veil is finally expressive—it "bodies-forth" meaning.[29] But we will recall Cassirer's observation that, conceived as a veil, language is never quite so transparent as to be wholly penetrable. And this seems particularly the case in a poetry whose words seek to turn in upon themselves—a phenomenon which St. Augustine decries as the worst sort of barbarism but which in other, perhaps more secular contexts is taken to be the emblem of high art. This was so among the troubadours of Provençal during the eleventh and twelfth centuries, for example, but a more powerful instance is to be found in the *Soledades* (ca. 1612–1613) of Don Luis de Góngora. For Góngora poetry is a formalist enterprise: it is an activity which fulfills itself in a concatenation of Latinate syntax, mythology, elaborate conceits, and (of course) sound:

> Sobre corchos después, más regalado
> sueño le solicitan pieles blandas,
>   que al príncipe entre holandas,
> púrpura tiria o milanés brocado.
> No de humosos vinos agravado
> es Sísifo en la cuesta, si en la cumbre
> de ponderosa vana pesadumbre,
> es, cuanto más despierto, más burlado . . .
> Durmió, y recuerda al fin, cuando las aves
> —esquilas dulces de sonora pluma—
>   señas dieron suäves
> del alba al Sol, que el pabellón de espuma
>   dejó, y en su carroza
> rayó el verde obelisco de la choza.[30]

Here language tends rather to be a medium for the poet's art than a medium for meaning. That the hero of the poem takes for himself a night of exquisite sleep is of less consequence than the ingenuity of the poet as he dilates upon the situation, thus to break up the surface of his poem among a diversity of extraordinary figures ("las aves—esquilas dulces de sonora pluma"). This is the "arte de ingenio," a defense for which is to be found not in Boccaccio or in Sidney but in Baltasar Grácian's *Agudeza y Arte de Ingenio* (1642; 1649), in which it is proposed that the mark of the true poet is the "agudeza," or acuteness of thought and speech. The "agudeza" is "an act of the mind which expresses the correspondence discovered between objects"—but with this difference, that the *concepto* which results is no simple trope but a "correlation ingeniously expressed." [31] For the poet of the "agudeza" is not content with the expression of truth but with the expressiveness of his art: he aspires toward the beauty of "intellectual symmetry," which is to say the beauty of form.[32] Góngora himself, it is true, leaned heavily upon the idea that the poet's language must be all but an impenetrable veil to conceal sacred and subtle truths from any but the adept; [33] but at bottom it is not so much the subtle truth as it is the subtlety of artifice that constitutes the end of his art.

The poetry of Góngora, of course, may with good and well-precedented reason be dismissed as trivial and even immoral; but it ought to be observed that it represents the working out of the same assumptions that underlie the humanist ideal of eloquence. It is clear, for example, that the "arte de ingenio" is an elaboration of the ancient concept of *technē*, according to which the knowledge which characterizes poetry (or any of the arts of language) is not knowledge of a truth but of a skill. In this sense the "arte de ingenio" is the concept of *technē* with an additional premium placed upon the execution of complex formal maneuvers, and thus it is essentially of a piece with the humanist idea of the *copia*—the *copia* as it is defined, for example, in Erasmus's *De Utraque verborum ac rerum copia* (1512), a handbook during the course of which Erasmus demonstrates one hundred fifty variations on the sentence, "Tuae literae me magnopere delecterunt," and two hundred variations on "Semper dum vivam tui meminero." [34] Here, as far as ingenuity is concerned, is God's plenty. Góngora and Erasmus would without question have disagreed upon the terms according to which poetry (or oratory) is to fulfill its moral function, or upon what finally constitutes decorous speech, but underlying both the *Soledades* and *De Utraque verborum* is the assumption that language is a material capable of being shaped into any given number of formations. Consider, after all, the disproportion between words and things which these two works imply: by what criterion, for example, would one choose among one hundred fifty or two hundred possibilities of expression, in order to articulate a single, utterly commonplace meaning? The answer, clearly, is provided by rhetoric, which is to say that the criterion must be a stylistic one. The point, at any rate, is that for both Góngora and Erasmus, mannerist and humanist, skill in speech fines itself down to a question of style, that is, to a thorough familiarity with the deviant forms of language, whose effect is finally to transform an utterance into an object—to create an utterance which is not only to be understood but to be contemplated for the brilliance of its design.

This question of design in speech extends, however, into fields other than rhetoric and poetry. The speaker who pursues the ideal of copiousness avails himself, to be sure, of distinct and isolatable forms—abstractions to be concretized in his utterance; but such figures as are to be found in theory or in traditional stylistic models are nevertheless forms *of language:* they are configurations which accentuate the patterns that constitute the very structure of language itself. The most abstruse conceit, after all, shows itself to be an act of predication, even as the most resonant and distracting scheme adumbrates a basic syntactical procedure. Thus it is that the "veil of words," however much it may work to conceal thought, is able at the same time to reveal what it conceals. Structure in speech, that is to say, makes signification possible. It is to this fundamental structure of language that we must now turn our attention, so as to discover to what extent the way in which this structure is conceived—the way it strikes the imagination—effects the way in which language is conceived to be significant.

How was language understood in the beginning? Many years ago, Bronislaw Malinowski observed that, when speaking of "primitive" languages, we should abjure "the conception of meaning as *contained* in an utterance," because for the primitive speech is not a mode of expression but a mode of action. "A word, signifying an important utensil, is used in action, not to comment on its nature or reflect on its properties, but to make it appear, to be handed over to the speaker, or to direct another man to its proper use. . . . The word therefore has a power of its own, it is a means of bringing things about, it is a handle to acts and objects and not a definition of them." [35] It would never occur to primitive man to regard the word as "a real entity, containing its meaning as a Soul-box contains the spiritual part of a person or thing" (p. 307). For the primitive, that is to say, the word is functional, not substantial: embedded as it is among objects and activities, the utterance is not a distinct and self-contained event; committed as it is to the fleeting world of sound, it is even less a "thinglike being." Yet the high incidence of speech-play in some so-called primitive societies suggests that for primitive man speech is not necessarily an undifferentiated part of his life. Speech-play suggests, indeed, that some primitive groups are capable of regarding the utterance as an activity which involves alterable relationships, that they are capable of attaching significance to the design of speech.[36]

Design in speech may be said to consist of relationships among diverse grammatical categories. How such categories are built up in any given language it is of course impossible to say with certainty; broadly speaking, grammatical categories are determined functionally, according to the social needs of a people. Thus we may suppose that in a primitive society the grammatical structure of the language will be relatively simple —as, to take a famous example, in the language of the Australian Arandas. The Aranda tribesman does not distinguish between things (as we usually think of them) and activities or states.[37] At the same time, however, the Aranda language is morphologically quite complex. According to T. G. H. Strehlow, there are available to the Aranda verb stem nearly a thousand combinations of suffixes. Thus, by a complex synthetic process, the basic verb *atakererama* ("to spread out roots") may be built up into *atakeri-takerereperelatanguna* ("to remain rooted down firmly for all time").[38] Quite obviously, the "word," as we think of it (namely, an isolatable element in a sentence), does not exist in the Aranda. The Aranda "word" is what used to be called a "holophrase." It was Jespersen's suggestion that the history of language generally is marked by the breaking-down of the holophrase into simpler morphological units: "The evolution of language," he wrote, "shows a progressive tendency from inseparable irregular conglomerations to freely and regularly combinable short elements." [39] The difficulty with such a principle is that it does not apply to a number of American Indian languages or to Chinese; [40] but it does describe the general "drift" of a number of Indo-European languages, most notably English and French, toward a more analytic morphological structure. Even Greek, which by comparison with English is synthetic in its structure, appears to have "drifted" according to a pattern of roughly this order. Thus R. H. Robins observes that in Greek "words were already 'institutionalized,' " even before the invention of the phonetic alphabet: "the Greek language had for generations been unconsciously and by usage analyzed into isolatable fragments that were called words." [41] It is this process of analysis that prefigures the more deliberate analysis called "grammar." But what is important to understand is that the breaking-down of the stream of speech into "isolatable fragments" is at the same time a breaking-down into *patterns*—into a subject-verb pattern, for example, if we are thinking of Greek, or into any number of formal patterns, which determine how the "fragments" are to enter into combination.

In preliterate societies, as Sapir has tried to show, such "isolatable fragments" as we call words are psychological entities; [42] but with the advent of the phonetic alphabet these fragments come to possess not merely a psychological but indeed an objective and spatial character. Language itself may be said to have assumed an objective and spatial character, in the sense that the effort to understand how words behave in relation to one another proceeds on the basis of a metaphorical description of language that is itself spatial and visual in character. Early grammar seems to have availed itself of just such a description, even though language was still conceived to be an oral–aural phenomenon, still a matter of sound, voice, and spirit. When we examine the *Organon* of Aristotle, for example, we find that in the *Topics* and in both the *Posterior* and *Prior Analytics* language is regarded as a system of *activities:* it is not something man has or uses but is a function of the mind, an *enunciation,* which is conceived to mark the fruition of thought. Knowledge, in its logical form, is a form of discourse. But in the *Categories* and particularly in the *De Interpretatione* Aristotle approaches language from the standpoint of the isolated word: from Plato's *Sophist* he takes over the distinction between *ónomata* and *rêmata,* subjects and predicates, but it is to be noticed that in Aristotle these are not so much logical as grammatical categories.[43] They have become the irreducible particles of a proposition, mere *pháseis* which cannot be further separated into parts. The *pháseis* are able to function only when combined into a *logos,* a *phonè semantikè* or significant utterance. There is reason to believe, however, that it is not the spoken utterance that Aristotle is thinking of here but the written sentence. As in the *Sophist,* the combination of nouns and verbs into a proposition is conceived to be a "stringing-together," as in the *symplokè onomatón* or "stringing-together of nouns." [44] Words thus appear to be regarded as so many atoms in space, available for combination into molecules according to a linear model. This linear model is clearly at work in Aristotle's discussion of diction in the *Poetics,* where he distinguishes, together with the letter, noun, and verb, the *syndesmos* and *árthron,* two anatomical terms meaning "ligament" and "joint." Such words (which approximate roughly our notions of conjunction and article) have only a purely grammatical function: they are "insignificant sounds," serving only to bind the parts of the sentence together [45]—or perhaps, as Dionysus Thrax was later to put it in his treatise on grammar, to "fill up the hiatuses of speech." [46] Finally, there is the important and decidedly spatial concept of *ptôsis,* or declension, according to which a word is said to "fall' or "bend" or "decline" into several positions.[47]

Particular attention ought to be paid to the concept of *ptôsis,* because it occupies a rather special place in ancient grammatical theory. The Stoics, following Aristotle's metaphorical lead, distinguished between *órthé* or *eùtheîa ptôsis,* the "upright" case, and *plagíai,* or "oblique" cases.[48] Roland Kent informs us that "the Greeks conceived the paradigm of the noun as the upper right quadrant of the circle: the nominative was the vertical radius, and the other cases were radii which 'declined' to the right." [49] Similarly, but with pointedly less concern for geometrical precision, Varro in *De Lingua latina* (first century B.C) explained that "as every offshoot is secondary by nature, because that vertical trunk from which it comes is primary, and it is therefore declined: so there is declension in words: *homo* 'man' is the vertical, *hominis* 'man's' is the oblique, because it is declined from the vertical." [50] The geometrical figure and Varro's organic simile serve well to illustrate the difference between the "analogists" and the "anomalists," that is, between those grammarians for whom language was a well-regulated whole whose parts were related according to definite structural laws, and those who found in language a great diversity of incongruous forms. What is of interest is that on both sides of the controversy (such as it was) the inclination appears to have been to regard language as a kind of world in little. For example, the effort on the part of the Alexandrian scholar Aristarchos (ca. 220–150 B.C.) to discover in language definite principles of order seems to have been nothing less than an effort to build up according to the model of a more or less perfectly organized cosmos a consistent and perhaps even self-contained linguistic system. For the Stoic Crates (fl. 120 B.C.), on the other hand, it is the richness and variety of the world which language appears to imitate, which is to say that the model for language is the physical world itself in all its diverse foliage, and not a universe harmonized by law.[51]

This matter of how language is designed, however, touches upon the relation of language to reality in other, more important ways. For the Stoics, it appears that language was not simply modeled after the physical world but belonged to it part and parcel. It was customary among the Greeks to identify the letters of the alphabet (and with them the indivisible sounds of speech) as *stoicheîa,* literally physical particles; but the Stoics extended the term to cover the parts of speech as well, so that noun and verb were understood to belong to the same order of things as the *stoicheîa* which compose the physical universe.[52] Such a shift in terminology could only be appropriate in the face of the conviction traditionally attributed to the Stoics that between word and meaning (or *lekton,* the what-is-said of an utterance) there prevailed a natural relationship. In this, of course, the Stoics were swimming upstream, for the whole movement of Greek thought had been to isolate speech from thought. Aristotle, for example, attributes to language a measure of independence that it does not have even in Plato. Plato, we recall, placed knowledge in a transcendent sphere beyond the reach of words; but he had in the *Theaetetus* and again in the *Sophist* identified thinking with silent speech: thought is the soul's *logos* with herself.[53] In Aristotle this identity appears to have been broken. As Harold Joachim observed in his *Logical Studies,* in Aristotle we find that "speech draws apart from, and is (not one with but) related to, the thought which it expresses or utters." [54] And this relationship between speech and thought is arranged by convention. No longer, as in Heraclitus, does a unity determined by universal law exist between language and the world: universal law has been replaced by cultural law. The word, that is, having long ceased to be a part of a luminous whole, is now no longer simply a natural extension of the world but is distinctly a creature of artifice in a world of its own. Indeed, things can no longer be properly said to *have* names; instead, men possess signs—artifacts by which to portion out into certain selected categories the elements of their existence.

Now it is when words have been thus drawn away from the meanings they are said to express, and when in turn they are conceived to exist as artifacts in a conventional relationship to those meanings, that the problem of meaning in language emerges into view. For Aristotle, of course, not words by themselves but only judgments are true or false: the value of an individual word is determined on a practical basis according to whether a significance that is communally shared can be attached to it. But if words possess no natural relationship to their meanings, then it is possible to argue that, however secure and practicable the convention which determines their use might seem, the significance of speech must always have about it something of a hypothetical and hence problematical character. It was this problematical character of language, as we have seen, of which Gorgias made so much and according to which he asserted the incommensurability of words and things. The Epicureans, according to Phillip De Lacy's exposition, appear to have made an effort to mitigate the problem of language by restricting, in the manner of the modern positivist tradition, the possibilities of linguistic meaning: "All language symbols refer ultimately to empirical facts," De Lacy explains. "Language has cognitive value only to the extent that it may be referred to objects of experience by a process of verification." [55] Here the convention which regulates speech is narrowed so as to operate only within the limits of what amounts to an investigative discipline. The language of poetry as well as that of logical propositions are merely admonitive, not indicative; such forms of speech have no traffic with the world of things. In the skeptic tradition, *all* forms of speech are reduced to a merely admonitive function. In the *Outlines of Pyrrhonism* Sextus Empiricus marshals a host of arguments against the belief that such things as indicative signs exist.[56] Indeed, the whole of the *Outlines* is a kind of prelude to a life of silence according to the example of Pyrrho, whose conviction it was that speech and wisdom are wholly incompatible.

The question to be considered at this point, however, is whether there is not some connection between this drawing away of speech from thought and the building up of a metaphorical description of language which gives to language a substantial identity. From a theoretical standpoint, an answer to this question would have as its principle theme the autonomy attributed, if only by implication, to language. Speech draws away from thought, and to the extent that language and the contents of the mind are in turn taken to be incommensurate, the significance of speech becomes less a fact than a problem, and language itself becomes more purely a world of words, a system of formally related but not always significant sounds. At the same time, there takes place a kind of "cul-

tural image" of language—the kind of image suggested, for
example, by the treatment of words in the *Ars Minor* of the
Roman grammarian Donatus (fl. A.D. 350):

> personae tertiae generis masculini numeri singularis ille illius
> illum ab illo, et pluraliter illi illorum illis illos ab illis; generis
> femini numeri singularis illa illius illi illam ab illa, et pluraliter
> illae illarum illis illas ab illis; generis neutri numeri singularis
> illud illius illi illud ab illo, et pluraliter illa illorum ab illis.[57]

This passage describes not an act of speech but the behavior
of language, not the articulation of thought but a spatial and
visual field in which discrete particles "fall away" from one
another according to a fixed design. Language, as it is
systematized by the grammarians, becomes a phenomenon of
quantity and extension; like all systems, it is perfectly self-
contained, its contact with the world of speech registered only
tangentially in such concepts as "person," "voice," and
"mood."

From a historical standpoint, however, our question is not
so easily answered. Against both the skepticism which reduces
human speech to a *flatus vocis* and the pedagogical spirit
which in the interest of mnemonics reduces speech to a set of
manageable objects, there prevails a common sense faith in
the ability of language to deliver man's judgment concerning
reality and a common sense experience of speech itself in
which speech shows itself to be not the system of the gram-
marians but the utterance of a living person. To test the
strength of this common sense tradition, one need only note
the attitude toward language in John of Salisbury's *Metalogi-
con* (1159). It was sufficient for John of Salisbury to believe
that names were "stamped on all substances," [58] that between
res and *verba*, ideas and words, there was an intelligible com-
munion, not, to be sure, as a matter of nature, but as a matter
of supreme reason—as a matter, quite simply, of divine ordi-
nation.

As the Middle Ages ran their course, however, this confi-
dence in the rationality of words began to lose its force. In

the fourteenth century William of Ockham, seeking finally to resolve Porphyry's question of whether *genus* and *species* have a real or a merely nominal existence, settled upon a distinction between two types of knowledge, intuitive and abstractive, and proposed that intuitive knowledge alone is "cognition that enables us to know whether the thing exists or does not exist." [59] This is to say that the only knowledge concerning which we can be certain is knowledge of concrete, particular objects: "Through abstractive cognition no contingent truth, in particular none relating to the present, can evidently be known" (p. 24). The business of recording the world of particular objects falls to the sign, of which there are three kinds: the written word (*terminus scriptus*), the spoken word (*terminus prolatus*), and the mental concept or image (*terminus conceptus* or *intentio animae*). The critical point is that all three types of sign refer to the same reality: individually existing things. "I say vocal words are signs subordinated to mental concepts," Ockham argues. "By this I do not mean that if the word 'sign' is taken in its proper meaning, spoken words are properly and primarily signs of mental concepts; I rather mean that words are applied to signify the very same things which are signified by mental concepts" (p. 47).

Aristotle's conception of the relation between language and thought is modified here in a way that is profoundly significant. Words (*verba*) refer, as they did for Aristotle and for John of Salisbury, to things (*res*), but whereas for Aristotle *res* meant *thing* as subject matter in a discourse, the content of an act of the mind, it came to mean for Ockham *thing* as object existing in the world.[60] The word, that is, refers to the thing in an empirical rather than logical sense. Language is in fact quite divorced from thought, in the sense that the word is no longer a sign of conception but runs—and on a subordinate level—parallel to conception. From Ockham's standpoint, we should be called upon to make a radical distinction between verbal and mental functions, and to understand that the one no longer reflects the other but hangs suspended, as though in a kind of imaginary space, between mind and world. The

word "man," for example, in its proper function no longer
signifies a concept but draws us out to the world of individu-
ally existing men—except that to utter the word "man" is not
to say what one means; on the contrary, it is to utter a fiction,
to substitute a purely verbal entity for a word ("men") which
would more accurately record the facts as they are. Thus the
power of the "veil of words" to body forth meaning is called
into question, and the ground is laid for Bishop Berkeley's
judgment that we need only draw this veil aside to behold
the tree of knowledge.

In other words, in Ockham we find the renewal of an an-
cient skepticism, but more than this we find that, cut loose
from the mind and viewed against a backdrop of a world of
particulars, language itself is particularized, in the sense that
the value of a given word is to be determined on the basis of
whether there exists for it a counterpart in the world of ex-
perience. Prefigured here is the sort of equation between word
and thing that Bishop Sprat was later to epitomize with the
exhortation "to return back to the primitive purity and short-
ness, when men deliver'd so many *things* almost in an equal
number of *words*." [61] Language, that is, is regarded less in the
context of human discourse than in a mathematical context, in
which the focus is not upon an utterance which describes a
mental process but upon discrete, precisely defined lexical
units.

There is a metaphorical equivalent for this attitude toward
language, and it is to be found in the work of François Rabelais
(ca. 1494–1553). For example, it is a hard fact in the world of
Gargantua and Pantagruel, but particularly in the world of
Pantagruel, that verbal communication is an end almost im-
possible to achieve. When Pantagruel first appears, early in
the second book, he encounters the young scholar Limosin,
whose "Latial verbocination" exasperates Pantagruel to the
point of violence.[62] Similarly, Panurge first greets Pantagruel
in a babel of tongues, some authentic, some nonsense; not
until Panurge speaks in French is communication established.
Kissbreech and Suckfist plead their cases unintelligibly before

Pantagruel, and Pantagruel, acting Solomon's part, justly repays them with an unintelligible though otherwise eloquent decision. By contrast, Panurge and the English scholar Thaumast appear to communicate with absurd ease in their wordless disputation, but Panurge's gestures, through which Thaumast, as he says, discovers " 'the very true well, fountain and abyss of the encyclopaedia of Learning' " (I, p. 393), are mostly obscene. Panurge's quest for advice concerning marriage in the *Tiers Livre* follows much the same pattern. The quest proves to be a play upon the ancient theme of the moral education. Panurge consults, among others, a sybil, a poet, an alchemist, a physician, a theologian, and a philosopher—a field of specialists whose function it has traditionally been to preserve and transmit human wisdom. But if such wisdom as Panurge seeks exists, it is cloaked by these wisemen in one or another kind of sophistry. This sophistry reaches a kind of apotheosis in the speech of Judge Bridlegoose, whose impenetrable jargon has nothing to do with the marriage question but is quite of a piece with the basic purpose of the *Tiers Livre,* insofar as it represents the voice of learning in what is perhaps its most intolerable form: " 'I very briefly,' quoth Bridlegoose, 'shall answer you according to the doctrine and instructions of *leg. ampliorem,* § *in refutatoriis C. de appella, which is conformable to what is said in gl. ff. quod. met. caus. Gaudent brevitate moderni' "* (II, p. 569). Words refer here not to a mind thinking but to an obscure text. Indeed, as a fictional character Bridlegoose is consumed by his own pedantry, inasmuch as he is reduced to a set of marginal ciphers against which no illusion of human speech (much less of mind) can survive.

The reduction of speech to a set of ciphers in the Bridlegoose episode is an illustration of one of the chief techniques of Rabelaisian satire; it is, in fact, a device in which Rabelais indulges himself at every turn, so enchanted does he seem to be by its effects. In the *Quart Livre,* for example, Pantagruel and his friends, while at sea, encounter sounds that appear to be without origin. The captain of the ship explains that they

are now " 'on the confines of the Frozen Sea, on which about
the beginning of last winter happened a great and bloody
fight between the Arimaspians and the Nephelibates.' " The
" 'words and cries of the men and women,' " together with the
assorted noises of war, " 'froze in the air; and now, the rigour
of winter being over, by the succeeding serenity and warmth
of the weather, they are melt and heard' " (II, p. 738). Panta-
gruel then throws

> on the deck whole handfuls of frozen words, which seemed to us
> like your rough sugar-plums, of many colours like those used in
> heraldry; some words *gules* (this means also jests and merry say-
> ings), some *vert*, some azure, some black, some *or* (this means also
> fair words); and when we had somewhat warmed them between
> our hands, they melted like snow and we really heard them, but
> could not understand them, for it was a barbarous gibberish.
> [II, p. 738]

The frozen words appear to be the debris left by a scholastic
disputation ("Nephelibates" means, literally, "cloud-dwel-
lers"), but the colors of the words suggest the figures of rhet-
oric. In any case, it is the image itself, apart from its function,
that is worth remarking, because a frozen word is an object,
not a sign. It is a word removed from the world of speech and
which refers to nothing beyond itself until it is returned to
that world through a process of melting. This frozen state is
another way of describing the condition of the written (and
particularly the printed) word, the word reduced to the ex-
tended, purely spatial mode of existence of the phonetic
alphabet. It was by means of the alphabet that man learned
how to fix the spoken word in space by transforming it into a
sequence of objects. To read the written or printed word, of
course, is simply to reverse this process: it is to re-create the
utterance, to return it from space into time. And it is this
re-creation which Pantagruel and his friends dramatize when
they warm the frozen word in their hands.

The episode of the frozen words becomes especially in-
triguing when we consider that the *Cinq Livres* of Rabelais is

a book which exploits the physical availability of words—
which exploits, that is to say, the ability of the printing press
to fix large numbers of words in purely spatial relationships,
so as to achieve a form of discourse (though it can hardly be
called that) that lies beyond the reach of the human voice. It
has been remarked of Rabelais that he had an "orator's ear,"
that his work owes much to the medieval sermon, and that,
although his book reached its audience in printed form, it
nevertheless grew out of a culture the medium of whose
literature was the speaking voice.[63] Unquestionably, the sound
of the speaking voice is one of the most perfectly achieved
illusions in the *Cinq Livres,* and perhaps for this reason it is
the more remarkable that Rabelais should seem so determined
to undermine this illusion by disengaging language from the
world of speech. Thus, for example, in the Prologue to the
Tiers Livre:

> And then again, in a mighty bustle, he bandied it, slubbered it,
> hacked it, whittled it, weighed it, darted it, hurled it, staggered it,
> reeled it, swinged it, brangled it, tottered it, lifted it, heaved it,
> transformed it, transfigured it, transported it, transplaced it, reared
> it, raised it, hoisted it, washed it, dighted it, cleansed it, rinsed it,
> nailed it . . . [I, p. 435]

and so on through some thirty additional items. One way to
describe this passage is to call it a parody of the rhetorical
habit of amplifying discourse, except that in this case dis-
course is amplified not by means of schemes and tropes but
simply by fixing words on the printed page as though they
were so many objects. A question raises itself, however, as to
whether the effect is finally not to amplify but to destroy dis-
course, to silence language by submerging reference and con-
text under the sheer physical presence of words. This annihi-
lation of discourse is clearly evident in the great catalogues. In
the *Tiers Livre* Friar John, who has been instructing Panurge
concerning cuckoldry, inquires:

> and, if so be it was pre-ordinated for thee, wouldst thou be so im-
> pious as not to acquiesce in thy destiny– Speak, thou jaded cod,

Faded c.	Musty c.	Senseless c.
Mouldy c.	Paltry c.	Foundered c.
Distempered c.	Grim c.	Exhausted c.
Bewrayed c.	Wasted c.	Perplexed c.
Inveigled c.	Inflamed c.	Unhelved c.

This list of epithets continues for several pages; it contains over four hundred items. Now it is quite obviously absurd to suppose that it is Friar John who utters each word of the list; Friar John has been effectively silenced—has in fact ceased to exist, even as the narrative itself has ceased to exist, precisely because the list destroys the illusion of someone speaking. The list enjoys its own peculiar existence, even as the words and cries of the Arimaspians and Nephelibates come to enjoy an independent, purely spatial existence when they freeze. The words of the list are, of course, authentic words, in the sense that they will bear definition; in another sense, however, they amount to little more than "barbarous gibberish." For the properly linguistic structure which gives significance to speech has been replaced by the empty space of the printed page, across which the words are geometrically placed like so many isolated stones.

Leo Spitzer has described this reduction of speech to a set of objects as the creation of a middle world between unreality and reality, a world of words the appearance of which is predicated "upon a belief in the reality of words, a belief which would have been condemned by the 'realists' of the Middle Ages. The belief in such vicarious realities as words is possible only in an epoch whose belief in the *universalia realia* has been shaken." [64] Thus William of Ockham begets Rabelais— and, according to Spitzer, not Rabelais only: "It is the belief in the autonomy of the word which made possible the whole movement of Humanism" and which helps to explain "the extraordinary development of mathematics in the sixteenth and seventeenth centuries—i.e., of the most autonomous language that man has ever devised." In Spitzer's view, Rabelais's chief antecedent is the Italian poet Luigi Pulci, in the word lists of whose *Morgante maggiori* (1481) "the Rabelaisian ten-

dency to let language encroach upon reality" makes its first
tentative appearance. In fact, however, the true antecedents
of Rabelais (and, indeed, of "the whole movement of Human-
ism") are to be found among the ancient and medieval gram-
marians, whose business it was to remove language from the
world of speech and to place it in a spatial and visual field
where its multiple forms could be arranged systematically into
a self-contained whole. The language of Donatus, in effect, be-
comes in Rabelais a kind of literary language, one which,
paradoxically, enunciates in concrete and parabolic terms that
skepticism which finds language to be an unwieldy instrument
for the formulation and expression of knowledge. In a sense,
Rabelais's belief in the autonomy of the word is a technical
matter. For the running satire against those forms of human
folly which dress themselves in empty speech is elaborated by
Rabelais into a satire against language itself: the reduction of
speech to a set of discrete particles is a comic maneuver,
diminishing what is commonly assumed to be a thing of rea-
son and spirit to a purely physical order of being. The heap-
ing up of words into a catalogue, freeing language as it does
from the human voice and from contexts of discourse, forces
the words themselves to bear the brunt of Pantagruelian sa-
tire: the word in its autonomy, isolated from what gives it
meaning, quite literally mocks itself.

Pantagruel himself, it is to be noted, announces that he pre-
fers the language of gesture to that of words, on the grounds
that it is "not counterfeit by the intermixture of some adulter-
ate lustre and affections" and is, therefore, less able to deceive
—unlike the speech of the oracles, which "through amphibol-
ogies, equivoques and obscurity of words" (i, p. 496) misleads
even men of wit and learning. Such a sentiment would appear
at first to contradict the Pantagruelist attitude, which is, after
all, built up out of a comic abundance of words. Yet it may
well be that Pantagruelism looks forward to the sanity of
measured speech. When the narrator in the episode of frozen
words suggests that some of the words be preserved, Panta-
gruel objects that " 'tis folly to hoard up what we are never

likely to want, or have always at hand, odd, quaint, merry and fat words of gules never being scarce among all good and jovial Pantagruelists' " (II, p. 739). We may indeed describe the Pantagruelist as the complete grammarian, a philologist of extraordinary scope and ability, to whom no word or phrase or linguistic form is unknown; but he is without question a profound skeptic as well, who treats the ancient *Logos* casually, or even with disdain, unwilling to regard the "veil of words" as sacred. Words are, for him, mere things, easily acquired and easily dismissed.

In short, Rabelais has inflated the traditional conception of language as a substantial medium—has isolated the image of language as an object of parts and extension and has underscored its density by exaggeration into comedy—in order to empty language of anything magical or sublime. His effort, like Ockham's before him, to demystify or demythologize language, constitutes a prelude to Bacon and the tradition of critical empiricism that sought to place language firmly upon the ground of reason and experience and in many cases to free reason and experience from language altogether. For what would become of the ideal of a knowledge grounded upon and verifiable by experience, if man's encounter with the world of things were perpetually interrupted by the intercessions of his speech? Hence the Enlightenment dreams of a Philosophical Language—dreams of the kind Bishop Wilkins sought to actualize by reducing human speech to a set of nonverbal but on that account precisely definable marks.[65] What is most interesting about this critique of language, however, is that its full flowering during the seventeenth and eighteenth centuries coincides with a renewed effort on the part of a number of poets and thinkers to invest language with a new mythological significance. The development of this new mythology of language is the subject of our next chapter.

2

Energeia: The Development of the Romantic Idea of Language

The difficulty with language, wrote John Locke, is that words "interpose themselves so much between our understandings, and the truth, which it would contemplate and apprehend, that like the *medium* through which visible objects pass, their obscurity and disorder does not seldom cast a mist before our eyes, and impose upon our understandings." [1] For Locke, it was enough to know that this difficulty existed and that one could, in the course of one's own thinking or in the examination of someone else's, take the danger of words into account and so avoid as much as possible those controversies that inevitably derive from the confusion of words and things. A more radical solution to the problem of language—a solution that grew out of the development of scientific method—called for the substitution of language by mathematics, on the grounds that, unlike the meaning of a word, the value of the mathematical sign can be measured with a precision that is very nearly absolute. Approximations to this scientific solution took such forms as the speculation concerning the possibility of a Philosophical Language, which is to say the development of a truly philosophical lexicon, one grounded upon an "alphabet of thought," in which the precise meanings of words would be established on the basis of a thorough analysis of the mind and all that issues into it by virtue of experience. [2] One thinks in this connection of more modest programs, such as the composition of dictionaries. Johnson said of his great work that he undertook it because he "found our speech copious without order, and energetick without rules: wherever I turned my view, there was perplexity to be disentangled, and confusion to be regulated; choice was to be made out of boundless variety, without any established principle of selection; adulterations were to be detected, without a settled test of purity; and modes of expression to be rejected or received, without the suffrages of any writers of classical reputation or acknowledged authority." [3] This need to rationalize language is a principal theme in Enlightenment thought, an expression of that magnificent critical intelligence which shook the whole of Western culture in order, paradoxically, to make it stable.

The theme of this chapter, however, is the "poetization" of language, a process that begins in the very heart of the Enlightenment, although one can locate the seeds whence it grew at a much earlier time. We can mark out the oppositions which define this process by comparing two passages, Pope's couplet from the *Essay on Criticism,* which we have already quoted:

> *Words* are like *Leaves;* and where they most abound,
> Much *Fruit* of *Sense* beneath is rarely found

and a portion of one of Coleridge's letters to Godwin:

> Is *thinking* impossible without arbitrary signs? and—how far is the word 'arbitrary' a misnomer? Are not words etc parts and germinations of the Plant? And what is the law of their Growth?— In something of this order I would endeavour to destroy the old antithesis of *Words* and *Things,* elevating, as it were, words into Things, and living Things too.[4]

There are perhaps a number of ways to describe the difference between Pope's *Leaves* and Coleridge's "parts and germinations of the Plant." One point to notice is that Coleridge wants to resurrect the ancient and even primitive conception of a natural relationship between words and things, the word "natural" taking on, in this context, a special significance: namely, that for Coleridge as for Pope the word is imagined to be a "thinglike being," but for Coleridge this "thing" is alive. It exists not by itself in a spatial and visual field but as part of a whole which itself exists temporally in a process of growth, that is, a process of unfolding from within, or expression. A second point is that for Pope words, being objects, tend to conceal the *Fruit* of *Sense;* but Coleridge would say that they are the fruition of sense because they incorporate and articulate meaning even as the "parts and germinations of the Plant" display the fundamental energy that marks the life of the whole.

I come round to the term "energy" by design, partly as a way of avoiding what may seem like an obvious point, that Coleridge's theory of language is organic in character. There is no disputing the importance of the organic analogy in Coleridge's thought or in the history of ideas generally, but so far as the idea of language is concerned—and particularly with respect to the understanding that developed during the eighteenth and early nineteenth centuries concerning the relationship between language and poetry—the concept of energy appears to be of primary significance. The term *energy* (or *energeia*) has a fascinating and important history. From its origins in Aristotle it becomes one of the traditional figures of rhetoric, and refers specifically to vigor or forcefulness of expression. Quintilian defines it as "the virtue of allowing nothing we say to be tame," and he goes on to observe that "such vigor is employed specifically for abuse, and is illustrated by Cassius Servius, who promised to outdo his abuser." [5] By the time of Julius Caesar Scaliger's *Poetices libri septem* (1561), however, *energeia* (used interchangeably with the Latin name *efficacia*) had become one of the four attributes of the poet [6]—a position for which it competed, curiously enough, with *enargeia* (or *evidentia*), or vividness of expression, by virtue of which a subject is said to be transformed into an image or a "speaking picture." For George Puttenham the two terms provided the occasion for a nice but important distinction. Of poetic ornaments, Puttenham tells us, there are "two sortes according to the double vertue and efficacie of figures":

One to satisfie & delight th'eare onely by a goodly outward shew
set vpon the matter with wordes, and speaches smothly and tun-
ably running: another by certaine intendments or sense of such
wordes & speaches inwardly working a stirre to the mynde: that
first qualitie the Greeks called *Enargia*, of this word *argos*, because
it geueth a glorious lustre and light. This latter they called *En-
ergia* of *ergon*, because it wrought with a strong and vertuous op-
eration: and figure breedeth them both, some seruing to giue
glosse onely to a language, some to geue it efficacie by sence.[7]

Puttenham departs here from the traditional interpretation of
enargeia. For him it is but a purely verbal phenomenon, de-
signed to "delight th'eare onely by a goodly outward shew set
vpon the matter with wordes," whereas for Quintilian and
indeed a whole generation of theorists who appealed to the
notion of a "speaking picture" to explain or defend the efficacy
of style, it means a use of language which displays its subject
to the eyes of the mind. But Puttenham's intention is to subor-
dinate *enargeia* to *energeia*, which touches not "th'eare onely"
but "by certaine intendments or sence of such wordes &
speaches inwardly [works] a stirre to the mynde." Indeed,
enargeia merely provides a "glosse" to one's language, whereas,
by contrast, *energeia* gives it "efficacie by sence" or force of
meaning.

Energeia, in other words, is the power by which a speaker's
utterance moves an audience not to delight only but to under-
standing. We shall see in a moment how the term is broadened
to include the function traditionally attributed to *enargeia*,
namely the formation of images. What is interesting, however,
is that within a century and a half after Puttenham *energeia*
is said to be as much a property of language itself as a virtue of
a particular utterance. Thus Richard Stackhouse, in *Reflec-
tions on the Nature and Property of Languages* (1731), ob-
serves that

a Language is . . . truly *Energick*, when the Terms and Expres-
sions of it make the Hearer conceive Things with the same Clear-
ness and Perspecuity, the same Extent and Profoundness, that the
Speaker has in his Mind, insomuch that at the very moment we

hear him speak, we seem to have before us the very same View and
Prospect of things, that he has.[8]

Notice that the rhetorical problem of intelligibility in speech
—that is, the ability of a speaker to communicate with his
audience—is transformed into a problem of language. For
Stackhouse's concern here is not simply with clarity or vivid-
ness of expression but with the power of language itself. This
fact becomes the more telling when we consider that Stack-
house associates this power of language—its *Energick* character
—with complexity of meaning. Energy, he tells us,

> arises from the Composition of Words; because *Simple* and *Primi-
> tive* Words can signify no more than one *Thing*, one single Idea,
> one Thought, and one Action: So that to swell the Signification
> of Words, we make use of such as are long and compound, which
> by their Length and Composition may enlarge our Ideas, and for
> this Reason, *Tongues* that abound with Words of this Kind have
> necessarily most *Force* and *Energy*. [pp. 100–101]

We can hardly miss the superb contrast here between Stack-
house and Bishop Sprat, who enjoined his colleagues in the
Royal Society "to return back to the primitive purity and short-
ness, when men deliver'd so many *things* almost in an equal
number of *words.*" We have here, it may be, something like an
Enlightenment version of the ancient conflict between philos-
ophy and poetry or rhetoric. For if Bishop Sprat stands unalter-
ably opposed to "all amplifications, digressions, and swellings
of style," [9] Stackhouse appears to regard style as a way of re-
leasing the energy present in language—as a way of making
language function more effectively by swelling "the Significa-
tion of Words." Thus, for example, "certain Phrases us'd in a
sprightly and judicious Composition . . . may be compar'd to
the several parts of [a] Machine, which when asunder have
no Force, but when conjoyn'd, can raise up the greatest
Weight" (p. 101). Just so, the conception of language as a sub-
stantial medium, a "thinglike being," is here significantly mod-
ified by the concept of energy. For the machine which Stack-
house has in mind is not simply an assemblage of parts; it is an

active agent: it possesses a functional rather than a strictly substantial unity, because it is principally in its operation that its unity and efficacy are revealed. The point is that the concept of energy, as it is applied to language, focuses upon what language does rather than upon what it is or upon how it is composed; it serves to define language in terms of its activity as a whole rather than in terms of the value of its constitutive elements.[10]

But what is worth remarking is Stackhouse's association of style and energy, which is to say the idea that, besides "long and compound" words, *"Figurative* Terms and ways of Expression are another Cause of this *Energy"* (p. 101). Stackhouse here anticipates the tradition which places poetry among the so-called energetic arts. In James Harris's *Three Treatises* (1744), for example, we are advised to

> call every *Production,* the *Parts of which exist successively,* and *whose Nature hath its Being or Essence in a Transition,* call it, what it really is, a *Motion* or an *Energy*—Thus a Tune and a Dance are Energies; thus Riding and Sailing are Energies; and so is Eloquence, and so is Life itself. On the contrary, call every *Production,* whose *Parts exist all at once,* and those *Nature depends not on a Transition for its Essence,* call it a *Work,* or *Thing Done,* not an *Energy* or Operation. Thus a House is a Work, a Statue is a Work, and so is a Ship, and so a Picture.[11]

It is this distinction between the arts of motion and those of space that forms the central theme of Lessing's *Laocoön* (1766), which is, among other things, a broad attack upon the concept of *enargeia* (upon which, as we have seen, the metaphor of the "speaking picture" is based), on the grounds that poetry is by nature opposed to painting, because poetry is an art of language, and language is a temporal rather than spatial and visual phenomenon, an action rather than a thing.[12] For language is not the language of the grammarians nor even of the logicians, but is to be identified with the act of speech itself: to use Saussure's distinction, it is to be understood not simply as *langue* (or *langage*) but as *parole.* Cassirer tells us that already in Giambattista Vico's *Principi di scienza nuova* (1725) "language was considered in terms of the dynamics of speech, which in turn was related to the dynamics of feeling and emotion." [13] Thus Vico writes that language at first "began to develop by way of onomatopoeia," but that for the most part words have been formed "from interjections, which are sounds articulated under the impetus of violent passions." [14] According to Vico, this original language was "natural," in the sense that it was neither a gift of God nor a consciously constructed system but arose spontaneously, even as authentic emotion arises spontaneously, from the human interior. What is more, this original language was poetic in character, which means that it was governed by what Vico calls "poetic logic," that figurative activity of mind that, "under the impulse of the most violent passions," seeks release in song (p. 151). For the minds of those first men "were not in the least abstract, refined, or spiritualized, because they were entirely immersed in the senses, buffeted by the passions, buried in the body" (p. 118)—and hence were able to think imaginatively only and not rationally.

Thus poetry comes to be understood as energetic speech; and, what is more, the concept of *enargeia,* understood as a speaking in images, is displaced (or perhaps subsumed) by the concept of *energeia,* insofar as passionate or energetic speech is said to be naturally figurative or imaginative. It is noteworthy, too, that energy should be set so clearly over and against reason—an opposition that becomes one of the premier commonplaces in a good many eighteenth- and early nineteenth-century discussions of language. We have already quoted Johnson's complaint that the English language as he found it was "energetick without rules," but more to the point would be Rousseau's remark in the "Essay on the Origin of Languages" (ca. 1749–1755) that the earliest known languages, the Oriental, "are not at all *systematic and rational. They are vital and figurative.* The language of the first men is represented to us as the tongues of geometers, but we see that they were the tongues of poets." [15] More telling still is a passage from Herder's "Essay on the Origin of Language" (1772):

> And even with us, where reason to be sure often displaces emotion, where the sounds of nature are dispossessed by the *artificial language of society*—do not with us the highest thunders of rhetoric, the mightiest bolts of poetry, and the magic moments of action [that is, drama], come close to the *language of nature* by imitating it? [16]

We should not overlook the imagery here of the electrical storm, nor ignore what it suggests concerning Herder's conception of poetic speech. It is well to remember, in this connection, that Herder was among the first to invest the organic analogy with the great significance it was to have for writers from Goethe and Kant to our own day. As applied to language, however, the organic analogy seems largely to codify and amplify an already established way of thinking about language. For during the eighteenth century the concepts of energy and vitality were already at work as part of a general redefinition of language—a redefinition that constitutes finally the emergence of an identifiably "romantic" view of language.

Thus, for example, in Wordsworth's 1800 Preface to the *Lyrical Ballads*, Vico's primitives ("who, without power of ratiocination, were all robust sense and vigorous imagination" [*Principi*, p. 116]) are modified into men of "humble and rustic life," whose speech is said to be "real" and "natural" as against "artificial" and "civilized." [17] What is significant about Wordsworth's Preface, however, is that in it the concept of language as energy becomes the ground for a rejection of the ancient concept of literary language—that is, language defined, as in Peacham's *Garden of Eloquence*, as a "tournying from the common manner and custom of wryting and speaking." Another way to put this would be to observe that what Wordsworth rejects is the old rhetorical concept of style, with its implication that language is a substantial medium, an object to be shaped according to an established system of stylistic forms and models. Style for Wordsworth is not something into which language deviates; it is, on the contrary, something that is (or should be) natural to speech, and particularly to impassioned speech. Accordingly, we are told that if the Poet's subject be judiciously chosen, it will naturally, and upon fit occasion, lead him to passions the language of which, if selected truly and judiciously, must necessarily be dignified and variegated, and alive with metaphors and figures. I forbear to speak of an incongruity which would shock the intelligent Reader, should the Poet interweave any foreign splendour of his own with that which the passion naturally suggests: it is sufficient to say that such addition is unnecessary. And, surely, it is more probable that those passages, which with propriety abound with metaphors and figures, will have their due effect, if, upon other occasions where the passions are of a milder character, the style also be subdued and temperate. [p. 22]

We have here something like a Viconian principle of decorum: passion, born naturally of a given subject, naturally (though evidently not automatically) begets its appropriate expression, one which "must necessarily be dignified and variegated, and alive with metaphors and figures." This decorum is grounded upon a unity of process—that is, upon a process of expression, which is conceived to be a continuous movement that possesses its own internal law of development, against which any external or "foreign splendour" can only seem incongruous. The poet, by such a process, reproduces what Wordsworth, in the 1802 Appendix to the Preface, calls "the original figurative language of passion" (p. 42). He does this by taking recourse not to "a family language which Writers in metre seem to lay claim to by prescription" (p. 18)—not, that is, to a history of literary texts—but to the world of actual speech, in which this "original figurative language of passion" has been maintained from those earliest days, when men "wrote naturally, and as men," and not as professional poets (p. 41).

This unity of process implies a unity of word and meaning. Indeed, Wordsworth neutralizes the old problem of how words can be signs for things by thinking of language not as a system of conventional words but as a functional activity that gives form and objectivity to an interior phenomenon, whether it be thought or feeling—or both, as in the case of the poet, that man of "more than organic sensibility," whose "overflow of powerful feelings" issues in a poem of value precisely because he did not merely feel but "also thought long and deeply" (p. 15). For Wordsworth, language is natural rather than conventional, in the sense that it belongs less to the human community than to the human interior, where it abides, together with thought and feeling, as a power of the human spirit. It is on this account that Wordsworth inveighs against

> The dangerous craft of culling term and phrase
> From languages that want the living voice
> To carry meaning to the natural heart;
> To tell us what is passion, what is truth,
> What is reason, what simplicity and sense.[18]

Language, that is to say, is not to be dissociated from the dynamics of speech, for to do so is to dissociate word and man —to isolate the word from that human reality whose life is revealed in the immediacy of thought and feeling.

It is interesting to know that when Wordsworth does, on one occasion, think of language apart from the activity of speech, he nevertheless continues to apply the concepts of force, activity, and spirit:

> Words are too awful an instrument for good and evil, to be trifled with; they hold above all other external powers a dominion over our thoughts. If words be not . . . an incarnation of thought, but only a clothing for it, then surely will they prove an ill gift; such a one as those possessed vestments, read of in the stories of superstitious times, which had power to consume and to alienate from his right mind the victim who put them on. Language, if it do not uphold, and feed, and leave in quiet, like the power of gravitation or the air we breathe, is a counter-spirit, unremittingly and noiselessly at work, to subvert, to lay waste, to vitiate, and to dissolve. [pp. 129–130]

The idea that words incarnate or embody thought is an ancient one, and Wordsworth employs it here to assert the virtual unity of word and meaning. As P. W. K. Stone has noted in this connection, "To the idea that language is the *incarnation* of thought, the idea that words are *constituents* of thought is a natural corollary" [19]—meaning that words and their "contents" are reciprocal and cannot function or even exist independently of one another. But Wordsworth goes beyond this traditional way of conceiving language and insists upon its *unsubstantial* nature, its discreet and invisible character. The analogy which Wordsworth establishes between language and the power of gravity makes of language something more than a coordinate of thought: it becomes a force for unity and order—a force which holds things together and so provides a virtual ground for our existence. Or, similarly, "like the air we breathe," it functions as a sustaining environment. The relationship of language to reality is thus not simply a relationship of objects—not an assemblage of connections between words and things that experience is required to validate. Language is rather a way of gaining and holding the world encountered in experience. By its mediation the world does not stand over and against man as a mere object; it becomes rather the theme of human expression—expression of a kind that gives to the world the stabilizing character of intelligibility.

Similarly may we find in Coleridge a traditional way of thinking about language: "Words are things," we are told in one of the *Philosophical Lectures.* "They are the great mighty instruments by which thoughts are excited and by which alone they can be [expressed] in a rememberable form." [20] Yet what characterize Coleridge's diffuse and periodic inquiries into the subject of language are the concepts of force and energy. In a notebook entry from February 1805, for example, Coleridge writes: "Reason, Proportion, communicable intelligibility intelligent and communicant, the Word—which last expression strikes me as the profoundest and most comprehensive Energy of the human Mind, if indeed it be not in some distinct sense *energma Theoparadoton*"—that is, God-given energy.[21] As with human imagination, human language is but a repetition in the finite mind of that "divine energy" which, in this same notebook entry, Coleridge identifies as the *Logos:* "The moment we conceive the divine energy," he says, "that moment we co-conceive the Logos." One point to make here is that, in contrast to Herder, Coleridge places the concept of language as energy against a supernatural rather than natural background: human language is born of the language of God, not the language of nature, the Johannine, not the Heraclitean Word.

In one of the Shakespeare Lectures, however, Coleridge remarks upon the opposition between human language and the languages of God and Nature. For human language, Coleridge says, is composed of arbitrary signs: "The sound *sun,* or the figures *s, u, n,* are purely arbitrary modes of recalling the object. . . . But the language of nature is a subordinate *Logos,* that was in the beginning, and was with the thing represented, and was the thing represented." [22] Here the Johannine Word is echoed in that original and perhaps magical word which, as a matter of nature, was identical with the world. In a moment we shall inquire further into this primitive or original language of nature; but what we should notice first is that, in Coleridge's view, the language of poetry aspires to this primitive condition in which word and world are one:

> Now the language of Shakespeare, in his *Lear* for instance, is a something intermediate between these two [human language and the language of nature]; or rather it is the former blended with the latter, —the arbitrary, not merely recalling the cold notion of the thing, but expressing the reality of it, and, as arbitrary language is the heirloom of the human race, being itself a part of that which it manifests. [p. 47]

Poetry, that is to say, is a way of destroying "the old antithesis of *Words* and *Things*" that characterizes ordinary human speech; it is a way of "elevating . . . words into Things." Students of Coleridge will recognize in the passage above the formula which Coleridge uses to describe the nature and function of the symbol, which is always "a part of that which it manifests." Just so, what distinguishes the language of

Shakespeare from ordinary speech is that it is rather more symbolic than arbitrary—more symbol than sign—and accordingly it works to induce that original, primitive condition of mind in which word and world appear to constitute a luminous and undifferentiated whole.

Precisely how the word is able to induce in the mind this primitive sense of unity with the world is a subject to which Coleridge devoted himself at least once:

> I do not know whether you are opticians enough to understand me when I speak of a Focus formed by converging rays of Light and Warmth in the *Air*. Enough that it is so—that the Focus exercises a power altogether different from that of the rays not converged—and to our sight and feeling acts precisely as if a solid flesh and blood reality were there. Now exactly such focal entities we are all more or less in the habit of creating for ourselves in the world of Thought. For the given point in the Air take any given *word*, fancy-image, or remembered emotion. Thought after Thought, Feeling after Feeling, and at length the sensations of Touch, and the blind Integer of the numberless numbers of the Infinitesimals that make up our sense of existing, converge in it— and there ensues a working on our mind so utterly unlike what any one of the confluents, separately considered, would produce, and no less disparate from what any mere Generalization of them all, would present to us, that I do not wonder at the unsatisfactoriness of every attempt to undeceive the person by analysis, however clear. The focal word has acquired a *feeling of reality*—it heats and burns, makes itself to be felt. If we do not grasp it, it seems to grasp us, as with a hand of flesh and blood, and completely counterfeits an immediate presence, an intuitive knowledge. And who can reason against intuition? [23]

Here the conception of the word as a locus of power is built up by an analogy with natural energy, that is, the focal point at which "rays of Light or Warmth" converge, as in the familiar experiment with the magnifying lens. Coleridge asks us to regard the word as a point at which the several elements that "make up our sense of existing" are drawn together. When this happens, Coleridge says, the "focal word" takes on *"a feeling of reality"*—a feeling so strong as to be impervious to reason or analysis. More than this, however, the word "heats and burns, makes itself to be felt. If we do not grasp it, it seems to grasp us, as with a hand of flesh and blood." This grasping, in Coleridge's view, is an act or moment of "intuitive knowledge," in which "reality" is encountered *mediately*, but with all the force and energy of an "immediate presence." Coleridge may have in mind here a Kantian moment, in which the mind synthesizes a world for itself out of the flow of undifferentiated sensation; or he may be thinking of a kind of epiphany, a moment of moments, in which reality of a very special kind is encountered. Whatever the case, the function of the word is clear: it is to mediate between mind and world, not simply to correlate the one to the other but to fabricate an *immediate* relationship between the two. It does so, moreover, by appearing to become the reality: the word is elevated into the thing, "a solid flesh and blood reality."

Indeed, the word becomes more *presence* than thing, and so takes on something like the power of an Ancient Mariner: "If we do not grasp it, it seems to grasp us, as with a hand of flesh and blood." The word in this sense is not merely alive; it is *personalized*—transposed by the image of "flesh and blood" from its isolation as a single "focal entity" to the world of the living person, where it exists not as an object but as an utterance. We may, in this connection, look to what Kathleen Coburn has called Coleridge's complaint against "the atomic use of language," in which words are treated as so many discrete and isolatable particles.[24] Coleridge once announced, by way of apology for his own prose style, his "aversion to the epigrammatic unconnected periods of the fashionable *Anglo-gallican* taste" and his preference for "the stately march and difficult evolutions, which characterize the eloquence of Hooker, Bacon, Milton, and Jeremy Taylor." [25] It is, he goes on to make clear, a preference for the orator over the essayist, the speaker over the writer. For, indeed, quite as much as Wordsworth, Coleridge is disinclined to dissociate the word from the act of speech.

Nor is he inclined to dissociate language from time and

history, for one of his chief preoccupations is with the idea of speech in its relation to the historical progress of a given language. In "An Outline of the History of Logic" (1799–1803), for example, Coleridge proposes that

> general talkativeness will mould the common language and give it strength, harmony, flexibility and copiousness even to the expression of the finest shades of meaning. Such a language may easily be made an instrument of deceit as well as of truth to a degree of which those languages must be unsusceptible in which, as in the Oriental, the forms of connexion are few and simple and express merely annexment and disjunction, not the niceties of cause and consequence, division and exception. You cannot fail to see how great an influence this must have on philosophy in general.[26]

By "general talkativeness" Coleridge means the act of speech considered as a cultural and historical activity—a collective act which, evidently as a matter of nature, moves toward greater precision of discourse and so becomes a formative process by which a language fit for philosophical thought is developed. In the *Philosophical Lectures* Coleridge calls this process "desynonymizing," according to which a language gradually constructs a universe of signification by building up distinctions among words "originally equivalent" in meaning. This concept implies an original Word, a primitive and undifferentiated totality of all possible utterances within which differences are historically and yet systematically established. From the standpoint of our own day this confluence of history and system is perhaps anomalous, but it is distinctively Coleridgean. It is clear, for example, that long before Saussure Coleridge was thinking of meaning not simply in terms of the classical theory of correspondence but diacritically in terms of the paradigmatic relations among words within a self-contained system. Thus he conceives the formation of the sign as a "breaking-off" of one word from another, and not as a "naming" that locks the word onto a referent. A sentence from Claude Lévi-Strauss provides an approximate gloss for what Coleridge had in mind: "The meaning of a word depends on the way in which each language breaks up the realm of meaning to which the word belongs; and it is a function of the presence or absence of other words denoting related meanings." [27] But Coleridge's "structuralism" is charged with energy: for him this "breaking-up" of the realm of meaning belongs to the diachronic order of events, and not to the modern structuralist's world of purely formal or worldless systems.

Coleridge knew that he had in this concept of "desynonymizing" a firm way of distinguishing between poetic and philosophic language. It is "the business of the philosopher," Coleridge says in the *Philosophical Lectures,* "to desynonymize words originally equivalent, therein following and impelling the natural progress of language in civilized societies" (p. 152). The philosopher in this case is clearly a romantic variation of Royal Society Man—one driven by what Coleridge once called "the instinctive passion in the mind for a *one word* to express a *one act* of feeling." [28] French—the French of Descartes, the Port Royalists, and the encyclopedists—is for Coleridge the prime example of a "desynonymized" language, whose words have begun to assume the quality of mathematical univocity. But French is, on this account, "wholly unfit for Poetry," which is rather the province of those "elder Languages [that] expressed only prominent ideas clearly, others but darkly"— languages, that is to say, which seemed to incorporate nature as she is in herself, in all her profusion of undifferentiated detail. In such a case, Coleridge explains, "the Mind in its simplicity gives itself up to a Poem as to a work of nature." [29] The nearest modern equivalent to an elder language, in Coleridge's view, is German, which in contrast to French and English is rather more synthetic than analytic in character. Thus Coleridge speaks, in connection with the German poet Klopstock, "of this superior power in the German of condensing meaning." It is this power which makes German a "more picturesque" language, one that "*depictures* images better." Prefixes in English, although they may convey "no separate or separable meaning to the mere English Reader, cannot possibly act on the mind with the force or liveliness of an original and homogeneous language, such as the German is." [30]

We thus come round once more to the central theme of Coleridge's discussions of language. In German the word is not simply a unit of meaning; it is, if anything, a unity of many meanings, but more importantly it is a unit of energy that acts with "force or liveliness" upon the mind. This energetic character marks German as an essentially poetic language, or at least one that has not progressed so far as more philosophical or analytical tongues from that original unity with the world that distinguishes man's primitive from his more rational state. It is this progress of language that makes philosophy possible, for philosophy seeks to give us a *mediated* experience of the world, in which the world appears to us in all its clarity and distinctness as an idea. But poetry seeks to return us to our mythic origins, in which the world is present in the word, not as an idea but as a reality—a reality because the word, being "energetic," acts upon us as though it were not a word at all but a thing, "and a living Thing too." It is at this point that Coleridge's discussions of language come nearest to the condition of a coherent theory. For it seems to have been Coleridge's impulse to regard poetry and philosophy as complementary rather than simply antithetical activities of discourse: philosophy reduces to order and intelligibility a reality which poetry tries to comprehend in the fulness of feeling. The two suggest in this sense a dialectic of departure and return, of analysis and synthesis, of thought and feeling, of reason and imagination—doubtless one could extend this list of opposites. Perhaps one can see in this dialectic, as in other collocations of Coleridge's prose, the outline of a system that was never brought to birth.

Let us cull from this unborn system the notion of an "original and homogeneous language," one in which all words converge toward the possibility of a single universal Word that subsumes all meanings. It is, clearly, a mythic notion. It is the more interesting, however, when we move it within the context of Shelley's several remarks on language. For if Coleridge conceived the "natural progress of language" to consist in a process of desynonymizing, according to which one Word becomes many and a single universal meaning becomes a multiplicity of particular significations, Shelley would reverse this process, thus to work toward the recovery of that primal utterance by which the unity of all things, the One, could be articulated. As it happens, Shelley is quite in concert with Coleridge on this matter, since for Coleridge the language of the poet is distinguished by its resemblance to that original language of nature—a language which mysteriously disallows distinctions between word and thing, subject and object, and so on.

Shelley is, among the chief romantic poets in England, the preeminent skeptic, but so far as language is concerned he appears to reverse the terms of typical Enlightenment skepticism. The problem is not, in his view, that language is incommensurate with the world of ordinary, sensible experience; the problem is rather that it is commensurate with nothing else, that by the very nature of its structure and the function of its parts it falsifies not the phenomenal world of things and activities, persons and places, temporal and spatial relations, but the transcendent world of the One. "How vain it is," Shelley writes in the "Essay on Life" (1812–1814), "to think that words can penetrate the mystery of our being!" [31] Thus, for example,

> the existence of distinct individual minds [is] . . . a delusion. The words *I, you, they* are not signs of any actual difference subsisting between the assemblage of thoughts thus indicated, but are merely marks employed to denote the different modifications of one mind.
>
> Let it not be supposed that this doctrine conducts to the monstrous presumption that I, the person who now write and think, am that one mind. I am but a portion of it. The words *I* and *you* and *they* are grammatical devices invented simply for arrangement, and totally devoid of the intense and exclusive sense actually attached to them. [p. 174]

The problem of language, in other words, is that it implies distinctions where none, in fact, exist; the problem is that the terms by which language is constituted are not sufficiently synonymous. For, given a "view of life" characterized by unity, language which as a matter of course breaks life down into diverse grammatical categories (subject and object, person and number) can only be of marginal value.

And so we should all be doomed to a life of error and delusion, were it not for the poet. For in contrast to ordinary language, which analyzes experience into grammatical parts, the language of poetry is synthetic, in the sense that, as we are told in the *Defence*, it

> is vitally metaphorical; that is, it marks the before unapprehended relations of things and perpetuates their apprehension, until the words which represent them, become, through time, signs for portions or classes of thoughts instead of pictures of integral thoughts; and then if no new poets should arise to create afresh the associations which have been thus disorganized, language will be dead to all the nobler purposes of human intercourse. [p. 278]

We can pass over the evident commonplace that languages die and need to be revitalized, in order to observe that the language of poetry constitutes for Shelley a way of seeing unity in diversity—that is, a way of gaining and holding in perception "the before unapprehended relations of things." Poetry thus aims at an original primitive habit of mind ("the copiousness of lexicography and the distinctions of grammar are the works of a later age" [p. 279]). Whereas we have grown accustomed to see the world grammatically, as a field of *disjecta membra*, poetry will enable us to see metaphorically and thus to sense, in the vast relatedness of things, the presence of the One. For "to be a poet is to apprehend [not merely relationships, but] the true and the beautiful, in a word, the good which exists in the relation subsisting, first between existence and perception and secondly between perception and expression" (p. 279). In this trinity of existence, perception, and expression the *Logos* of Shelley is to be found. Such a *Logos* provides the ground for a transcendental point of view, according to which all things may be observed to disappear in the luminescence of the whole.

We can amplify this discussion of Shelley's idea of the *Logos* in the following way: It is clear that there is a radical separation between the *Logos,* conceived as a transcendental synthesis of being, percept, and word, and ordinary language, which Shelley conceives to be grammatical or analytical. We see how Shelley understands this separation in Act I of *Prometheus Unbound,* when Prometheus asks Earth to speak once more his curse of Jupiter:

> Speak, Spirit! from thine inorganic voice
> I only know that thou art moving near
> And love. How cursed I him?
>   *The Earth.*   How canst thou hear
> Who knowest not the language of the dead?
>   *Prometheus.* Thou art a living spirit; speak as they.
>   *The Earth.* I dare not speak like life, lest Heaven's
>   fell King
> Should hear, and link me to some wheel of pain
> More torturing than the one whereon I roll.
> Subtle thou art and good, and tho' the Gods
> Hear not this voice, yet thou art more than God,
> Being wise and kind: earnestly hearken now.
>   *Prometheus.* Obscurely thro' my brain, like shadows
>   dim,
> Sweep awful thoughts, rapid and thick, I feel
> Faint, like one mingled in entwining love;
> Yet 'tis not pleasure.
>   *The Earth.*   No, thou canst not hear:
> Thou art immortal, and this tongue is known
> Only to those who die.[32]

The opposition here is between the language of the One, or Prometheus—a language shared by the gods and by all "living spirits"—and the language of men, which in this case is "the language of the dead," or of "the inarticulate people of the dead" (I, 183). It is the part of Shelley's theme, of course, that it is not in the destiny of mankind to speak this "inorganic" language. Indeed, part of the liberation that Prometheus will effect will be precisely the liberation of man from ordinary

speech. In Act ii, for example, we learn that upon the estab-
lishment of the new dispensation Prometheus and Ione will

> like lutes
> touched by the skill of the enamoured wind,
> Weave harmonies divine, yet ever new,
> From differences sweet where discourse cannot be. . . .
>
> [iii, iii, 36–39]

These "harmonies divine," Prometheus goes on to say, will
evoke by way of response "The echoes of the human world,
which tell / Of the low voice of love" (iii, iii, 44–45); and they
will evoke, too, those "lovely apparitions,"

> the progeny immortal
> Of Painting, Sculpture, and rapt Poesy,
> And arts, though unimagined, yet to be
>
> [iii, iii, 54–56]

This dialogue between gods and men contrasts sharply with
the opposition in Act i between the languages of the living
and the dead. What this dialogue implies, of course, is a trans-
formation of human language into something approximating
the language of the gods. And this transformation is precisely
what is celebrated in Act iv. So far as the New Man is con-
cerned, Earth tells us, language is no longer "inorganic" or
dead; on the contrary,

> Language is a perpetual Orphic song,
> Which rules with Daedal harmony a throng
> Of thoughts and forms, which else senseless and
> shapeless were.
>
> [iv, 415–417]

The language of the New Man is the language of the god,
Orpheus; it is poetry. What is to be marked, however, is that
this language harmonizes the once inchoate "thoughts and
forms" of the human world, which means that its function
is synthetic rather than analytic, and so it approximates, even
shares in, the transcendental synthesis of the *Logos*. As Shelley
puts it in the *Defence*, "A poet participates in the eternal, the

infinite, and the one; as far as relates to his conceptions, time and place and number are not. The grammatical forms which express the moods of time, and the difference of persons, and the distinctions of place, are convertible with respect to the highest poetry without injuring it as poetry" (p. 279). The poet is, in this sense, a mediator between the many and the One; or, better, he is the mediator between ordinary speech and the *Logos* of the gods.

Indeed, the idea of the synthetic function of language involves necessarily the activity of mediation. Just this point is made repeatedly by Wilhelm von Humbolt (1767–1835), to whose philosophy of language we can now turn. It is worthwhile to have Shelley in mind as we read the following, from *Ankündigung einer Schrift über die vaskische Sprache und Nation nebst Angabe des Gesichtspunktes und Inhalts derselben* (1812):

> Language everywhere mediates, first between infinite and finite nature, then between one individual and another. Simultaneously and through the same act it makes union possible and itself originates from it. . . . It is something which is given by the idea of union, of the reconciliation of what for us and our way of thinking must always be opposites, and it is a something which is given only in this connection.[33]

This union of opposites, moreover, is not simply a grammatical connection—not simply a union of predication; on the contrary, it is, in the most primitive sense, natural:

> One must free oneself of the notions that language can be separated from that which it designates, as, for example, the name of a person from the person, and that it is a product of reflection and agreement, an agreed-upon code, as it were, or in fact that it is any work of man at all (in the common sense in which one takes that phrase), not to mention the work of some individual. A true, inexplicable miracle, it breaks loose from the mouth of a nation, and—no less marvellous, though seen by us every day with indifference—it breaks through the gurgle of any baby. It is the brightest trace and the surest proof of the fact (leaving out for a moment the celestial relatives of mankind) that

man does not possess an absolute, segregated individuality, that 'I' and 'Thou' are not merely interrelated but—if one could go back to the point of their separation—truly identical concepts, and that there exist, therefore, only concentric circles of individuality, beginning with the weak, frail single person who is in need of support and widening out to the primordial trunk of humanity itself. [p. 236]

One could argue that in this passage the whole "romantic" idea of language is contained. At least we are confronted with a collocation of familiar themes: the idea of language as an activity which reconciles opposites; the idea of the identity of word and thing; and (hardly to be missed) the Shelleyan notion that "man does not possess an absolute, segregated individuality, that 'I' and 'Thou' are not merely interrelated but [in a distinctly primordial way] truly identical concepts." Between Shelley and Humboldt there is, of course, this difference, that for Humboldt there is no transcendental *Logos,* no language of the gods, to be set over and against human speech, nor is there any transcendental unity of all men in the One, but rather a cultural unity grounded upon the fundamental mediative activity of language.

Humboldt's masterwork in the philosophy of language is the general introduction to his study of the Kwai language, *Über die Verschiedenheit des menschlichen Sprachbaues und ihren Einfluss auf die geistige Entwicklung des Menschengeschlechts* (1830–1835). Central to this work is Humboldt's insistence upon the definition of language in terms of the dynamics of speech:

Language, taken as real, is something which constantly and in every moment passes away. Even its preservation in writing is only an incomplete mummified depository which needs, for full understanding, an imaginative oral reconstitution. Language is not a work (*ergon*) but an activity (*energeia*). Its true definition can therefore only be a genetic one. For it is the ever-repetitive work of the spirit to make articulated sound capable of expressing thought. Taken directly and strictly, this is the definition of each act of speaking, but in a true and intrinsic sense one can look upon language as but the totality of all spoken utterance. [p. 280]

This conception of the identity of language and speech is predicated, as it was in Vico and Wordsworth, upon a greater identity between language and the human interior. We should notice that, no sooner does Humboldt formulate his distinction between *ergon* and *energeia,* than, curiously, he goes on to describe language as "the ever-repetitive work of the spirit." He explains, however, that "to designate languages as works of the spirit is completely correct and adequate expression, if only because the existence of the spirit can only be imagined in the form of activity" (pp. 280–281). Language is not an artifact of the spirit but the very form in which the life of the spirit is realized. Indeed, Humboldt makes it clear that without language there would be no life of the spirit, for language does not simply articulate the already formed contents of man's interior; on the contrary, it is the activity by which man's inner life takes on form and meaning.

And not man's inner life only but his very world as well. Humboldt places language squarely in the wake of Kant's "Copernican Revolution," according to which knowledge is no longer understood as a relationship between an internal image or idea and an external object; rather, the flow of undifferentiated sensation that constitutes immediate experience is said to be reconstituted by the mediation of imagination and understanding as a world of objects and events, qualities and relations, and so on. Humboldt offers a somewhat simplified version of this process:

> In thinking, a subjective activity forms itself an object. For no type of imaginative representation may be considered a merely receptive apperception of an already existent object. The activity of the senses must be synthetically joined with the inner action of the spirit. From their connection the imaginative representation tears itself loose, becomes objective in relation to subjective energy, and then returns to it, having first been perceived in its new, objective form. [p. 289]

Thinking, in this sense, is "a yearning from darkness to see the light." For what is subjective and hidden is literally brought out into the open, made "objective in relation to subjective energy," which means that it becomes at last an object for knowledge. What is important to understand, however, is that in Humboldt's view "language is indispensable" to this process. "Just as no concept is possible without language," he writes, "so no object is possible without it, since even external ones receive their intrinsic substance only through language" (p. 293). Language, that is to say, is an expressive movement which carries the ingredients of human experience into the open and establishes them there as a world of objects.

What this means, of course, is that man's world is fundamentally linguistic in character. "Man surrounds himself by a world of sounds in order to take into himself the world of objects and operate on them," Humboldt says. "Man lives with his objects mainly, in fact exclusively . . . as language turns them over to him. The same act which enables him to spin language out of himself enables him to spin himself into language, and each language draws a circle around the people to whom it adheres which it is possible for the individual to escape only by stepping into a different one" (p. 294). This is to say, for example, that the world of objects actualized for man by the activity of language cannot be objects in the strict empiricist sense of assemblies of sensible phenomena. They are rather objects which seem to come into being in an already interpreted form: they are intelligible objects, possessed of identities assumed in the very process of expression by which they were brought out into the open. The natural world is thus not set over and against man as some distant and alien universe; rather, by means of language it is integrated into the human community. The world becomes in this way preeminently a world for man, which is to say that it takes on reality for him as part of his cultural existence: it is not a world of objects only, but a world of meanings.

In a sense, of course, Locke's problem yet remains: words interpose themselves between man and the world—except that in Humboldt's view they are no longer "the medium through which visible objects pass" but rather the medium by means of which objects are made visible. Doubtless a staunch empiricist must remain unsatisfied by such a formulation, for what Humboldt's theory of language gives up once for all is the possibility of experiencing the pure immediacy of the world—the world untouched by the activity of the human spirit. Nature gives way to culture, for what the activity of man renders visible is in part his own inner world, the universe of signification. Precisely for this reason, however, Humboldt's theory of language becomes of great value for the poet—who, as we shall see in chapter 8, lays claim to such a view of language as a way of defining the nature of poetry and indeed as a way of restoring the poet to his role as the primordial speaker, whose power of language undergirds the world, thus to provide man with a dwelling-place.

PART TWO

Literature as a Problematics of Language

3

From Intransitive Speech to the Universe of Discourse: The Formalist Theory of Literary Language

We saw in the first chapter that in Henry Peacham's stylistic manual *The Garden of Eloquence,* figurative speech is understood to be a "tournying from the common manner and custom of wryting and speaking." Similarly, for George Puttenham, the figures of rhetoric are "in sorte abuses or rather trespasses in speach, because they pass the ordinary limits of common vtterance." [1] This notion of "tournying from the common manner and custom of wryting and speaking," or of passing "the ordinary limits of common vtterance," forms the basis for what might be called the traditional rhetorical conception of literary language. The literary or stylistic use of language, that is to say, is defined as a "deviant utterance," according to which the language of everyday speech no longer functions for the poet or orator simply as a medium for discourse, but constitutes rather a point of departure for the creation of literary art. This means that the very motivation for the act of speech lies to some extent in language itself: language has its own value, quite apart from its function, which is to say its transitive purpose. To be sure, poet and orator remain committed to the act of speech understood as a transitive act, that is, as a form of signification, and even more importantly as a medium

71

for communication, but their commitment is inclined to be tempered by style, which transforms language in a way that gives the act of speech an intransitive character.

One must take care, however, not to speak so simply and definitely about the traditional rhetorical idea of literary language—and this is so for a number of reasons. For one thing, traditional rhetoricians were less ready to distinguish sharply between ordinary and literary discourse than to catalogue and describe the different kinds of style by which the texture of ordinary speech might be transformed. What is more, distinctions between ordinary and literary uses of language were often drawn upon grounds that were not simply linguistic or stylistic but moral as well. Puttenham, for example, is compelled to describe figurative speech in terms of its "power to deceiue the ear and also the minde," thus to imply that such speech must of necessity be immoral and can be redeemed only by being subordinated to some higher end. This means that the figures of rhetoric may be utilized within a discourse whose character is essentially transitive—a discourse, that is to say, which is directed toward an end beyond itself. From such a point of view, epideictic or display oratory constitutes an egregious form of utterance. We have already seen that such distinction as Puttenham draws between figurative speech and the common utterance serves mainly as a way of articulating a mimetic theory of language. The common utterance maintains, if only approximately, an ideal union of word and thing; figurative speech, by contrast, amplifies the distance between word and thing, drawing as it does so the mind away from reality into a merely verbal universe. Puttenham's conception of literary language is, in this sense, predicated less upon a distinction between the literary and the ordinary than upon their fundamental unity: the speech of the poet or orator, in other words, must conform to the standards or limits which govern the common utterance.

There is, however, a more important theme that runs through traditional discussions of literary language. What Puttenham finally opposes, and what many writers from

Dante through the seventeenth century argued strenuously against, is the idea that the common utterance is in any real sense unliterary. Indeed, the central distinction drawn during the Renaissance was not between the literary and the ordinary but between languages of antiquity and the vernacular, and the prevailing argument, in England for example, was that in its poetic or expressive power—its capacity, in Sir Philip Sidney's phrase, for "vttering sweetly and properly the conceits of the minde"—English was "neere the Greeke [and] fare beyond the Latine." [2] Such a view of the vernacular constitutes an early variation on the theme which we explored in the last chapter: namely, that poetry, so far from being an artificial form of discourse contrived out of language by the devices of style, is a quality inherent in the language, which is to say that certain languages, at least, are to be considered naturally poetic, as against those which, once poetic, have developed the capacity for philosophical utterance. Thus one finds, for example, that the term "literary" is often applied, not to poetry or oratory or any stylistic use of language, but to language itself—as in Bacon's distinction, in *De Augmentis Scientiarum* (1623), between two kinds of grammar, "whereof the one is Literary, the other Philosophical. The one is merely applied to Languages, that they may be more speedily learned; or more correctly and purely spoken. The other in a sort doth minister and is subservient to Philosophy." [3]

What I wish to come round to, however, as a way of uncovering the subject of this chapter, is the fact that the effort to define the literary utterance in terms of its difference from or even opposition to ordinary speech—and, following from this, the effort to define the nature of literature in terms of this difference—is finally an identifiably modern phenomenon, at least in the sense that such a definition, so far from receiving merely isolated formulations, itself helps to define the position of a group of writers who form what we might call the formalist (or perhaps formalist-structuralist) tradition. Actually, this tradition is composed, and roughly so, of three groups: the Russian Formalist critics, who flourished during the second and third decades of this century; the members of the Linguistic Circle of Prague, or Prague Structuralists, who dominated European linguistics for nearly a quarter of a century prior to World War II; and a number of contemporary French literary critics, whose writings draw not only upon the Russian and Slavic schools but upon a native formalist tradition whose *daimon* is Mallarmé and whose master is Ferdinand de Saussure. The importance of this so-called formalist tradition for the understanding of literary language cannot be too greatly emphasized. Certainly, not since classical rhetoric has the language of literature received the sort of systematic attention that these writers have given it. What is more important, however, is that these writers go far beyond the classical tradition and tend to make of language a reality that transcends even the reality of literature itself.

Broadly speaking, the achievement of Russian Formalist criticism lies in the development of two related concepts: the so-called principle of perceptible form, and the idea of the functional or structural significance of literary content.[4] These concepts received their earliest and perhaps most important formulation in two studies by Victor Shklovský, *Voskresěnie slova [The Resurrection of the Word]* (1914), a work composed to provide a theoretical ground for certain experiments in verse attempted by a number of Russian Futurist poets, and "Iskusstvo kak priëm [Art as Technique]" (1917), which is perhaps the central document among those treatises composed between 1916 and 1919 by members of *Opojaz,* the Society for the Study of Poetic Language, which Shklovský helped to organize in 1914.[5] Shklovský's argument in these studies turns upon a distinction between "automatized" and aesthetic forms of perception. "If we start to examine the general laws of perception," he writes in "Art as Technique," "we see that as perception becomes habitual, it becomes automatic." [6] Our daily lives, that is to say, are composed of repeated and unnumerable encounters with the world, such that our perception of the world in these encounters tends to become less than fully conscious. Indeed, so habituated do we become to the presence of the world, so familiar do we become with our environment and all that it contains, that we fall into what Shklovský calls an " 'algebraic' method of thought" (p. 11), according to which the world comes to be perceived not as a world of objects but as a world of ciphers and outlines:

> By this "algebraic" method of thought we apprehend objects only as shapes with imprecise extensions; we do not see them in their entirety but rather recognize them by their main characteristics. We see the object as though it were enveloped in a sack. We know what it is by its configuration, but we see only its silhouette. The object, perceived thus in the manner of prose perception, fades and does not even leave a first impression. . . . The process of "algebraization," the over-automatization of an object, permits the greatest economy of perceptive effort. Either objects are assigned only one proper feature—a number, for example—or else they function as though by formula and do not even appear in cognition. [pp. 11–12]

All life, in other words, is a life of "prose perception." Things are known, even as the meanings of words are gleaned from an utterance in prose; but things are not perceived: they are like words which disappear before the meanings they transmit. To put it another way, our world is a world of essences abstracted from a sensible landscape. So automatic is this process of abstraction that the world of things no longer registers upon our senses. "And so life is reckoned as nothing," Shklovský goes on to say, and, in a wonderful *aperçu*, he adds: "Habitualization devours works, clothes, furniture, one's wife, and the fear of war" (p. 12).

Over and against a life of prose perception, however, lies the world of art, which "exists that one may recover the sensation of life; it exists to make one feel things, to make the stone *stony*. The purpose of art is to impart the sensation of things as they are perceived and not as they are known" (p. 12). As it happens, however, Shklovský is less concerned with the end or purpose of art than with the way art accomplishes this purpose; that is, he is concerned principally with the *technique* of art, whose function "is to make objects 'unfamiliar,' to make forms

difficult, to increase the difficulty and length of perception be-
cause the process of perception is an aesthetic end in itself and
must be prolonged." Shklovský's discussion here takes a subtle
but important turn. The rediscovery of objects in their sensible
form is made possible through the process of *defamiliarization,*
but for Shklovský this process transforms perception into a kind
of transcendent activity. Art itself, however much it may help
us to "recover the sensation of life," remains altogether un-
worldly. Or, again, if art is a medium for an authentic percep-
tion of the world, it paradoxically renders perception an *in-
transitive* act, precisely to the extent that "the process of per-
ception is an aesthetic end in itself." Indeed, Shklovský em-
phasizes this point by condensing it into a formula: *"Art is a
way of experiencing the artfulness of an object; the object is
not important"* (p. 12).

It is worth inquiring here into the meaning of the word "art-
fulness." In the French edition of Russian Formalist critical
essays, *Theorie de la littérature,* Tzvetan Todorov translates
Shklovský's formula as follows: *"L'art est un moyen d'éprouver
le devenir de l'object, ce qui est déjà 'devenu' n'importe pas
pour l'art."* [7] Art is a way of experiencing the "becoming" of
an object, which is to say its *formation.* We shall see in a mo-
ment the preeminence which this concept of the experience
of formation has in the poetics of Paul Valéry. In Shklovský's
case, the point to observe is that the process of defamiliar-
ization is one by which the object is lifted out of the field of
ordinary or prose perception and placed within a network of
relationships that constitutes the work of art. What is impor-
tant to understand, however, is that this is not a simple trans-
position but a transformation of the object—indeed, a recon-
stitution of the object as a formal element that has its own
special function within the total structure of the work. From
one point of view, of course, the object exists in the work as an
image of what exists in the world of experience, but against
this view Shklovský stands firmly opposed. His essay is in part
a polemic against the mimetic theory of art, or against any
theory which takes the image to be the basic constituent of
the work. For Shklovský, the meaning of an image is not to be

derived from its relation to a world of objects; its meaning lies rather in its relation to the work as a whole, in which it functions as a structural device, *a technique of formation,* not as an instance of representation. Accordingly, he observes that "poets are much more concerned with arranging images than with creating them" (p. 7), for it is not the content of images that is of principal significance but rather the system of relationships into which they are organized.

To the extent, therefore, that imagery in a work of art assumes a formal rather than strictly referential intelligibility, the act of perception enters an unfamiliar and, on the face of it, hardly intelligible world. For the meaning of the work must assume, on this basis, a problematical character. As Shklovský puts it, "The meaning of a work broadens to the extent that artfulness and artistry diminish" (pp. 12–13). Now it is upon this axiom—this idea of the opposition between form and meaning—that Shklovský balances his conception of poetic language. For Shklovský, meaning is a function of the prose utterance: it is a process of abstracting the known from the perceived—of recognizing the "essences" of words as distinct from their sensible form. The function of the poetic utterance, by contrast, is to disrupt this process of abstraction. "The language of poetry," Shklovský says, "is . . . difficult, roughened, impeded language" (p. 22).[8] Or, again, "We can define poetry as *attenuated, torturous* speech. Poetic speech is *formed speech.* Prose is ordinary speech—economical, easy, proper, the goddess of prose [*dea prosae*] is a goddess of the accurate, facile type, of the 'direct' expression of the child" (p. 23). The point is that our experience of language, quite as much as our experience of the world, is habitual and to that extent tends to be automatized. But poetry is a use of language which is not automatized, because it is a deviation from the norm, or from that system of expectations which supervises the use of language in everyday speech. Poetry is defamiliarized language, whose formations, so far from being simply formations of meaning, are aesthetic structures—a system, that is to say, of intransitive relations.

The implication here, of course, is that in poetry the aesthetic experience is finally an experience of language itself. It is this idea of poetry which was taken up and developed on a systematic basis by the Prague Structuralists, who extended the traditional theory of linguistic functions or purposes (referential, conative, emotive) so as to include those utterances in which language is used intransitively. In place of Shklovský's ambiguous distinction between prose utterances and poetic speech (that is, between "tortured" and "easy" discourse), the Prague Structuralists, particularly Bohuslav Havránek and Jan Mukařovský, formulated a distinction between those utterances in which language is "automatized" according to the economy of everyday speech, and those in which language is "foregrounded." Foregrounding, according to Havránek, is "the use of the devices of the language in such a way that this use itself attracts attention and is perceived as uncommon, as deprived of automatization, as deautomatized, such as a live poetic metaphor (as opposed to a lexicalized one, which is automatized)." [9] Thus, for example, Noam Chomsky's happy line, "Colorless green ideas sleep furiously," is a foregrounded utterance. Although, as it happens, the sentence is perfectly grammatical—Chomsky composed it to show that meaning is not a necessary effect of "grammaticalness"—it is afflicted or, like many lines of poetry, blessed with a dissonance between lexicon and syntax that renders it impervious to whatever effort we may make to impose an interpretation upon it.[10] The structure of words by which Chomsky's utterance is constituted occupies, that is to say, that "foreground" of the utterance that is ordinarily the special domain of meaning.

The idea of foregrounding is not only important as a linguistic concept; it pushes linguistics to the brink of a poetics. According to Mukařovský, "The function of poetic language consists in the maximum foregrounding of the utterance." More than this, "In poetic language foregrounding achieves maximum intensity to the extent of pushing communication into the background as the objective of expression and of being used for its own sake; it is not used in the services of communication but in order to place in the foreground the act of expression, the act of speech itself" (p. 19). Just so, the first prin-

ciple of Paul Valéry's poetics—indeed, the theme which he re-
lentlessly pursues in almost all of his writings on poetry—is
that "ordinary language is a practical tool. It is constantly solv-
ing immediate problems. Its task is fulfilled when each sen-
tence has been completely abolished, annulled, and replaced
by the meaning. Comprehension is its end. But on the other
hand, poetic usage is dominated by personal conditions, by a
conscious, continuous, and sustained musical feeling." This
"musical feeling" transforms the whole structure of language,
and indeed its whole function, for in poetry "language is no
longer a transitive act, an expedient. On the contrary, it has
its own value, which must remain intact in spite of the oper-
ations of the intellect on the given propositions. Poetic lan-
guage must preserve itself, through itself, and remain the same,
not to be altered by the act of intelligence that finds or gives
it a meaning." [11] The poetic act, that is to say, has for its pur-
pose the creation of what Valéry variously calls "the universe
of language," "the musical universe," or the "poetic state"—a
world of words whose intelligibility is not semantic but formal,
in the sense that words no longer function as differentiations of
meaning but as "units of sonority [that] tend to form clear
combinations, successive or simultaneous implications, series,
and interactions" (p. 66), in short a system of pure relations, as
against a system of syntactical relations that one finds in
ordinary linguistic constructions.

Like Shklovský, Valéry thus conceives the structure of poetic
language in terms of an opposition between meaning and form,
but in Valéry's analysis this opposition provides a way of de-
scribing the peculiar dynamism of poetic speech. For Valéry,
poetry is a system of departures and returns, in which language
functions essentially as a point of repose:

> Think of a pendulum oscillating between two symmetrical points.
> Suppose that one of these extremes represents *form:* the concrete
> characteristics of language, sound, rhythm, accent, tone, move-
> ment—in a word, the *Voice* in action. Then associate with the
> other point, the acnode of the first, all significant values, images
> and ideas, stimuli of feeling and memory, virtual impulses and
> structures of understanding—in short, everything that makes the

content, the meaning of the discourse. Now observe the effect of poetry on yourselves. You will find that at each line the meaning produced within you, far from destroying the musical form communicated to you, recalls it. The living pendulum that has swung from *sound* to *sense* swings back to its felt point of departure, as though the very sense which is present to your mind can find no other outlet or expression, no other answer, than the very music which gave it birth. [p. 72]

Understood in this way, the opposition between meaning and form in poetry is harmonized—although not, as the axiom that form and content are indissolubly one would have it, abolished. For poetry thus conceived becomes a use of language in which a set of semantic components takes on structural value, or in which a set of semantic components takes on meaning precisely as it communicates the form by which it is articulated. This formulation is actually less paradoxical than it seems. It is true that all utterances, all uses of language, involve in some sense a synthesis of phonetic and semantic components, but it is Valéry's point that in poetry this synthesis is finally of a different order from the kind ordinarily accomplished in acts of speech. It is a synthesis achieved on behalf of language itself. Language, of course, is not simply a system of sounds but a system of signs, but in poetry these signs no longer function simply in a process of signification but rather in a process of formation in which phonetic and semantic components, sound and sense, possess equal value and, so to speak, become mutually symbolic. They become mutually symbolic, that is, in the sense that words in poetry not only mean, but that meanings in poetry refer back to the words themselves, so that, as Valéry puts it, "at each line the meaning produced within you, far from destroying the musical form communicated to you, recalls it"—recalls it, thus to establish it as the very subject of the poem, the very reason for the being of the poem, which is to say its motivation.

We might pause here to note that Valéry's conception of poetic language differs sharply from those diverse conceptions found in the New Criticism, which (largely under the impetus

of I. A. Richards) approach the problem of the literary ut-
terance from the standpoint of a distinction between science
and poetry, one that resolves itself into a distinction between
referential and emotive statements, or, less simply, between
those statements which are referential and those which are
contextual, in which words refer not to things but to each
other, thus to compose a self-contained system of meanings
that cannot be expressed by any other arrangement of words.[12]
Whatever the case, discussions of poetic language among the
New Critics tend to be apologetic and polemical insofar as
their fundamental motive is to argue on behalf of poetry as a
form of signification that is the equal of science and, from the
human point of view, even superior to it. For Valéry, however,
poetry is a form of signification only to this extent, that the
meaning of a poem is reflexive and instrumental—that "the
thoughts uttered or suggested by the text of a poem are by no
means the unique and chief objects of its discourse—but
means which combine equally with the sounds, cadences,
meter, and ornaments to produce and sustain a particular ten-
sion or exaltation, to engender within us a *world*, or *mode of
existence*, of complete harmony" (p. 147).

The question is, How can meaning function as a *means?*
What, after all, does it mean to say that meaning in poetry is
reflexive and instrumental? Any answer to this question must
focus upon the nature of linguistic structures in poetic speech.
Mukařovský attacks this problem by observing that, in poetry,
maximum foregrounding of the utterance is achieved not on a
quantitative basis—not, that is, by foregrounding each and
every component of the utterance; rather, it is an activity
which proceeds selectively and systematically, for what is fore-
grounded in poetic speech is a complex of multiple interrela-
tionships among linguistic components. Mukařovský amplifies
and clarifies this point as follows:

> There is always present, in communicative speech . . . the poten-
> tial relationship between intonation and meaning, syntax, word
> order, or the relationship of the word as a meaningful unit to
> the phonetic structure of the text, to the lexical selection found

in the text, to other words as units of meaning in the context of
the same sentence. It can be said that each linguistic component
is linked directly or indirectly, by means of these multiple inter-
relationships, in some way to every other component. In com-
municative speech these relationships are for the most part merely
potential, because attention is not called to their presence and
to their mutual relationship. [pp. 20–21]

In ordinary speech, the manifold of relationships among the
linguistic components of an utterance is present largely as a
structural possibility; it is the function of poetic speech, by
contrast, to actualize this possibility—to bring this manifold
of relationships into the foreground.

It is worth noting, in this connection, that in a famous
essay, "Linguistics and Poetics," Roman Jakobson singles out
the formation of this manifold of relationships among linguis-
tic components as "the empirical linguistic criterion of the
poetic function [of language]." Jakobson observes that all
uses of language are governed by two activities: selection and
combination. Poetry differs from ordinary speech, however, in
the way that these two activities are related. In ordinary
speech, selection proceeds on the basis of what Jakobson calls
"the principle of equivalence," whereas combination proceeds
on the basis of contiguity. Thus, for example, "If 'child' is the
topic of the message, the speaker selects one among the extant,
more or less similar nouns like child, kid, tot, youngster, all of
them equivalent in a certain respect, and then, to comment on
this topic, he may select one of the semantically cognate verbs—
sleeps, dozes, nods, naps." Poetic usage, however, is governed
by the principle of equivalence, not simply in its selection of
words, but in their combination as well. In Jakobson's formu-
lation, *"The poetic function projects the principle of equiv-
alence from the axis of selection onto the axis of combina-
tion."* This means that the poetic line will be organized not
only horizontally, in a semantically contiguous sequence or
predication, but vertically as a system of equivalences among
linguistic components: "In poetry one syllable is equalized
with any other syllable of the same sequence; word stress is
assumed to equal word stress, as unstress equals unstress;

prosodic long is matched with long, and short with short; word boundary equals word boundary, no boundary equals no boundary; syntactic pause equals syntactic pause, no pause equals no pause. Syllables are converted into units of measure, and so are morae or stresses." [13]

But whereas Jakobson describes this structure of equivalences spatially, according to a model of intersecting axes, Mukařovský regards it as a temporal structure—as does Valéry, for whom poetry is to be understood according to the traditional nineteenth-century analogy with music. In Mukařovský's view, the relationships among linguistic components by which a poetic work is constituted are organized according to principles of "subordination and superordination." This means that in a given work the whole will be governed by a "dominant" component, which is "that component which sets in motion, and gives direction to, the relationships of all other components" (p. 20). The point here is that the "dominant" is defined in terms of its *dynamic* function: it "sets in motion, and gives direction to," the whole structure, which is to say finally that poetic structure is essentially a dynamic system. The linguistic components of a work are not simply interrelated; their interrelationships are constituted as a system of interactions.

It is possible to illustrate this point by observing how the parts of a poem act upon one another. Consider, for example, Wallace Stevens's "Bantams in Pinewoods":

> Chieftain Iffucan of Azcan in caftan
> Of tan with henna hackles, halt!
>
> Damned universal cock, as if the sun
> Was blackamoor to bear your blazing tail.
>
> Fat! Fat! Fat! Fat! I am the personal.
> Your world is you. I am my world.
>
> You ten-foot poet among inchlings. Fat!
> Begone! An inchling bristles in these pines,
>
> Bristles, and points their Appalachian tangs,
> And fears not portly Azcan nor his hoos.[14]

This poem is dominated by phonetic equivalences, or by what Mukařovský would call "the foregrounding of intonation" (p. 20). So, indeed, is virtually all poetry, but "Bantams in Pinewoods" is an exaggeration of sound. It builds up a powerful system of assonances and alliteration which, as it plays off against the formation of semantically contiguous sequences or predications, displaces these sequences to the background of the poem. One can see to what radical extent this is so, by observing that the meaning of the poem is developed less by the formation of semantically contiguous relationships than by the formation of an opposition between two images: "Chieftain Iffucan," an exotic "universal cock," and a fearless, bristling inchling, whose territory the cock has evidently invaded and who sings out his defiance as he brandishes a tuft of pines in his defense. Fortunately, this opposition is weighted—indeed, interpreted for us—by the epithet which defines the cock as a "ten-foot poet," and which by implication figures the inchling as a lesser or minor poet. Accordingly, it may be that the prosaic "I am the personal" further defines the inchling as a private or subjective poet, in contrast to the objective or "universal" character of the cock. Hence the theme of solipsism in the line, "Your world is you. I am my world."

However, these prosaic, even philosophical utterances do not simply serve to thrust a thematic statement through the sound of the poem; they provide as well something like a center of repose around which the phonetic unity of the text is organized. To this extent they illustrate the fact that no one linguistic component in the poem exists as a self-contained or isolatable unit: it is never simply itself but is always in the process of becoming some other component. The semantic metamorphoses into the phonetic, quite as though the poem were constituted as a system of transformations, by virtue of which differences among linguistic components become difficult to define. Consider, for example, that syntax in "Bantams in Pinewoods" is not simply a means of combining words into predications; it organizes the poem according to the imperative mood, which, articulating as it does the inchling's de-

fiance, generates the basic opposition between cock and inch-
ling upon which the imagery of the poem turns. More than
this, however, is the fact that the rhythmic structures in the
poem tend to be syntactical rather than metrical, which is to
say that an additional function of syntax is to coordinate the
rhythms of the poem in such a way that the more purely
phonetic devices of meter, assonance, and alliteration are
absorbed into the patterns of a speaking voice. Indeed, the
fundamental image in the poem is finally that of a speaking
voice, and it is in accordance with this image that the
phonetic equivalences which dominate the poem assume a
semantic function, becoming, as the poem develops, no longer
simply a free play of sounds but the melodious cry of an out-
raged inchling—or even, to the extent that the inchling is a
poet and "Bantams in Pinewoods" a poem about poetry, typi-
cal formations of poetic speech and therefore part of the very
subject of the poem.

In "The Noble Rider and the Sound of Words," Stevens
wrote: "Those of us who may have been thinking of the path
of poetry, and those who understand that words are thoughts
and not only our thoughts but the thoughts of men and
women ignorant of what it is that they are thinking, must be
conscious of this: that, above everything else poetry is words;
and that words, above everything else, are, in poetry, sounds." [15]
One need hardly be conscious to utter a thought; one needs
only to speak. But poetry is a very different sort of speech from
the utterance of a thought: it requires an act of the mind
which transforms thought into sound—sound which displays
its meaning, not as idea, but simply as sound. Stevens is hardly
to be identified as a formalist poet, but throughout his writ-
ings on poetry there recurs an identifiably formalist theme—
as in the "Adagia": "Bringing out the music of the eccentric
sounds of words is no different in principle from bringing
out their form and its eccentricities (Cummings): language as
the material of poetry not its mere medium or instrument." [16]
Stevens's allusion here could as easily have been to Valéry as
to Cummings, for his adage adumbrates Valéry's central

thesis: that in poetry the sounds of words so modify the act of speech that this activity itself becomes an integral part, perhaps even the essential part, of the meaning of the work.

Conventions of literary history normally fix both Valéry and Stevens within or near the later reaches of what is called the "symbolist" tradition. We shall see in a later chapter how far Stevens exceeds such a tradition, but it is clear in any case that a view of poetry which places a heavy premium upon what Valéry calls "the physical, the concrete part [of language], the very act of speech" (p. 65), must finally be radically unsymbolic, or (to borrow a formulation from Susanne Langer) symbolic only in an "unconsummated" sense. Music, Langer tells us, "is an unconsummated symbol. Articulation is its life, but not assertion; expressiveness, but not expression. The actual function of meaning, which calls for permanent contents, is not fulfilled." [17] Just so, articulation is for Valéry the life of poetry—articulation in which the function of signification, as in music, remains unconsummated. Repeatedly throughout his writings Valéry expresses his envy of the "nonrepresentational arts," whose " 'pure' methods are not encumbered with personalities and events drawn from everything arbitrary and superficial in observable reality. . . . On the contrary, they exploit, they compose and organize the values of each power of our sensibility, free of all reference, of all function as a *sign.*" Thus the musician "finds himself as it were faced with a number of possibilities upon which he can work without reference to a world of things and people" (p. 110). Unlike the musician, however, the poet is imprisoned by the sign: he is enclosed within a semiotic system (enclosed, Stevens might say, within the thoughts of other people), and cannot on this account bring poetry into being without at the same time activating in some way those processes of signification by which the system functions. His only recourse, according to Valéry, is to become "a maker of deviations" (p. 172), which means in effect that he must impose upon the language a special grammar of his own making—a musical grammar, so to speak—thus to generate utterances in which "the sound, the rhythm, the physical proximity of words, their effects of induction or their mutual influences . . . dominate at the expense of their capacity for being consummated in a defined and particular meaning" (p. 157).

Valéry amplifies this theme of a musical grammar most fully in his reflections upon his own poetry. "Certain of the poems I have written," he tells us, "had as a starting point merely one of these impulses of the 'formative' sensibility which are anterior to any 'subject' or to any finite, expressible idea. *La Jeune Parque* [one of Valéry's most famous poems] was, literally speaking, an endless research into the possibility of attempting in poetry something analogous to what in music is called 'modulation' " (p. 111). Or, again: "I had left my house to find, in walking and looking about me, relaxation from some tedious work. As I went along my street, which mounts steeply, I was *gripped* by a rhythm which took possession of me and soon gave me the impression of some force outside myself. Another rhythm overtook and combined with the first, and certain strange *transverse relations* were set up between them" (p. 112). These passages suggest the working of something like a formalist muse, whose transcendent "theme" can only be constructed, not expressed. "If I am questioned," Valéry wrote in a preface to a detailed analysis of one of his poems, Gustave Cohen's *Essai d'explication du Cimetière marin* (1933), "if anyone wonders . . . what I 'wanted to say' in a certain poem, I reply that I did not *want to say* but *wanted to make,* and that it was the intention of *making* which wanted what I said" (pp. 147–148). Poetry in this sense literally ceases to be an act of meaning, insofar as the intentionality of the utterance is so thoroughly of a technical order. Indeed, Valéry pushes this point relentlessly to its conclusion: "It is an error contrary to the nature of poetry, and one which may even be fatal to it, to claim that for each poem there is a corresponding true meaning, unique and comformable to, or identical with, some thought of the author's" (pp. 155–156). Nor is Valéry's argument simply that it is fallacious to equate the meaning of a text with the inten-

tions of its author; on the contrary, the argument is much
more radical: namely, that it is in the very nature of poetry
to pose an extreme hermeneutical problem, because in poetry
"there is no true meaning to a text" (p. 152). In poetry, that
is to say, meaning is characterized by the condition of inde-
terminacy, which means that limits cannot be placed upon
the meanings that can be construed from a text.[18] In Valéry's
words, "A work is an object or event of the senses, whereas the
various values or interpretations it suggests are the conse-
quences (ideas or affections) which cannot alter it in its en-
tirely material capacity to produce quite different ones" (pp.
157–158).

The sort of poetry Valéry has in mind, of course, is his own:

> Cette main, sur mes traits qu'elle rêve effleurer,
> Distraitement docile à quelque fin profonde,
> Attend de ma faiblesse une larme qui fonde,
> Et que de mes destins lentement divisé,
> Les plus pur en silence éclaire un coeur brisé.
> La houle me murmure une ombre de reproche,
> Ou retire ici-bas, dans ses gorges de roche,
> Comme chose déçue et bue amèrement,
> Une rumeur de plainte et de resserrement . . .
> Que fais-tu, hérissée, et cette main glacée,
> Et quel frémissement d'une feuille effacée
> Persiste parmi vous, îles de mon sein nu? . . .
> Je scintille, liée à ciel inconnu . . .
> L'immense grappe brille à ma soif de désastres.[19]

One way to describe these lines (the first extended verse
paragraph of *La Jeune Parque*), is to observe that they present
a sequence of perceptions—perceptions of objects or events:
a doting and seemingly disembodied hand, a surge of the sea
and its descent into a grotto (movements which mysteriously
form an utterance), the fluttering of a heart, the scintillation
of an "I" and an attendant cluster of stars. These perceptions
reflect an emotional center, the young Fate herself, who is
meditating (or about to meditate) upon a melancholy destiny

which she has devised and for which the surge of the sea evidently reproaches her. The reproach is subtle ("La houle me murmure un ombre de reproche / . . . Une rumeur de plainte et de resserrement"), the more so by virtue of the simile ("Comme chose déçue et bue amèrement") around which it is organized. It may be, however, that the reproach is sufficient to startle the young Fate—

> Que fais-tu, hérissée, et cette main glacée,
> Et quel frémissement d'une feuille effacée
> Persiste parmi vous, îles de mon sein nu?

—thus to induce perhaps the surprise of self-discovery that is at the same time an instance of self-admiration: "Je scintille. . . ."

In a sense, however, the passage is more interesting for the way it resists this sort of paraphrase. The formation of meaning in a given utterance depends upon the capacity of its diverse linguistic units to integrate themselves into larger units, that is, into sentences and contexts. In this passage, however, care has been taken to impede or disrupt this process of integration. The first five lines, for example, are organized as so many systems of inversion and apposition, which tend to isolate individual words and to obscure their syntactical function. Thus "Cette main . . . Attend . . . une larme" emerges as an utterance characterized by what Albert Cook has called the principle of "diffusion," a method of composition that "puts the parts of a poem to some degree apart, rather than together, the expected practice not only in poems but in language generally." [20] This point is the more worth remarking because the movement of these first five lines turns upon an act of displacement, whereby "Cette main . . . Attend" gives way to the transformation of "une larme" into the subject of "qui fond / Et que . . . éclaire un coeur brisé." Indeed, "une larme" becomes the key word in the whole utterance, for it undergoes a metaphorical change as well as a change in its grammatical function, thus to take on meaning as "le plus pur" of those destinies which the young Fate has devised. What is interesting, however, is that Valéry constructs this metaphor not by predication but by apposition—

> une larme qui fond,
> Et que de mes destins lentement divisé,
> Le plus pur . . .

—which means that the reader must, so to speak, retrieve the metaphor from what linguists have come to call the "deep structure" of the utterance.[21] The critical problem, however, is not simply to discover how the metaphor was constructed; it is rather the hermeneutical problem of determining the sense in which the metaphor can be understood. As it happens, "a tear, which is the purest of my destinies," is a locution which seems not to contain within itself the reason why it is so and not otherwise, nor is it articulated within a context in terms of which its meaning can be established. It is in its own case the purest of locutions, an indeterminate figure—an instance, we should observe, of a phenomenon to which Valéry gives considerable attention in his writings on poetry: namely, that type of poetic utterance "in which relations between meanings [are] themselves perpetually similar to harmonic relations, in which the transmutation of thoughts into each other [appear] more important than any thought" (p. 192).

We are thus opened more precisely to Valéry's understanding of the relationship "between the form and the content, between the sound and the sense, between the poem and the state of poetry" (pp. 72–73). For the "harmonic relations" between words as signs executes something like a decorum with the "harmonic relations" between words as phonetic units. The passage quoted from *La Jeune Parque* is constituted, that is to say, not only as so many systems of inversion and apposition but as a complex system of assonances: each line (the classic alexandrine of French prosody) contains its own pattern of phonetic duplications—"Distraitment docile a quelque fin profonde"—as does, indeed, each couplet:

> Que fais-tu, hérisée, et cette main glacée,
> Et quel frémissement d'une feuille effacée.

Accordingly, what is generated is a poem governed by the principle of diffusion, which establishes distances between words that are syntactically related—a poem, however, which at the same time emerges as a tightly organized whole, a structure of combinations among words that are phonetically equivalent. It is clear, moreover, that the one functions on behalf of the other, that the diffusion of syntax is a technique by which Valéry achieves what he calls "the conservation of form" (p. 157), for it is precisely by means of diffusion that syntactic relations are held in abeyance—purified, so to speak —and so brought into harmony with those pure relations which constitute the phonetic unity of the text.

In "Fragments des mémoires d'une poème," Valéry remarks that in writing "the main thing is to oppose thought, to arouse resistance to it," for by doing so one creates or discovers "the illusion of proceeding toward the formation of an 'object' with its own consistency, very clearly separated from its author" (p. 131). It is upon this illusion of a self-composed "object," of a poem that seems to develop of itself, according to laws peculiarly its own, that Valéry predicates the value of poetry. The illusion is the poet's own: it is, so to speak, the *content* of his experience of the act of writing. For Valéry, in other words, the value of poetry lies in the process of creation, which is to say in the relationship between the poet and the poem—hence his insistence that "work interests me far more than the product of that work" (p. 183). Obviously, however, such a view calls into question the relationship between the poet and his audience, or between poem and reader. Valéry, for his part, clearly distrusts this relationship. Repeatedly he alludes to the problem of value that his conception of poetry and his own poetic work will impose upon a reader who assumes that poetry is a form of signification and that the poetic work has in one way or another been composed for him. Paradoxically, however, it appears to be precisely this distrust of his audience that moves Valéry to project his poetics beyond that private space in which poetry can have value only for the poet. Indeed, his writings on poetry amount finally to so many efforts to create an audience that will seek in poetry that very experience of formation which Valéry identifies as the content of the act of writing. For the curious fact in Valéry's poetics is that the meaning of poetry is invariably described as an *experience of poetry*—an experience, that is to say, of "a universe of language that is not the common system of exchanging signs for acts or ideas" (p. 98). Hence the tautology in the formulation which defines the dynamics of poetic structure as an oscillation "between the form and the content, between the sound and the sense, *between the poem and the state of poetry*." The point is that if Valéry considers the process of "work itself as having its own value, generally much superior to that which the crowd attaches only to the product" (p. 177), he nevertheless insists that "a poet's function . . . is not to experience the poetic state: that is a private affair. His function is to create it in others" (p. 60).

Similarly, Valéry's famous concept of "pure" or "absolute" poetry is defined with a view toward the poet's audience, that is, in terms of "the varied and multiform relations between language and the effects it produces on men" (pp. 185–186). Interestingly, Valéry describes these effects by contrasting them with the effects generated by a novel:

> Watch the reader of a novel plunge into the imaginary life his book shows him. His body no longer exists. He leans his forehead on his two hands. He exists, moves, acts, and suffers only in the mind. He is absorbed by what he is devouring; he cannot restrain himself, for a kind of demon drives him on. He wants the continuation and the end; he is prey to a kind of madness; he takes sides, he triumphs, he is saddened, he is no longer himself, he is no more than a brain separated from its outer forces, that is, given up to its images, going through a sort of *crisis of credulity*. [pp. 210–211]

Anxiety, hallucination, demonic possession, the dissolution of the self: it is as though narrative duplicated in the most intense fashion the ravages of insanity. Poetry, by contrast, induces repose—a harmony not only of the interior but of the body and the spirit:

> If poetry really affects someone, it is not by dividing him in his nature, by communicating to him illusions of a fancied and purely mental life. It does not impose on him a false reality that demands the docility of the mind and hence the absence of the body. Poetry must extend over the whole being; it stimulates the muscular organization by its rhythms, it frees or unleashes the verbal faculties, ennobling their whole action, it regulates our depths, for poetry aims to arouse or reproduce the unity and harmony of the living person, an extraordinary unity that shows itself when a man is possessed by an intense feeling that leaves none of his powers disengaged. [p. 211]

Valéry's point is that there exist psychological and even physiological equivalents for the system of harmonic relations that characterizes poetry. The poet's task, Valéry says, "if he is aiming at the heights of his art, can only be to introduce some stranger's spirit to the divine duration of his own harmonious life, in which all forms are composed and measured, and responses are exchanged between all his sensitive and rhythmic powers" (p. 215). Poetry, that is to say, establishes in the reader a system of interactions, an exchange of responses between powers comparable to the dynamism of its own structure. But what is especially to be noted here is Valéry's remark that poetry "frees or unleashes the verbal faculties" of the reader: it is a stimulus to speak, for it generates a specifically poetic emotion, which Valéry describes as "an emotion characterized by the spontaneous power of expression" (p. 215). We have here a unique conception of the relationship between the poet and his audience, for the poetic universe is grounded for both poet and reader upon the will to speak—not the will to say this or that ("It is indeed nonusage—the *not saying* 'it is raining'—which is [the poet's] business" [p. 98]), not the will to predication but the desire to free oneself from all points of

reference in the world of experience and to give oneself
wholly up to language.

We converge here upon a theory of expression, whose mean-
ing can perhaps be summed up in a single principle: The
motive for speech does not lie outside of language but is to
be discovered within the language itself. By all traditional
conceptions of human speech, this seems a radical and imperti-
nent principle, and yet it will serve us well to examine it a
little more closely. Such a principle is perhaps already implied
in the famous axiom formulated by Coleridge to answer
the problem of whether meter is a necessary constituent of
poetry: "Nothing can permanently please which does not
contain in itself the reason why it is so and not otherwise." [22]
This axiom anticipates the Russian Formalist concept of
motivation, according to which any element that is included
in a work of art derives its justification—its reason for being
in the work—from its relation to the structure of the whole
and not from anything outside the work.[23] According to
Mukařovský, this principle holds true even for works of
realistic fiction, in which the subject matter appears to be the
foregrounded component of the work: "Even for works and
genres of poetry in which the subject matter is the dominant,"
Mukařovský says, "the latter is not the 'equivalent' of a reality
to be expressed by the work as effectively (for instance, as
truthfully) as possible, but . . . is part of the structure, is
governed by its laws, and is evaluated in terms of its relation-
ship to it" (p. 23). Mukařovský is here arguing against the
notion that the language of fiction, unlike the language of
poetry, is essentially transitive, in the sense that, as Simon
O. Lesser puts it, the fictional utterance "quickly and effec-
tively transmits almost any kind of material without requiring
the reader to put what he understands into words." [24] For
Mukařovský, the function of language in a work of fiction does
not consist in the *transmission* of fictional material but in its
formation. The difficulty is that we habitually think of nar-
rator, plot, and character as substances or entities within a
novel, when in fact it may well be the more accurate to think

of them as formations within a totality of linguistic structures; or, indeed, insofar as we find this totality to be a dynamic system, it may be a point of even greater accuracy to think of them neither as entities nor simply as formations but as activities—activities of narration, plotting, and characterization. From this decidedly formalist point of view, the subject matter of a novel comes to be defined, not on the basis of its relationship to any "extralinguistic" reality but as the system of techniques by which a novel is actualized. To understand the subject matter of a work of fiction in this way is, moreover, to be reminded that of these activities narration is of primary importance. It is the activity out of which the novel grows; it is the "dominant," so to speak, which "motivates" the other activities, so that plotting and characterization become, in this sense, functions of narrative activity.

Mukařovský's argument does not, of course, carry him into a poetics of the novel. His point is simply that "in a work of poetry of any genre [whether lyric or narrative] there is no fixed border, nor, in a certain sense, any essential difference between the language and the subject matter" (p. 22). Thus the distinctive feature of narration is the fact that it is preeminently an act of speech, one that generates its own referent but one which is at the same time an essential part of the structure in which its referent inheres. For in any work of fiction, as it is now commonplace to observe, the narrator, even when radically impersonal or when situated outside of the "story," remains internal to the work. What this means, however, is that any work of fiction contains its own center, its own point of origination, even as it contains its own referent— namely, the fictional world, which exists nowhere but in the work.

Narration in this sense can be regarded as an activity of what in traditional grammar is known as the "middle voice." In a recent essay, the French critic Roland Barthes has touched upon this theme as part of what he calls a "diathetical analysis of the modern verb *to write.*" As Barthes uses it, the term "diathetical" (which means, literally, "placed between") refers to the now largely vestigial category of grammar that describes such oddities as the sentence, "It is raining," in which the subject is neither active nor passive but is rather the purely grammatical agent of a self-motivating activity. We cannot ask what it is that rains, except as a way of observing that "It is raining" possesses a phantom or mythical subject. Barthes's contention is that the sentence "I am writing" is comparable to "It is raining," insofar as the writer (or, as Barthes prefers, *scripteur*) is situated "inside the writing, not as a psychological subject"—that is, not as the subject of any predication—"but as the agent of the action." [25] This contention turns upon and indeed derives its full significance from a historical judgment (one that Barthes insists upon everywhere in his criticism) concerning the differences between "classical" and "modern" writing.[26] Traditionally, the verb *to write* was active or transitive in character: a writer did not write, purely and simply; he composed a book, expressed an idea, championed a cause. In modern writing, by contrast, the opposition between active and passive, or between transitive and intransitive, is neutralized by an increasing tendency to define the writer in terms of the *act* of writing rather than in terms of the *product* (we have already remarked upon this tendency in Valéry). Barthes might also have called up as an example the diverse theories of impersonality in literature and the critical convention that is their issue: namely, that we no longer think of the speaker in a poem or the narrator in the novel as the author who exists outside the work as a transcendent originator of meanings; we think of him instead as a nameless and departed god, an irrelevance, and in his stead we attend to the figure whose identity is found precisely in the activity by which the poem or novel unfolds. In Barthes's words, "the distance between the writer and the language diminishes asymptomatically" in modern literature: the writer is no longer anterior to the activity of writing; he is interior to it as an implicated agent.[27]

The point to mark, however, is that Barthes here projects the formalist conception of the primacy of language to its furthest extension. The reason for the disappearance of the writer within the activity of writing, Barthes says, is that "modern literature is trying, through various experiments, to establish a new status in writing for the agent of the writing. The meaning or goal of this effort is to substitute the instance of discourse for the instance of reality (or of the referent), which has been, and still is, a mythical 'alibi' dominating the idea of literature." [28] As we have seen, formalist criticism abandons this "alibi" in the very establishment of its premises. It abandons, that is to say, the traditional relationship between signifier and signified and focuses upon the act of speech as a process which runs its course according to its own laws of development. Formalist thought thus coincides with the tendency (already apparent in Saussure's *Cours de linguistic générale*) to think of language as a system without a center— without, that is, an internal equivalent of that Origin whence all utterances were once understood to take their departure and to which they were expected to refer for their meanings. [29]

Thus, for Saussure, language is a system in which the meanings of words are derived "not positively on the basis of their content, but negatively on the basis of their relationships with other words in the system." [30] Words are not signs for things, nor do they "possess" meanings in and of themselves; on the contrary, words are "diacritical," which means that the function of a word in the process of signification depends upon its unique phonetic structure, by virtue of which it is able to signify not a meaning but its difference from other words. Words, after all, are not self-subsistent entities; they do not exist and cannot function as signs except in relationship with other words. As Saussure says, the value of a word derives from the synchronic nature of language, which is to say the "simultaneous presence" of other words. [31] Language in this sense is a negative system: there are no significations as such in a language, only differences of signification. Accordingly, the act of speech itself may be defined as an act of differentiation. As Merleau-Ponty describes it, we do not, in forming an utterance, "simply choose a sign for an already defined signifi-

cation, as one goes to look for a hammer in order to drive a
nail or for a claw to pull it out"; rather, the choice of a sign
requires that we "evoke some of the other expressions which
might have taken its place and were rejected, and we must
feel the way in which they might have touched and shaken
the chain of language in another manner and the extent to
which this particular expression was really the only possible
one if that signification was to come into the world." [32] Speech
is thus an event which takes place not simply by means of
language but *within* it. "Language is much more like a sort
of being than a means," Merleau-Ponty writes. "Its opaque-
ness, its obstinate reference to itself, and its turning and fold-
ing back upon itself, are precisely what make it a mental
power; for it in turn becomes something like a universe, and
it is capable of lodging things themselves in this universe—
after it has transformed them into their meanings" (p. 43).

This inclination to hypostatize language, as we have already
seen, is an ancient and venerable habit. But in this context
the conception of language as a being or universe takes on new
importance and becomes, so to speak, less clearly metaphorical.
For the point is that meaning is now understood to be a
phenomenon that is interior to language. The relationship be-
tween signifier and signified, between word and world, can no
longer be adequately described as a relationship between an
"inside" and an "outside." Quite the contrary, language makes
a claim to divine definition as a circle whose center is every-
where and whose circumference is nowhere. No longer faced
with what Jacques Derrida calls a "transcendental and privi-
leged signified," [33] this divine circle, this universal and in-
clusive system of differences, becomes transcendent in its own
right, an overarching horizon beyond which we need not and
perhaps cannot go in search of what is real. It is, moreover,
precisely on the basis of such a conception that language
provides that new "mythical 'alibi'" for literature of which
Barthes speaks. "For literature," Barthes says, "language can
no longer be the convenient instrument or the superfluous
backcloth of a social, emotional, or poetic 'reality' which pre-
exists it, and which it is language's subsidiary responsibility to

express, by means of submitting itself to a number of stylistic rules. Language is literature's Being, its very world; the whole of literature is contained in the act of writing, and no longer in those of 'thinking,' 'portraying,' 'telling,' or 'feeling.' " [34] No longer, that is to say, does literature express itself through language; it is rather language which now expresses itself through literature.

It is important to know that this radical theme is not Barthes's private formulation but is to be found at the same time in a remarkable book by Michel Foucault, *Les Mots et les choses.* Foucault examines the tendency in traditional empiricist or scientific thought to reduce language to the status of an instrument and beyond that (with the development of linguistics) to the status of a mere object. It is part of Foucault's purpose, however, to argue that language seeks to compensate for this reduction by taking possession of literature, and through it to articulate its own transcendence. For "at the beginning of the nineteenth century, at a time when language was burying itself within its own density as an object and allowing itself to be traversed, through and through, by knowledge, it was also reconstituting itself elsewhere, in an independent form, difficult of access, folded back upon the enigma of its own origin and existing wholly in reference to the pure act of writing." For Foucault, the importance of this concept of "the pure act of writing" is that it displaces the classical system of *genres* by which language once articulated its diverse relationships with the world. Under the dominance of this new category, writing itself, "literature becomes progressively more differentiated from the discourse of ideas, and encloses itself within a radical intransitivity." It no longer serves the narration of hypothetical events or the expression of specialized forms of feeling; instead, literature becomes, by virtue of its intransitivity,

a manifestation of a language which has no other law than that of affirming—in opposition to all other forms of discourse—its own precipitous existence; and so there is nothing for it to do but to curve back in a perpetual return upon itself, as if discourse could have no other content than the expression of its own form; it addresses itself to itself as a writing subjectivity, or seeks to re-apprehend the essence of all literature in the movement that brought it into being; and thus all its threads converge upon the finest of points—singular, instantaneous, and yet absolutely universal—upon the simple act of writing. At the moment when language, as spoken and scattered words, becomes an object of knowledge, we see it appearing in a strictly opposite modality: a silent, cautious deposition of the word upon the whiteness of a piece of paper, where it can possess neither sound nor interlocutor, where it has nothing to say but itself, nothing to do but shine in the brightness of its being.[35]

We are brought, by this allusion to the word silently deposed upon the whiteness of paper, to the threshold of our next chapter: to Mallarmé, for whom language is similarly a mythic creature, whose mode of existence (or mode of expression—the terms become interchangeable) is a kind of magic alphabet. Indeed, in the next three chapters our subject will be language as it takes possession of literature, thus to speak nothing but itself, in order to "shine in the brightness of its being."

I cannot help thinking here of that remarkable and unsettling story by Jorge Luis Borges, "The Library of Babel," in which man's universe is imagined to be a labyrinth of letters —letters arranged (perhaps systematically, perhaps not) in numberless books gathered into a system of indefinitely extended hexagonal galleries. The troubled narrator of this story, curiously enough, defines the Library as "a sphere whose exact center is in any one of its hexagons and whose circumference is inaccessible." [36] It is an apt formula, for the universe thus conceived is entirely a universe of discourse, an infinite combination of alphabetic differences which contains (and therefore supersedes and renders useless, or intransitive) the totality of possible human utterances. As Borges's narrator puts it, "This wordy and useless epistle already exists in one of the thirty volumes of the five shelves of one of the innumerable hexagons—and its refutation as well." [37] It is a notion which brings one abruptly to silence.

4

Mallarmé: The Transcendence of Language and the Aesthetics of the Book

The notion of language as a circle whose circumference is nowhere and whose center is everywhere might well have been impossible to conceive, had it not been for the dark inquiries of Stéphane Mallarmé, whose conviction it was that "all earthly existence must ultimately be contained in a book." [1] Taken by itself, this conviction seems merely to amplify a *fin-de-siècle* commonplace: that the creation of the world is not complete until the world comes to exist within the work of art. One could adjust this context slightly, thus to say that the world cannot exist by itself but only (according to the poet) in language: the ideal unity of word and being constitutes the condition of the world's possibility, which only the poet can actualize. This view of poetry suggests the Orpheus myth and the figure of the poet-magus whose song calls the world into being, and this in turn recalls Mallarmé's claim, in the *Autobiographie,* that the book of which he dreams will constitute the "Orphic explanation of the earth" (*M*, p. 15; *Œuvres*, p. 633). But if Orpheus is the poet whose song establishes the world in being, Mallarmé, by contrast, emerges as the poet who seeks to return the world to the original void, for his dream of the book rests not upon the unity of word and being but upon their radical separation. For him, the poetic act fulfills itself in a process of annihilation which releases language from its bondage to the world and establishes the word in the pristine universe of nothingness, in which impossible sphere, Mallarmé was sure, the essence of beauty is to be found.

In a famous passage from "Crise de vers" (1895), for example, Mallarmé writes: "Why should we perform the miracle by which a natural object is almost made to disappear beneath the magic waving wand of the written word if not to divorce that object from the direct and the palpable, and so conjure up the pure idea?" (*M*, p. 42; *Œuvres*, p. 368). Such a notion of language recalls Hegel's idea that all representational thinking is essentially an act of negation, in the sense that the object present to the mind is abolished and replaced by a concept. But Mallarmé appears to have interested himself in language as a process which annihilates the world purely and simply, in order to go beyond those forms of experience that push man up against the material world. "When I say: 'a flower!' then from that forgetfulness to which my voice consigns all floral form, something different from the usual calyces arises, something all music, essence [aroma], and softness: the flower which is absent from all bouquets" (*M*, p. 42; *Œuvres*, p. 368). Speech here is a way of purifying the word, a way of emptying sensation of any external point of reference; it is a gesture toward the condition of absence.

It was in 1866, during the now legendary Tournon-Avignon "crisis," that Mallarmé first discovered what value lay for the poet in this condition of absence. Mallarmé's early poetry had turned upon the romantic and paradoxical theme of its own impossibility—the impossibility, that is to say, of executing an act of creation conceived as a flight across infinite space toward a transcendent ideal, *l'Azur*. But in March of 1866 *l'Azur* seemed to give way to space itself. Mallarmé wrote to Henri Cazalis that, while struggling to compose the *Hérodiade*, "I came upon twin abysses which drove me mad. The first was nothingness, which I found without any prior knowledge of Buddhism,[2] and I am still too heartsick to bring myself to believe in my own poetry . . . [or] to get back to the work that I had to abandon in the face of this overwhelming vision"

(*M*, p. 88; *C*, i, p. 207). Mallarmé's genius, however, was such that he could translate this "overwhelming vision" into an aesthetic experience: "I am traveling," he wrote to Cazalis in July 1866, "but in unknown lands, and if I have fled from the fierce heat of reality and have taken pleasure in cold imagery, it is because for a month now I have been on the purest glaciers of esthetics; because, after I had found nothingness, I found beauty" (*M*, pp. 89–90; *C*, i, p. 220). For beauty is no longer an attribute of being; it is rather an attribute of *le Néant*—a beauty purified of content, which displays itself in the very condition of nonexistence.

Such a notion of beauty, as Mallarmé's commentators have often observed, is roughly Hegelian in character. For Hegel, beauty conceived as an absolute cannot be the predicate of any object. For "the absolute," as Hegel wrote in the *Encyclopedia* (1817), "negates all things that are not absolute. It is their nothing or negativity. The absolute pervades all finite and definite positions; ruling out the metaphysical value of all positivisms, and thereby affirming its sovereign *freedom*. It is unutterable, unpredictable." [3] The absolute emerges only upon the annihilation of all that is not absolute; its possibility rests upon negation, absence, the void. For Mallarmé, the same (he discovers) can be true of poetry, which can become an art of the beautiful only upon a process of negation; its possibility can only rest upon the void, nothingness. So much, indeed, is made clear in a letter that Mallarmé wrote to Villiers de L'Isle-Adam in September 1867:

> Beneath a wave of sensitiveness, I was able to understand the intimate relation of poetry to the universe; and, to make poetry pure, my design was to divorce it from dreams and chance and link it to the idea of that universe. But, unfortunately, since my soul is made for poetic ecstasy alone, I had no mind at my disposal (as you have) to clear the way for this idea. And so you will be terrified to hear that I have discovered the idea of the universe through sensation alone—and that, in order to perpetuate the indelible idea of pure nothingness, I had to fill my brain with the sensation of absolute emptiness. [*M*, p. 91; *C*, i, p. 259]

Mallarmé reveals himself here to be less a Hegelian than an eclectic; he proceeds not by reason but by experience, and to describe his experience (and by this same token to suggest the kind of poetry he would like to write) he appropriates language that is originally Hegel's. Let us mark, however, that the idea of the universe of which Mallarmé speaks is nothingness. Poetry, we are told, aspires to unity with this idea—but how is this aspiration to be realized? The answer, it appears, is by a process (or, better, by processes) of negation.

Notice that Mallarmé attains to his idea of the universe by means of purgation: he empties himself of all that betokens an external world. For his own part, Mallarmé thought of this process as a kind of death, as though by purging his interior he could destroy himself as an experiencing subject. In May 1867 he had written to Cazalis: "My thought has thought itself through and reached a pure idea. What the rest of me has suffered during that long agony, is indescribable. But, fortunately, I am quite dead now." What we have here, as Mallarmé makes clear in this same letter, is the theory of impersonality in art conceived in its most radical form: "I am impersonal now, not the Stéphane you once knew, but one of the ways the spiritual universe has found to see itself, unfold itself through what used to be me" (*M*, pp. 93–94; *C*, I, pp. 240–242). The "unfolding" of the idea has (once more) a Hegelian resonance; but, once more, the point is not philosophical but part of an emerging poetics. The contemplation of the void is a process of self-annihilation, which process is of the first importance if the creation of poetry is to be possible. For if poetry aspires to the condition of nothingness, and so by its purity to display the idea of the universe; or, again, if it seeks by its purity to participate in the very nature of beauty, the poem must on this account become a closed system—a structure of words closed above all to the poet himself, since it is by his mediation that the world of things and events, ideas and emotions, seeks to make its way into the poem. That expressive movement by which a world of experience becomes objectified in language must be abolished, so that what seems an utterance will finally emerge as an object—a structure that appears to occupy its own world and to display its own laws of development. "If a poem is to be pure," Mallarmé wrote in "Crise de vers," "the poet's voice must be stilled and the initiative taken by the words themselves, which will be set in motion as they meet unequally in collision. And in an exchange of gleams they will flame out like some glittering swath of fire sweeping over precious stones, and thus replace the audible breathing in lyric poetry of old—replace the poet's own personal and passionate control of verse" (*M*, pp. 40–41; *Œuvres*, p. 336). Creativity seems to be envisioned here as a kind of alchemical process, in which words no longer function as signs in an act of speech but become instead objects with physical and, indeed, magical properties. The poem, that is to say, is no longer a human utterance, for expression has been displaced by the very substance of language—language as a reality transcendent in the purity of nothingness, articulating, according to a dynamism peculiarly its own, the pure poem.

And so it was, indeed, Mallarmé's conviction that the language of poetry must be isolated from the language of ordinary speech (*M*, pp. 42–43; *Œuvres*, p. 368). Poetry is not expression; its intelligibility rests upon other, more purely formal grounds. Mallarmé sought to enforce this distinction between the poetic art and the act of speech by aligning poetry with music. "Crise de vers," in fact, appears to take its cue from Richard Wagner's belief that poetry had in the nineteenth century reached a critical juncture in its development: it could now evolve either toward science or toward music— toward the exact signification of scientific discourse or toward the pure expressiveness of the symphony.[4] In "La Musique et les lettres" (1894), Mallarmé makes it clear what he thinks the poet's choice must be. "Nature exists," he writes. "She will not be changed, although we may add cities, railroads, or other inventions to our material world." This being so, the poet's only recourse is "to seize relationships and intervals"—that is, to seek out the hiatuses in nature, the spaces between objects. For we must understand that to create is no longer to evoke substances in pursuit of *la belle nature;* on the contrary,

> to create is to conceive an object in its fleeting moment, in its absence.
>
> To do this, we simply compare its facets and dwell lightly, negligently upon their multiplicity. We conjure up [not the object but] a scene of lovely, evanescent, intersecting forms. We recognize the entire and binding arabesque as it leaps dizzily in terror or plays disquieting chords; or, through a sudden digression (by no means disconcerting), we are warned of its likeness unto itself even as it hides. Then, when the melodic line has given way to silence, we seem to hear such themes as are the very logic of our soul. [*M,* pp. 48–49; *Œuvres,* pp. 647–648]

We may recall here the passage quoted earlier: "Why should we perform the miracle by which a natural object is almost made to disappear beneath the magic waving wand of the written word . . . ?" Not, as in Hegel, to replace it with a meaning, but to "conjure up a scene of lovely, evanescent, intersecting forms." To create is to conceive an object in its absence, that is, to negate it; but whatever ideal content cognition might then ordinarily pursue is superseded, in Mallarmé's view, by "relationships and intervals"—by an "arabesque" whose movements, as Mallarmé goes on to say, mark the "creation of idea —creation perhaps unseen by man, mysterious, like some harmony of perfect purity" (*M,* p. 49; *Œuvres,* p. 648).

The difficulty is that this creation of the pure idea, this evocation of "some harmony of perfect purity," must be accomplished by means of language. We have already observed, in connection with Valéry's use of the analogy between poetry and music, that the poet lacks the freedom of the musician. For the musician, freedom lies in the undifferentiated character of his material, which is sound, and which, being undifferentiated, lends itself without bias to formation according to an infinity of possible structures. The poet's material is not sound but language, which is never undifferentiated but rather is given to the poet as a system already structured for signification. This is to say, in effect, that the poet is, quite as a matter of nature, drawn by his material into a universe of meaning.

But Mallarmé resists this pull of language toward meaning. What he proposes is the isolation of the word between the poet and the world—the fixing of the word in empty space.

Critics have long been intrigued by Mallarmé's experiments with syntax in the four lyrics that make up *Plusieurs sonnets* (1887). We might consider briefly the last of these poems:

> Ses purs ongles très haut dédiant leur onyx,
> L'Angoisse, ce minuit, soutient, lampadophore,
> Maint rêve vespéral brûlé par le Phénix
> Que ne recueille pas de cinéraire amphore
>
> Sur les crédences, au salon vide: nul ptyx,
> Aboli bibelot d'inanité sonore,
> (Car le Maitre est allé puiser des pleurs au Styx
> Avec ce seul objet dont le Néant s'honore).
>
> Mais proche la croisée au nord vacante, un or
> Agonise selon peut-être le décor
> Des licornes ruant du feu contre une nixe,
>
> Elle, défunte nue en le miroir, encor
> Que, dans l'oubli fermé par le cadre, se fixe
> De scintillations sitôt le septuor.

> [*Œuvres*, pp. 68–69]

This poem is characterized by the sort of diffusion of parts that we observed in Valéry's *La Jeune Parque*. Words which are meant to function together syntactically (for example, "L'Angoisse . . . soutient . . . Maint rêve vespéral") are dispersed by the intervention of other words. More than this, however, the period of which "L'Angoisse . . . soutient . . . Maint rêve vespéral" forms the (apparently) central syntactical structure is designed in such a way as to allow the insertion of additional but by no means subordinate material:

> . . . brûlé par le Phénix
> Que ne recueille pas de cinéraire amphore
> Sur les crédences, au salon vide.

For its part, "nul ptyx, / Aboli bibelot d'inanité sonore" is held in place less by syntax than by typography, and so remains structurally independent of the whole—a condition reinforced somewhat by the parenthetical account of the shell's absence and of its enigmatic relation to "le Néant."

In "Ses purs ongles," in short, the ordinary function of syntax has been appreciably deflected: so far from organizing words into a unified utterance (one capable of bearing the weight of meaning), its activity here seems to have been radically subordinated to another principle of unity. For if words do not unite syntactically, they are inclined to do so thematically: they suggest, most of them, images of absence—an empty urn, an empty room, an absent shell, a departed master, nothingness, an empty window through which one may observe the death throes of the evening, a dead nymph reflected in a mirror whose frame encloses forgetfulness. Indeed, the poem creates a void within which, for unknown reasons, "se fixe / De scintillations sitôt le septuor." What we are left with, however, is not an utterance but a motif—a musical rather than a truly linguistic structure, one which, as Elizabeth Sewell has shown in her analysis of *Plusieurs sonnets,* moves freely among still more strictly musical relationships. Sewell urges us to consider that "the principle of construction of this poetry is to use the elements [words] not for any intrinsic meaning but to mark positions in a relation system." [5] This system, she says, is built up from what she calls the "sound-look" properties of words, which is to say that it is marked by the interplay of physical equivalences ("Aboli bibelot d'inanité sonore"; "De scintillations sitôt le septuor") and not by an interplay of significant functions. The words of the poem, that is, do not come together on the basis of any unified movement of meaning such as one finds in a system of utterances organized according to identifiably syntactic procedures; instead, one discovers somewhat more easily relations formed among separate meanings (as in the diverse images of absence in "Ses purs ongles") and on the basis of similar phonetic and even orthographic constructions. Thus the poem, whatever possibilities of meaning it may present to the reader, suggests at the same time and indeed with greater force the presence of a system of pure relations.

What is more, the poem is an example of how Mallarmé worked to actualize his theory of impersonality. For the effort to displace the structural laws that govern speech (and which govern as well traditional poetic usage) by structural laws that belong to the world of music serves to diminish the illusion of a speaker, that is, the illusion of a presence behind or beneath the words, whose voice provides the rhythm of their organization. It is helpful to recall here Barthes's notion of the middle voice—of the *scripteur* who is present in the poem not as a persona but as an agent of the pure act of writing. "Ses purs ongles" is preeminently the written poem, the creation of "the magic waving wand of the written word." Just so, Mallarmé attaches a great premium to the written or printed word—the word not as a functional element in a discourse but as an object existing in a spatial and visual field. We shall see in a moment the great importance which this spatial and visual field—the white page—has for Mallarmé. For now, however, we should look to Mallarmé's remark, in "Le Mystère dans les lettres" (1895), that "Mystery is said to be music's domain. But the written word also lays claim to it," precisely as the written word is able to induce those "supreme" and heart-rending musical moments [which] are born of fleeting arabesques"— that is, when the word, by its diverse "movements" upon the white page, describes not an utterance but a structure of pure relations. Mallarmé describes such movements as follows:

> The sentence may seem to stammer at first, hold back in a knot of incidental bits; then it multiplies, takes on order, and rises up in a noble harmony, wavering all the while in its knowing transpositions.
>
> For those who may be surprised and angered by this broad application of my words, I shall describe the revels of this language.
>
> Words rise up unaided and in ecstasy; many a facet reveals its infinite rarity and is precious to our minds. For our mind is the center of this hesitancy and oscillation; it sees words not in their usual order, but in projection (like the walls of a cave), so long as that mobility which is their principle lives on, that part of

speech which is not spoken. Then, quickly, before they die away, they all exchange their brilliancies from afar; or they may touch, and steal a furtive glance. [*M*, pp. 32–33; *Œuvres*, p. 385–386]

We should notice here that language appears to have been returned to the world of myth, for in "the revels of this language" words take on a life of their own—an independent mobility that perhaps asserts once for all their liberation from the laws of ordinary speech and, indeed, from the agency of a speaker. Words themselves are the agents of the Mallarmean utterance: they "rise up unaided and in ecstasy"; they move ("not in their usual order") like so many objects projected upon a wall; "they all exchange their brilliancies from afar; or they may touch, and steal a furtive glance." Words contain their own principle of motivation, by virtue of which, as Mallarmé puts it in "La Musique et les lettres," language is able to adumbrate "certain orchestral phrasings in which we hear, first, a withdrawal to the shades, swirls and uneasy hesitation, and then suddenly the bursting, leaping, multiple ecstasy of brilliance, like the approaching radiance of sunrise" (*M*, p. 49; *Œuvres*, p. 648). And by this means language—written or printed language—lays claim to mystery: that is, mystery in its ancient (and, indeed, mythical) sense of revelation. The purity of form displayed by the "hesitancy and oscillation" of language marks it as the proper vehicle for beauty—the idea. Indeed, the "winding and mobile variations of the idea . . . are the prerogative of the written word" (*M*, p. 49; *Œuvres*, p. 648).

Mallarmé's use of the music–poetry analogy thus contains a paradoxical variation: music belongs to the world of sound, as does the spoken utterance, but for Mallarmé poetry lays claim to the domain of music by way of the written word, which belongs not to sound but to space. This paradox lies at the heart of Mallarmé's conviction that the present task of modern poets "is to find a way of transposing the symphony to the book: in short, to regain our rightful due. For, undeniably, the true source of music must not be the elemental sound of brasses, strings, or wood-winds, but the intellectual and written word in all its glory—music of perfect fulness and clarity—the totality of universal relationships" (*M*, p. 42; *Œuvres*, pp. 367–368). The book here is Mallarmé's great work—the book in which all earthly existence must one day be contained. The poet's task, in this case, would be as follows: to transpose objects into words, and to gather those words not into structures of meaning that will refer us back to the world of things but into "the totality of universal relationships"—into a musical structure whose circumference is nowhere and whose center is everywhere.

How to accomplish such a task? Mallarmé proceeds by renewing the art of the ancient scribe, whose special vocation grew out of the discovery that the world of objects and events, ideas and emotions, could be reduced to a set of physical particles, only twenty-four in number, yet capable of being combined in an infinite number of ways. It is well known that many ancient and medieval grammarians, and with them those curious initiates of the Cabalist tradition, invested the letters with mystical significance. In *Mallarmé's Un Coup de dés*, R. G. Cohn has shown how far Mallarmé went toward re-creating this myth of the alphabet.[6] Letters, Mallarmé says in some notes on language and method, are "purely hieroglyphic" characters, that is, ciphers whose significance is a matter of shape (*Œuvres*, p. 855). But in these notes and elsewhere he seems finally less concerned with the content of these hieroglyphs than with their function. In "La Musique et les lettres," for example, he identifies the letters of the alphabet as "our ancient heritage from the ancient books of magic," and he explains that their value is that "they provide us with a method of notation which spontaneously becomes literature" (*M*, p. 47; *Œuvres*, p. 646)—spontaneously, that is, as if by magic, according to which the words themselves become the agent of the literary act. We seem every inch now in a mythical universe. The point to mark, however, is that in the letters Mallarmé finds the possibility of his great book, because, as he says in "Le Livre, instrument spirituel" (1895), the letters are "gifted with infinity": "Everything [the totality of earthly existence] is caught up in their endless variations," which is to say in their capacity for forming an infinite variety of combinations—"the totality of universal relationships" (*M*, p. 26; *Œuvres*, p. 380).

It is in terms of the power of letters, Mallarmé goes on to say, that "typography becomes a rite" (*M*, p. 26; *Œuvres*, p. 380). For "the book, which is a total expansion of the letter, must find its mobility in the letter; and in its spaciousness must establish some nameless system of relationships" (*M*, pp. 26–27; *Œuvres*, p. 380). "Nameless" is indeed the appropriate word here. For the world, existing, as it does for the poet, in words, is by the rite of typography to be displayed not as a field of objects nor as a world of experience but as a totality of relations among a set of lexical structures. There is no question here of poetry involving itself in mere representation. In "Crise de vers" Mallarmé remarks that "the inner structures of a book of verse must be inborn"—rather like an innate idea, or perhaps like those of several principles deduced by Kant, whereby the mind is understood to organize the undifferentiated material of sensation into structures which, so far from corresponding to an outside world, ground their intelligibility upon their own laws of development. Whereas Kant's world is phenomenal and significant, however, Mallarmé's is at once typographic and musical:

> From each theme, itself predestined, a given harmony will be born somewhere in the parts of the total poem and take its proper place within the volume; because, for every sound, there is an echo. Motifs of like pattern will move in balance from point to point. There will be none of the sublime incoherence found in the page-settings of the romantics, none of the artificial unity that used to be based on the square measurements of the book. Everything will be hesitation, disposition of parts, their alterations and relationships—all contributing to the rhythmic totality, which will be the very silence of the poem, in its blank spaces, as that silence is translated by each structural element in its own way. [*M*, p. 41; *Œuvres*, pp. 366–367]

Not substance but form: not the imagining of a totality of objects but the unfolding, typographically, of a manifold of pure activities—"hesitation, disposition of parts, their alternations and relationships"—all contributing to a "rhythmic totality" that, paradoxically, constitutes "the very silence of the poem."

"Silence" here is, in one sense, the silence that attends the written or printed word. But for Mallarmé silence takes on special importance from the standpoint of his aesthetic as a whole. Silence, we may say, signals for Mallarmé the presence of beauty; or, again, in silence the mystery of nothingness— the idea—breaks in upon man. Consequently, in reading, Mallarmé tells us in "Le Mystère dans les lettres,"

> we must bend our independent minds, page by page, to the blank space which begins each one; we must forget the title, for it is too resounding. Then, in the tiniest and most scattered stopping-points upon the page, when the lines of chance have been vanquished word by word, the blanks unfailingly return; before, they were gratuitous; now they are essential; and now at last it is clear that nothing lies beyond; now silence is genuine and just.
>
> It is a virgin space, face to face with the lucidity of our matchless vision, divided of itself, in solitude, into halves of whiteness; and each of these is lawful bride to the other at the wedding of the idea.
>
> Thus the invisible air, or song, beneath the words leads our divining eye from word to music; and thus, like a motif, invisibly it inscribes its fleuron and pendant there. [*M*, pp. 33–34; *Œuvres*, p. 387]

The spatial field across which the poet casts his words (or, rather, across which the words arrange themselves) is gratuitous in traditional verse, but here it must be understood to be an integral part of the poem itself, in the same way that silence forms an essential part of any musical composition. "Music is born, develops, and realizes itself within silence," writes Gisèle Brelet: "upon silence it traces out its moving arabesques, which give a form to silence, and yet do not abolish it. A musical work, like all sonority, unfolds between two silences: the silence of its birth and the silence of its completion. In this temporal life where music perpetually is born, dies, and is born again, silence is its faithful companion." [7] Just so, for Mallarmé, will written language trace out its "moving arabesques," upon the white page, executing, like so many words in the void, splendid variations of the idea before it is consumed, like music, by the silence of the page. Just so will written language "give a form to silence," thus to articulate the mystery of the universe that it seeks to contain.

What is remarkable, perhaps, is how accessible Mallarmé considers this mystery finally to be. For, "in reading, a lonely quiet concert is given for our minds, and they in turn, less noisily, reach its meaning. All our mental faculties will be present in this symphonic exaltation; but, unlike music, they will be rarefied, for they partake of thought. Poetry, accompanied by the idea, is perfect music, and cannot be anything else" (*M*, p. 27; *Œuvres*, p. 380). That is to say, in the afterglow of our encounter with the written word, it is given to us to share the mystery of Mallarmé's poetry: our minds, "rarefied"—emptied, doubtless, of all but "the sensation of absolute emptiness"—"partake of thought." We come to share, in other words, that elemental experience of the idea upon which Mallarmé grounds his poetry and in particular his dream of the book.

Such a dream, understandably, proved impossible to realize —although it is clear from the documents published by Jacques Scherer in 1957 under the title *Le "Livre" de Mallarmé* that Mallarmé went some distance in planning the book —in planning, that is to say, its physical dimensions, for nearly half of the notes are composed of mathematical computations, and very few are concerned with the kind of work the book was finally to be. Thus we are told, for example, that "the intellectual armature of the poem [is to be] concealed . . . in the space which isolates the strophes amid the white of the paper; significant silence which is not less beautiful to compose than the verse." [8] Or, again: "The volume, despite [its] fixed impression, becomes by this play [of pages], mobile." [9] But these and a handful of other, similar statements merely adumbrate the themes which Mallarmé develops in his prose. It remains the case that he could only rest content, as he says in "Crise de vers," that "certain recent publications have heralded this sort of book," which is to say that certain "young poets have seen what an overwhelming and harmonious totality a poem must be, and have stammered out the magic concept of the great work" (*M*, p. 41; *Œuvres*, p. 367). Thus, perhaps, does the book emerge as a kind of mythic subject: not the work of one poet but of many, it attains to a cultural dimension, which is to say that it becomes the subject of a cultural activity and so becomes not a book to be realized once for all in a single creative outburst but instead one to be approximated in successive typographic rituals—a book the totality of which is never fully to be grasped but only to be glimpsed in the luminescence of its several parts.

In this way we may interpret *Un Coup de dés* as a part which mysteriously evokes the whole, for in this poem Mallarmé seeks to actualize not the book itself but its constitutive principles. For in *Un Coup de dés* typography replaces syntax as a way of establishing relationships among words—that is, as a way of organizing the material of the poem. Syntactical structures are everywhere to be found, but they are radically diffused by the way the words are positioned on the page. The importance of this displacement or subordination of syntax has already been suggested: syntax describes a movement in time, but what Mallarmé seeks is the illusion of objects moving in space. "We avoid narrative," he writes in his preface to *Un Coup de dés,* for his aim is to "space out" our reading of the poem so that as we move from word to word and from one group of words to another, we will do so within "a simultaneous vision of the page" (*Œuvres,* p. 455). The page, not the line, is the unit of Mallarmé's verse, and within the unit words appear and disappear "according to the mobility of the writing." As we have seen, it is principally the release of language from the conventional maneuvers of syntax that makes possible the kind of movement that Mallarmé has in mind—the "withdrawals" and "prolongations" of words that betoken a musical structure (*Œuvres,* p. 455). Hence a line of verse falls in variable movements from left to right across "halves of whiteness," its apparently discontinuous but finally carefully modulated mobility controlled by the white space, which, like silence in music, intervenes to give the line a formal as against a strictly linguistic intelligibility. One has evidently to imagine a visual experience of music, the movement of free, visible forms, in order to comprehend fully what Mallarmé seeks to achieve.

The differences in points of type in the poem play an integral role in this effort toward the illusion of visual music—the illusion of the symphony transposed to the book. The title and main theme, "Un coup de dés jamais n'abolira le hasard," is printed in 48-point type and is dispersed throughout the poem. In his preface Mallarmé identifies it simply in terms of its structural function: it is "the latent conductor wire" which holds the poem together and through which, as through a concealed spine, the energy of the poem runs its course. Subordinate themes, printed in various smaller points and faces of type, exist simultaneously with the main theme, which they surround and punctuate, occupying "variable positions" in relation to it, finally to constitute what Mallarmé, again thinking of his poem in terms of a visual experience, calls "prismatic subdivisions of the idea" (*Œuvres*, p. 455).

"Idea" here is once more the pure idea which the poem seeks to actualize structurally. The themes shadow this idea in the harmony—the "rhythmic totality"—which their mobility suggests. But the themes are also accessible to paraphrase, and from them it is possible to deduce the "fiction" which underlies the poem and which evidently articulates the "idea" along the lines of a more traditional (that is to say, mimetic) literary utterance. As in "Ses purs ongles," the significance of the fiction appears to turn upon the idea of absence—or nothingness. In "Ses purs ongles," the motif of absence gives way at the end to "De scintillations . . . septuor"—to a septet of stars, or constellation. The same pattern is present in *Un Coup de dés*, except that here the idea of absence is developed dramatically, that is, through the representation of "l'acte vide." [10] A "master," at a critical moment in his life, seeks to test the efficacy of the human will.

By a throw of the dice—an act of choice which, paradoxically, utilizes the forces of chance—he will abolish chance, and thus establish himself as the master of his own fate. The moment is prepared for, but the theme which courses through the poem in 14-point type advises us that "rien . . . n'aura eu lieu"—nothing will have taken place. A throw of the dice will never abolish chance. Just so, nothing does take place, "EXCEPTÉ . . . PEUT-ÊTRE . . . UNE CONSTELLATION," which (as in "Ses purs ongles") emerges enigmatically at the end, "froide d'oubli et de désuétude"—cold from forgetfulness and disuse. One might speculate, nevertheless, that the act has efficacy still, that if it is indeed empty and so disintegrates in "du vague en quoi tout réalité se dissout," it creates at the same time, as though *ex nihilo,* a purely formal structure such as the constellation implies—implies, the more so as the arrangement of stars against the blackness of the void becomes something like a negative image of *Un Coup de dés* itself, with its words strewn like so many stars across the white space of the page.

Mallarmé's vision, then, is of the transcendent word—of language which belongs neither to the world of things nor to the human world of speech but rather to primordial emptiness, in which the splendor of beauty exists as a sheer presence, a pure quality unpredicated of any reality but the word. Mallarmé's, indeed, is the song of Orpheus in his absence—

> Vaste gouffre apporté dans l'amas de la brume
> Par l'irascible vent des mots qu'il n'a pas dits,
> Le néant à cet Homme aboli de jadis:
> 'Souvenirs d'horizons, qu'est-ce, ô toi, que la Terre?'
> Hurle ce songe; et, voix dont la clarté s'altère,
> L'espace a pour jouet le cri: 'Je ne sais pas!'
>
> [*Œuvres,* p. 294]

UN COUP DE DÉS

JAMAIS

QUAND BIEN MÊME LANCÉ DANS DES CIRCONSTANCES

ÉTERNELLES

DU FOND D'UN NAUFRAGE

SOIT
    que

          l'Abîme

blanchi
      étale
         furieux
                sous une inclinaison
                    plane désespérément

                              d'aile

                         la sienne
                              par

avance retombée d'un mal à dresser le vol
                    et couvrant les jaillissements
                              coupant au ras les bonds

            très à l'intérieur résume

l'ombre enfouie dans la profondeur par cette voile alternative

                    jusqu'adapter
                        à l'envergure

            sa béante profondeur en tant que la coque

                    d'un bâtiment

                penché de l'un ou l'autre bord

LE MAÎTRE

surgi
    inférant

de cette conflagration

que se

comme on menace

l'unique Nombre qui ne peut pas

hésite
cadavre par le bras
plutôt
    que de jouer
        en maniaque chenu
            la partie
        au nom des flots
un

naufrage cela

                    hors d'anciens calculs
          où la manœuvre avec l'âge oubliée

                        jadis il empoignait la barre

à ses pieds
                de l'horizon unanime

prépare
      s'agite et mêle
            au poing qui l'étreindrait
un destin et les vents

être un autre

                    Esprit
                          pour le jeter
                                  dans la tempête
                          en reployer la division et passer fier

écarté du secret qu'il détient

envahit le chef
coule en barbe soumise

direct de l'homme

          sans nef
                n'importe
                        où vaine

ancestralement à n'ouvrir pas la main
                                        crispée
                              par delà l'inutile tête

        legs en la disparition

                                    à quelqu'un
                                            ambigu

                        l'ultérieur démon immémorial

ayant
        de contrées nulles
                              induit
le vieillard vers cette conjonction suprême avec la probabilité

                                            celui
                                                son ombre puérile
caressée et polie et rendue et lavée
                                assouplie par la vague et soustraite
                        aux durs os perdus entre les ais

                                            né
                                                d'un ébat
la mer par l'aïeul tentant ou l'aïeul contre la mer
                        une chance oiseuse

                                                        Fiançailles
dont
        le voile d'illusion rejailli leur hantise
        ainsi que le fantôme d'un geste

                                chancellera
                                s'affalera

                                    folie

N'ABOLIRA

COMME SI

Une insinuation

au silence

dans quelque proche

voltige

simple

enroulée avec ironie
                    ou
                        le mystère
                                précipité
                                        hurlé

tourbillon d'hilarité et d'horreur

autour du gouffre
                    sans le joncher
                                ni fuir

        et en berce le vierge indice

                                COMME SI

plume solitaire éperdue

sauf

que la rencontre ou l'effleure une toque de minuit
et immobilise
au velours chiffonné par un esclaffement sombre

cette blancheur rigide

dérisoire
en opposition au ciel
trop
pour ne pas marquer
exigüment
quiconque

prince amer de l'écueil

s'en coiffe comme de l'héroïque
irrésistible mais contenu
par sa petite raison virile
en foudre

soucieux

     expiatoire et pubère

                 muet

          La lucide et seigneuriale aigrette
              au front invisible
       scintille
         puis ombrage
     une stature mignonne ténébreuse
       en sa torsion de sirène

     par d'impatientes squames ultimes

rire

que

SI

de vertige

debout

le temps
de souffleter
bifurquées

un roc

faux manoir
tout de suite
évaporé en brumes

qui imposa
une borne à l'infini

$$C'ÉTAIT$$
issu stellaire

$$CE\ SERAIT$$
pire

non

davantage ni moins

indifféremment mais autant

LE NOMBRE

EXISTÂT-IL
autrement qu'hallucination éparse d'agonie

COMMENÇÂT-IL ET CESSÂT-IL
sourdant que nié et clos quand apparu
enfin
par quelque profusion répandue en rareté
SE CHIFFRÂT-IL

évidence de la somme pour peu qu'une
ILLUMINÂT-IL

LE HASARD

Choit
la plume
rythmique suspens du sinistre
s'ensevelir
aux écumes originelles
naguères d'où sursauta son délire jusqu'à une cime
flétrie
par la neutralité identique du gouffre

RIEN

de la mémorable crise
ou se fût
l'événement

accompli en vue de tout résultat nul
                                         humain

                          N'AURA EU LIEU
                  une élévation ordinaire verse l'absence

                                              QUE LE LIEU
inférieur clapotis quelconque comme pour disperser l'acte vide
                          abruptement qui sinon
                              par son mensonge
                                  eût fondé
                                la perdition

dans ces parages
                      du vague
                              en quoi toute réalité se dissout

EXCEPTÉ
    à l'altitude
        PEUT-ÊTRE
            aussi loin qu'un endroit

fusionne avec au delà

                    hors l'intérêt
              quant à lui signalé
                                en général
selon telle obliquité par telle déclivité
                                de feux

        vers
            ce doit être
                le Septentrion aussi Nord

                            UNE CONSTELLATION

            froide d'oubli et de désuétude
                              pas tant
                        qu'elle n'énumère
                sur quelque surface vacante et supérieure
                          le heurt successif
                                    sidéralement
                d'un compte total en formation

veillant
        doutant
                roulant
                    brillant et méditant

                            avant de s'arrêter
                à quelque point dernier qui le sacre

                Toute Pensée émet un Coup de Dés

5

Flaubert, Joyce, and
the Displacement of Fiction

In *Fundamentals of Language,* Roman Jakobson takes up the theme of "the bipolar structure of language," and he observes that, in any given instance, a discourse may develop along a vertical axis, in which one topic leads to another according to the principle of similarity or metaphor, or it may develop along a horizontal or, as some linguists call it, a syntagmatic axis, according to the principle of contiguity or metonymy. To illustrate these processes, Jakobson refers us to the familiar psychological test in which "children are confronted with some noun and told to utter the first verbal response that comes into their heads." [1] Inevitably, these responses take either of two forms, corresponding to the metaphoric and metonymic (or syntagmatic) poles of language: a substitutive response, in which the given noun is replaced by a synonym or antonym; or a predicative response, in which the given noun is placed within a syntactic formation, that is, made to function within a sentence. Any act of speech involves an interplay between substitution and predication, or between metaphoric and metonymic processes, but what is interesting is that Jakobson sees in this bipolar structure a way of distinguishing, on a specifically linguistic basis, between the language of poetry and the language of fiction—especially the language of realistic fiction or the novel. Thus, for example, "following the path of contiguous relationships, the realistic author metonymically digresses from the plot to the atmosphere and from the characters to the setting in place and time," and by this means he builds up a system of details whose coherence is comparable to that of ordinary experience, in the sense that (to follow the implications of Jakobson's argument) our world is organized as a horizon within which things and events, persons and activities, present themselves to us on a contiguous basis.[2]

Poetic speech, by contrast, plays the syntagmatic order of discourse off against a network of phonetic, semantic, and syntactic (or, as Jakobson says, "positional") equivalences—as, for example, in Dylan Thomas's lines:

> Death is all metaphors, shape in one history;
> The child that sucketh long is shooting up,
> The planet-ducted pelican of circles
> Weans on an artery the gender's strip;
> Child of the short spark in a shapeless country
> Soon sets alight a long stick from the cradle;
> The horizontal cross-bones of Abaddon,
> You by the cavern over the black-stairs,
> Rung bone and blade, the verticals of Adam,
> And, manned by midnight, Jacob to the stars.[3]

Notice that the predications in this passage are not immediately accessible to interpretation: the syntagmatic order of speech is structured in a way that makes it difficult to follow the line of semantic contiguity that normally forms the content of an utterance. It is structured, that is to say, as an interplay of equivalences: "The child that sucketh long" is mirrored in "the planet-ducted pelican" that "weans on an artery the gender's strip"; the "child of the short spark . . . sets alight," by contrast, "the long stick"; "the horizontal cross-bones of Abaddon" are duplicated by "the black-stairs," which is to say "the verticals of Adam." More than this, the opposition in the first two lines between death and the ascension of life ("The child that sucketh long is shooting up") is repeated, on perhaps a higher order of being, in the last four lines, in which "cross-bones" are set over and against an allusion to Jacob's Ladder.

One could go on to observe, besides these semantic equivalences, phonetic and positional similarities as well. But the question I wish to raise has rather to do with the language of fiction: What happens to the work of prose fiction when its language shifts from the metonymic to the metaphoric pole of discourse? The question has, obviously, historical as well as theoretical value, and I mean to underscore the historical nature of the problem by attending to the work of Gustave Flaubert and James Joyce, who call the very nature of fiction into question by their transformation of its language.

We can begin to test the theoretical ground of this matter by looking to a number of Flaubert's letters, and particularly one which deserves to be read in connection with Jakobson's distinction between metaphor and metonymy. In April of 1852, shortly after beginning work on *Madame Bovary,* Flaubert wrote to his mistress, Louise Colet:

> I've imagined a style for myself—a beautiful style that someone will write someday, in ten years' time maybe, or in ten centuries. It will be as rhythmical as verse and as precise as science, with the booming rise and fall of a cello and plumes of fire; it will be a style which penetrates the idea for you like a dagger-thrust and from which at last thought is sent sailing over smooth surfaces as a boat glides rapidly before a good wind. Prose was born yesterday—this is what we must tell ourselves. Poetry is preeminently the medium of past literatures. All the metrical combinations have been tried but nothing like this can be said of prose.[4]

Flaubert here elaborates, for the first time, his doctrine of *le mot juste,* but what is interesting (and what is seldom observed) is that his conception of *le mot juste* is bipolar: it is not only that, in a given fictional context, the right word will contribute to the exact presentation of an object; it must at the same time form an integral part of a more purely formal structure. Language, that is to say, is understood by Flaubert to function along two axes: a vertical axis, according to which language duplicates "the booming rise and fall of a cello and plumes of fire"; and a horizontal axis, according to which it "penetrates the idea for you like a dagger-thrust and from which at last thought is sent sailing over smooth surfaces as a boat glides rapidly before a good wind." What Flaubert appears to have in mind is something like a unity or balance of the metaphoric and metonymic poles of discourse, whereby the act of speech takes on, without compromising its essentially transitive function, the musical character of the poetic utterance. The "rhythm of verse," the foregrounding of phonetic and syntactic similarities, is to be adequated to the precision of scientific description; the "booming rise and fall" of the formal line must be actualized without (somehow) disrupting the "smooth surface" across which the fictional utterance propels its imagined world.

The problem is, however, that metaphor and metonymy are not inert but (let us say) magnetic poles. As Jakobson explains, "A competition between both devices, metonymic and metaphoric, is manifest in any symbolic process," and accordingly a given act of speech will find its own peculiar harmony in the dominance of one or the other of these processes of articulation.[5] This theoretical linguistic problem confronted Flaubert in its most immediate and practical form: "no one," he wrote, "has ever conceived a more perfect type of prose than I; but as to the execution, how weak, how weak, oh God!" (*SL*, p. 139; *C*, II, p. 469). For what Flaubert understood—and what he most deeply felt—was the polarized nature of his undertaking. We see this polarity everywhere in the *Correspondance*. Thus, for example, Flaubert considered *Madame Bovary* to be "essentially a work of criticism, or anatomy," but he hoped at the same time that no one would take notice of "all the psychological work hidden under the form" (*SL*, p. 167; *C*, IV, p. 3). Similarly, he remarks that "actually I feel at home only in analysis—in anatomy, if I may call it such," and yet he adds that "the books I most long to write are precisely those for which I am least endowed. *Bovary*, in this sense, is an unprecedented tour de force (a fact of which I alone shall ever be aware): its subject, characters, effects, etc.—all are alien to me" (*SL*, pp. 139–140; *C*, III, p. 3). Or, again, he expresses his admiration for Homer, Rabelais, and Shakespeare on the grounds that "their form is whole, crammed full of substance to the bursting point" (*SL*, p. 150; *C*, II, p. 150). Elsewhere, however, he wonders whether a book, "quite apart from what it says," might not be able to produce the sort of aesthetic experience that is generated by "one of the walls of the Acropolis, a wall that is completely bare" (*SL*, p. 252; *C*, VII, p. 294).

More telling, however, is his conviction that "there are in me, literally speaking, two distinctive persons": one "who digs and burrows into the truth as deeply as he can, who likes to treat a humble fact as respectfully as a big one, who would like to make you feel almost *physically* the things he reproduces"; and another who dreams of writing "a book about nothing, a book dependent on nothing external, which would be held together by the strength of its style, just as the earth, suspended in the void, depends on nothing external for its support; a book which would have almost no subject, or at least in which the subject would be almost invisible, if such a thing is possible" (*SL*, pp. 127–128; *C*, II, pp. 343–345). Two Flauberts, anatomist and formalist, the one seeking to duplicate our experience of the world in all its immediacy, the other seeking a transcendence comparable to Mallarmé's *le Néant*—what this suggests is that there exists in Flaubert a psychological basis for his bipolar conception of *le mot juste,* that metaphor and metonymy are modes of discourse that open onto a competition of identities.

We know very well the history of this competition—"My accursed Bovary is harrying me and driving me mad. . . . No one will be able to say that I haven't experienced the agonies of art!" (*SL*, p. 127; *C*, II, p. 339). We might inquire, however, into the logic by which this famous agony runs its course. After *Madame Bovary* began to appear serially in the *Revue de Paris*, Flaubert wrote to the editor, Léon Laurent-Pichat:

Do you think that this ignoble reality, so disgusting to you in reproduction, does not oppress my heart as it does yours? If you knew me better you would know that I abhor ordinary existence. Personally, I have always held myself as aloof from it as I could. But aesthetically, I desired this once—and only this once—to plumb its very depths. Therefore I plunged into it heroically, into the midst of its minutiae, accepting everything, telling everything, depicting everything, pretentious as it may sound to say so. [*SL*, pp. 179–180; *C*, IV, p. 125]

"I abhor ordinary existence": as the anatomist abhors his specimen, and as the formalist abhors whatever will violate the purity of his art. The point here is that the impulse to ' expose the Bovarian world for what it is, and the impulse to annihilate that world by submerging its analogue beneath the stylistic virtuosity of an absolute book, are finally different expressions not of "two distinct persons" but of a unified sensibility.

We can glimpse something of the character of this sensibility by observing that, for the lover of beauty, the writing of fiction—the heroic plunging into the minutiae of ordinary existence—has about it a structural resemblance to the ritual of penance:

Art, like the Jewish God, wallows in sacrifices. So tear yourself to pieces, mortify your flesh, roll in ashes, smear yourself with filth and spittle, wrench out your heart! You will be alone, your feet will bleed, an infernal disgust will be with you throughout your pilgrimage, what gives joy to others will give none to you, what to them are but pinpricks will cut you to the quick, and you will be lost in the hurricane with only beauty's faint glow visible on the horizon. But it will grow, grow like the sun, its golden rays will bathe your face, penetrate into you, you will be illumined within, ethereal, all spiritualized, and after each bleeding the flesh will be less burdensome. [*SL*, pp. 161–162; *C*, III, p. 306]

Flaubert gives us here an elaborate metaphor for the agony of composing a work of fiction: it is a pilgrimage toward beauty, during the course of which the pilgrim mortifies himself with

the waste of existence. More than this, however, the pil-
grimage is finally a process of redemption, whereby the writer
is liberated from the world and transfigured by the light of
beauty. The way down, it appears, is the way up: to plunge
into the world of ordinary existence becomes a way of tran-
scending it, as though the anatomy performed upon the world
were, however disgusting in itself, a necessary adjunct to art,
a means to aesthetic salvation. The writing of fiction, con-
ceived as an anatomy, is thus not so much an art in its own
right as an activity that makes art possible. The writing of
fiction, that is to say, provides the occasion for the art of lan-
guage—for pursuing, as Flaubert puts it, "a certain manner of
writing and a certain beauty of language" (*SL*, p. 134; *C*, II,
p. 443). Thus Flaubert converges upon what was later to be
a central theme in Valéry's poetics: that "life must be con-
sidered as a means, nothing more" (*SL*, p. 256; *C*, VIII, p. 136).

The anatomist thus plays Servant to a formalist Master. The
important point of inquiry, however, is how this drama of
Master and Servant is played out in the writing itself. It is
perhaps reflected most clearly in the famous violation of de-
corum by which Flaubert executes his judgment against or-
dinary existence, for the turgid character of Emma Bovary's
world is transcended everywhere by the splendid artifice
within which that world is brought into being. Few commenta-
tors on Flaubert have failed to note this divergence of art and
life in *Madame Bovary*, but fewer still have observed that it
was Flaubert who first pointed it out: "My characters are com-
pletely commonplace," Flaubert explained to Louise Colet,
"but they have to speak in a literary style" (*SL*, pp. 142–143;
C, III, p. 25). Exigencies of art require, that is to say, that or-
dinary speech give way to a literary idiom. Hence Flaubert's
development of "le style indirect libre," a form of reported
speech that situates the drift of a character's utterance or
meditation within the locutions of the narrator and so medi-
ates, as in the case of *Madame Bovary*, between creatures of
elemental sensibility and the master stylist who, "like God in
creation, invisible and all-powerful . . . [is] everywhere felt,

but nowhere seen" (*SL*, p. 195; *C*, IV, p. 164). Indeed, the characters of *Madame Bovary* are surrounded and penetrated by the divine speech of the Master. Near the end of Part One, for example, we read the following:

> Mais c'était surtout aux heures des repas qu'elle n'en pouvait plus, dans cette petite salle au rez-de-chaussée, avec le poêle qui fumait, la porte qui criait, les murs qui suintaient, les pavés humides; toute l'amertume de l'existence lui semblait servie sur son assiette, et, à la fumée du bouilli, il montait du fond de son âme comme d'autres bouffées d'affadissement. Charles était long à manger; elle grignotait quelques noisettes, ou bien, appuyée du coude, s'amusait, avec la pointe de son couteau, à faire des raies sur la toile cirée.[6]

Not only bitterness and domestic squalor but the euphony and assonance of Flaubert's language attend Emma at her meal. The passage is dominated by the imperfect tense, which functions, however, not only grammatically but stylistically as a way of organizing words into a system of phonetic equivalences: "c'était," "pouvait," "rez-de-chaussée," "fumait," "criait," "semblait," "fumée," "montait," "bouffées." This "motif" is traversed, moreover, by other clusters of phonetic equivalences—"Mais c'était surtout," "toute l'amertume," "semblait servie sur son assiette"—as well as by syntactic formations that fall neatly into rhythmic patterns: "avec le poêle qui fumait, la porte qui criait, les murs qui suintaient, les pavés humides."

Even more significant than these schemes of rhetoric, however, is Flaubert's figurative ingenuity. Emma's emotional state is actualized not simply by an image but by an elaborate conceit that organizes her interior and her situation into a momentary drama: "toute l'amertume de l'existence lui semblait servie sur son assiette, et, à la fumée du bouilli, il montait du fond de son âme comme d'autres bouffées." Like all conceits, perhaps, this one poses a problem as to its precise function. It testifies, certainly, to the quality of Emma's life, which in this instance coalesces with the elemental character of the Bovary kitchen and stimulates in Emma an elemental response: steam emerges from the boiled meat, thus to be transformed into the fumes of bitterness that well up from the depths of Emma's soul. But if the conceit thus objectifies Emma's interior, it nevertheless exceeds its transitive purpose and reaches a complexity that does not form the ground of any complexity in Emma's emotion. In his analysis of this conceit in *Mimesis,* Erich Auerbach observes that Flaubert bestows "the power of mature expression upon the material which [Emma] affords," but between the expression and the material there is a dissonance, an absence of decorum, which underscores the poverty of Emma's sensibility.[7] The conceit in this sense testifies not only to the quality of Emma's life; it testifies *against* it—testifies against it, what is more, on behalf of the power of expression which it displays.

In *Madame Bovary,* in other words, the competition of which Jakobson speaks between the metaphoric and metonymic processes of discourse takes on a special significance: it becomes a competition no longer merely linguistic, but in fact a competition between language and reality, or between art and life. It is interesting to know, in this connection, that Flaubert's revision of the first draft of *Madame Bovary* consisted in the amplification of metaphoric devices over and against the metonymic development of the narrative. The phonetic equivalences that characterize the passage quoted above, for example, are only roughly adumbrated in the original version:

First Draft Version	*Final Version*
Aux heures repas, il fallait descendre manger dans la salle. Elle n'avait pas faim. Charles mangeait lentement. Le poêle fumait, et la porte de la cuisine criait toute les fois que Félicité entrait, des vens coulis passaient par les carreaux, les páves étaient froids.	Mais c'était surtout aux heures des repas qu'elle n'en pouvait plus, dans cette petite salle au rez-de-chaussée, avec le poêle qui fumait, la porte qui criait, les murs qui suintaient, les pavés humides.

Similarly, the conceit examined above was originally much less complex, and indeed was hardly a conceit at all:

Accoudée sur la toile cirée de la table, tout le dégoût de la vie lui semblait servi dans son assiette, a la fumée du bouilli, il lui montait des bouffées funèbres, devant cette petite table à toile cirée, chargée d'un plat et de deux salières, face à face avec cet homme, entre ces murs.[8]

toute l'amertume de l'existence lui semblait servie sur son assiette, et, a la fumée du bouilli, il montait du fond de son âme comme d'autres bouffées d'affadissement.

There were at least three revisions of the entire passage, but it was in the first that the major changes were established: namely, the building up of phonetic equivalences and rhythmic and figurative structures, and (significantly) the deletion of details and phrases to form a more tightly organized unit of syntactical relations. Flaubert's revision comprised a double movement toward formal complexity and economy in the presentation of detail. The earliest version is a plain prose presentation of a scene; in the finished version, by contrast, it is clear that the passage is no longer simply a fictional utterance but has become of kind of space within which the master stylist has assembled a system of verbal effects.

This passage is typical of the whole, for in revision Flaubert shifts the act of writing from the metonymic to the metaphoric axis—and radically so. To quote Albert Béguin (whose words describe in order to lament the process of revision), Flaubert abandons himself to the "tyrannical law of the verbal cadence," which now supersedes and, indeed, "stifles the deeper rhythm, the multiple rhythm of the flesh, the image, and time," that characterized the original development of the narrative. "Detached henceforth from the deeper realities which he had begun to discover," Béguin continues, "the novelist's only concern is to perfect what he now merely considers a mass of sound that demands to be ordered . . . a heavy and shapeless mass that demands to be modeled into shape in order to represent not life itself but an ideal model, an aesthetic canon of perfection." [9] For Flaubert, *Madame Bovary* becomes, after the first draft, "a book about nothing"—a book to be "held together by the strength of its style." This suggests that, even as there are two Flauberts, so are there two *Madame Bovarys*, one a representation of life, a tour de force in the realistic mode, the other an adumbration of an impossible book—a book which, given the nature of language as a semiotic system, cannot exist in a pure state but only in a relationship of competition with the reality which language seeks conventionally to articuate. One is reminded here of Valéry's observation that "the essence of prose is to perish—that is, to be 'understood' —that is, to be dissolved, destroyed without return, entirely replaced by the image or impulse that it conveys according to the conventions of language." [10] It is certainly true that Emma Bovary's world takes on meaning and the color of reality within a universe of prose; but the point is that in his revision of *Madame Bovary* Flaubert took pains to ensure that his prose would not perish, that it would not exhaust itself in the formation or transmission of a fictional reality but would maintain itself in being over and against that reality and even work to diminish it—to place it in its proper, which is to say subordinate, relationship to the art of language.

One is reminded also of an essay by Maurice Blanchot, "Le Langage de la fiction," in which it is proposed that the essence of fiction is not to be found in an image of reality but, on the contrary, in the poverty or absence of reality, or what Blanchot calls "le monde de l'irréalité." Blanchot's point is that any work of fiction, however realistic it may seem in its presentation of detail, will nevertheless force us to confess to the absence of that imaginary world which forms its content. Our perception that a work of fiction is a fabrication of language, is a perception of its "irreal" nature.[11] The more a writer moves us, by the several devices of his language, to acknowledge the artificial character of his writing, the more securely does he situate his work in an "irreal world"—the more does he increase the distance between the world of his writing and the world of actual objects and real events. Blanchot thus provides us with a way of defining the function of Flaubert's style: it is to distance the work from the world represented in the work. It is as though, in composing the first draft of *Madame Bovary*, Flaubert has called into imaginary being a reality which he was prepared to eradicate by amplifying, during the course of revision, the more purely formal properties of language. We may, therefore, think of *Madame Bovary* as a kind of incomplete "book about nothing," on the grounds that what this ideal book would have required for its creation is a process of revision of the kind that Flaubert brought to bear upon *Madame Bovary,* but one which would need to be continued beyond the point at which Flaubert stopped. For revision as Flaubert practiced it can be defined (following Blanchot) as a process of "irrealization"—a process which propels the work an infinite distance into that void in which all the inaccessible ideals of absolute art may be supposed to dwell.[12]

As soon as we begin to think of Flaubert's dream of "a book about nothing" in this way, as a kind of ultimate book implicit in the way Flaubert revised *Madame Bovary,* we begin to see how Flaubert anticipates Joyce. That Joyce continued what Flaubert had begun is a historical judgment that seems always to have been acknowledged, but usually the judgment is rendered broadly by such concepts as "the cult of style" or "encyclopedic realism." [13] The point I wish to move toward here is that the revisions of *Madame Bovary* and the hypothetical "book about nothing" look forward to the composition and revisions of *Ulysses,* and particularly to *Finnegans Wake,* in which the art of fiction is displaced almost entirely by what Barthes called the pure "act of writing."

There is at least one important difference between Joyce and Flaubert that ought to be recognized at once: the language of Flaubert is in good measure a departure from the language of ordinary speech ("My characters are completely commonplace, but they have to speak in a literary style"), whereas the language of Joyce, as Hugh Kenner observes, is in each of his works grounded upon the illusion of the speaking voice. From *Dubliners* ("At last the children grew tired and sleepy and Joe asked Maria would she not sing some little song before she went, one of the old songs") to *Finnegans Wake* ("It was of a night, late, lang time agone, in an auldstane eld, when Adam was delvin and his madameen spinning watersilts"), we are in the presence of a storyteller, one whose gift is perhaps less for storytelling, however, than for mimicry.[14] But precisely because Joyce executes so well the illusion of speech, his efforts to undermine this illusion seems the more remarkable. For as Joyce's career progresses beyond *Dubliners,* the sound of the human voice articulates a language that bears increasingly little resemblance to any known medium of human discourse.

This is so because for Joyce as for Flaubert language exists in a relationship of competition to the art of fiction. Thus, for example, the language of the *Portrait* works not only to actualize Stephen's mind and the world which penetrates it; at the same time it arranges itself into forms dictated by the sort of sensibility that Stephen happens to possess: "Emerald and black and russet and olive, it moved beneath the current, swaying and turning. The water of the rivulet was dark with endless drift and mirrored the highdrifting clouds. The clouds were drifting above him silently and silently the seatangle was drifting below him; and the grey warm air was still: and a new wild life was singing in his veins." [15] This is the language of Yeats's Michael Robartes stories; that is to say, it is the execution of an artificial form of discourse, one clearly meant to represent the peculiar stylistic *œuvre* to which Stephen is susceptible. The point to mark, is that in *Stephen Hero* this mannered prose appears only in the form of quotations by Stephen from Yeats's *Tables of the Law* and *Adoration of the Magi.* In the *Portrait,* however, this prose has taken over the activity of storytelling. Similarly in his revisions of *Madame Bovary* did Flaubert reorganize the language of fiction into an artifice of eternity. But notice that in the *Portrait* there is no violation of decorum, no superiority of style to that which it describes; on the contrary, we have what has been variously called "expressive" or "imitative" form, in which Joyce, as A. Walton Litz says, "seeks to establish a direct correspondence between substance and style." [16] Style, that is, becomes symbolic of the content, in the sense that the configurations of the prose take on meaning by analogy with the subject matter.

We converge here upon a conventional point in Joyce criticism: that Joyce complicates the art of storytelling by transposing his fictional material to the surface of his prose. It was precisely this transposition which governed the so-called great revision of *Ulysses,* which Litz has compared to Henry James's monumental rewriting of his early work but which, in terms of the nature and direction of the revision, is rather more comparable to the revisions of *Madame Bovary.* In any case, in 1918, with some thirteen chapters completed and seven in print (in the *Little Review*), Joyce decided to transform *Ulysses* into a literary work whose chief distinction would be the formal expressiveness of its language. Thus in the "Sirens" episode Joyce's prose performs the gyrations of a fugue, even as it articulates for us the scene in the bar, a songfest, Bloom's mind, and the peculiar relationship between the singing and Bloom's unconscious. Such analogies between style and content appear in all eighteen episodes of *Ulysses.*

In a sense, however, it is misleading and perhaps incorrect to speak of "analogies between style and content" in *Ulysses.* For it seems clear that if style is indeed symbolic, it is not merely ornamental, nor even expressive of a subject already transmitted by conventional means, but rather an entirely new form of discourse, one which tends to transform the content in a radical way by (at times literally) abolishing the narrative. Here it will be helpful to recall Flaubert's prose and its capacity to maintain itself in being and, indeed, transcend its emerging subject. Like Flaubert's prose, Joyce's does not perish; on the contrary, so far from being replaced by the image which one looks for it to convey, it is inclined to annihilate the image and to displace entirely the fictional world that is the substance of the storyteller's art. Expressive or imitative form is, to be sure, significant form, insofar as it appears to be grounded upon a world of images—in this case Bloom's world—that has a structure and a significance of its own. But the fact is that in *Ulysses* the expressive form tends to purify itself. The demands of the form are so great that the fictional world whence the form derives by analogy its significance emerges only at a distance and as though by implication. As David Hayman puts it in connection with "Oxen of the Sun," Joyce's language "hacks away at the very possibility of cor :-munication" because it displaces the very thing to be communicated.[17] Consider, for example, what happens in "Ithaca":

> Were there obverse meditations of involution increasingly less vast?

> Of the eons of geological periods recorded in the stratifications of the earth: of the myriad minutiae entomological organic existences concealed in cavities of the earth, beneath removable stones, in hives and mounds, of microbes, germs, bacteria, bacilli, spermatozoa: of the incalculable trillions of billions of millions of imperceptible molecules contained by cohesion of molecular affinity in a single pinhead: of the universe of human serum constellated with red and white bodies, themselves universes of void space constellated with other bodies, each, in continuity, its universe of divisible component bodies of which each was again divisible in divisions of redivisible component bodies, dividends and divisors ever diminishing without actual division till, if progress were carried far enough, nought nowhere was never reached.[18]

We can say of this particular passage that it is an exaggeration of Bloom's encyclopedic mind; or, alternately, that it is a parody of the catechetical method of instruction, or of scientific discourse, or of the kind of mathematicized speech the movement of whose parts, in the absence of any external point of reference, proceeds systematically toward zero. Or, again, we can say of "Ithaca" generally that its arcane questions and answers specify with great point and clarity the nature of the relationship between Bloom and Stephen: collocations of words and things irrelevantly supersede human intercourse. Language conspires against the world of persons by forcing human speech into patterns of discourse that hack away at the possibility of communication, if only because it ridicules that possibility. Indeed, the language of "Ithaca" executes, in a manner similar to the Pantagruelian feast of words in Rabelais, its own special comedy, so that finally what is satirized is not this or that category of utterance but human speech itself.

There remains, after these and other possible speculations begin to lose their attraction (as inevitably they do), the hard question of who is speaking in the "Ithaca" episode. The question is of importance, not only with respect to "Ithaca" but so far as all of *Ulysses* is concerned. Each episode of *Ulysses* has, we may say, its own narrator, but these narrators are repeatedly displaced by uses of language which require us to seek motivations of discourse other than narration. Accordingly, David Hayman, for example, postulates the figure of an "arranger"—"a figure who can be identified neither with the author nor with his narrators, but who exercises an increasing degree of overt control over his increasingly challenging materials." [19] It is the arranger who composes the fugue in "Sirens," who heaps up the great Rabeliasian catalogues of words and things in "Cyclops," who performs the history of style in "Oxen of the Sun," who constructs the closet drama of "Circe," who formulates the dialectic of questions and answers in "Ithaca"—who is, in short, responsible generally for the foregrounding of language that repeatedly displaces the fiction of *Ulysses*. The arranger in this sense is an instance of Roland Barthes's *scripteur* (or *l'écrivain*): he is not a distinct persona; he speaks rather in the middle voice as the agent whose identity is implicated in the pure act of writing. He functions, that is to say, not in any transitive sense, except as the mediating figure for language itself. Let us recall here Barthes's remark that "the whole of literature is contained in the act of writing, and no longer in those of 'thinking,' 'portraying,' 'telling,' or 'feeling.'" Just so, *Ulysses* is essentially an *œuvre de l'écriture*, in which language itself replaces reality as the motive, the "mythical 'alibi,'" of the creative act.

One is tempted by this line of thinking to generalize upon Joyce's creative life and to define it as an effort to purify the act of writing of those traditional effects of " 'thinking,' 'portraying,' 'telling,' or 'feeling.' " To be sure, so far as *Ulysses* is concerned, it remains possible, despite the energies of the "arranger," to speak of Bloom's world as an authentic fictional universe. The metonymic activity of discourse undergirds *Ulysses,* however much it may serve, as it did in *Madame Bovary,* to provide a point of departure for an act of speech that proceeds vertically toward a universe of language. Yet, if it remains possible to speak of Bloom's "world," it makes manifestly less sense to speak of Earwicker's "world." As a referent for the act of writing, Earwicker's "world" exists only as a radically backgrounded component of *Finnegans Wake.* Indeed, it is extremely difficult to speculate upon, much less to identify, the referent for the act of writing in the *Wake.* Doubtless the conventional hypothesis is sufficient to our needs, that in composing the *Wake* Joyce hoped to dramatize the dynamics of the dream state, not by representing that state in the form of a fictional universe but by modifying language in a way that would allow the development of discourse to suggest, by analogy, the morphology of the unconscious mind. The virtue of this hypothesis is that at least it tells us how to read this book. We should not, for example, assume that beneath Joyce's language there lies a narrative which, once discovered or reconstructed, will open to us the meaning of the work. There is no getting rid of the words, no displacing language by the conventional structures of fiction, however clear it may be that Joyce's prose adumbrates those structures by constant allusion to character and event. On the contrary, we should understand that, because Joyce organizes his prose as a system of equivalences and recurrences—because his discourse develops almost solely on a metaphoric rather than metonymic basis—the key to the reading of the *Wake* must lie in our ability to make connections among equivalents and to interpret words and phrases (or, as it happens, words within words and phrases within phrases) in terms of the patterns or motifs that they form.

We can examine Joyce's mode of discourse in the *Wake* by considering the following passage:

> Bygmester Finnegan, of the Stuttering Hand, freemen's maurer, lived in the broadest way immarginable in his rushlit toofarback for messauges before joshuan judges had given us numbers or Helviticus committed deuteronomy (one yeasterday he sternely struxk his tete in a tub for to watsch the future of his fates but ere he swiftly stook it out again, by the might of moses, the very water was eviparated and all the guenneses had met their exodus so that ought to show you what a pentschanjeuchy chap he was!) and during might odd years this man of hod, cement and edifices in Toper's Thorp piled buildung pon the banks for the livers by the Soangso. [p. 4]

Jakobson writes that "in the combination of linguistic units there is an ascending scale of freedom. In the combination of distinctive features into phonemes, the freedom of the individual speaker is zero; the code has already established all the possibilities that may be utilized in the given language." Nevertheless it is exactly on this fundamental level of linguistic activity that Joyce asserts his freedom—hence the word "struxk" in the passage above. Jakobson goes on to say that "freedom to combine phonemes into words is circumscribed, it is limited to the marginal situations of word-coinage." [20] In the *Wake*, however, word-coinage is not marginal but central, for Joyce develops his discourse out of a reconstituted lexicon. In William I. Thompson's formulation, Joyce's lexicon is *prehensive* in character, which means that the word as Joyce reconstitutes it becomes two or several words (often from diverse languages) and thus functions "as a bringing together of several happenings." [21]

When we say that the reconstituted word functions in this way, however, what exactly do we mean? We may say that a given word as Joyce touches it assumes multiple identities, and that these multiple identities work to enrich with multiple meanings the contexts in which they appear. Doubtless this is so. But if, for the moment, we consider the matter in terms of the act of reading itself, and not from the standpoint of exegesis, such an explanation is not altogether to the point. The point is rather that Joyce's reconstitution of words dominates his prose: his prose, we may say, is characterized by the foregrounding of a prehensive lexicon, which generates the effect of utterances superimposed upon one another, as in "he sternely struxk his tete in a tub for to watsch the future of his fates but ere he swiftly stook it out again." Before we observe how these allusions to Sterne, *Tale of a Tub*, and Swift function in the context of the passage as a whole, we should first inquire as to their effect upon the sentence in which they appear. For it is clear that Joyce's design is to displace the horizontal or syntagmatic order of discourse, that is, its predicative axis, in order to liberate words from the closed system that syntactical structures inevitably form. Accordingly, words occupy syntactical positions, but their function as units of signification is transposed at the same time onto a vertical axis of metaphorical equivalences. Indeed, the unity of the passage is determined less by the process of predication—less, that is, by the statement made about "Bygmester Finnegan"—than by the organization of words into motifs, as in the sequence, "joshuan judges," "numbers," "Helviticus" [Leviticus], "deuteronomy," "moses," "pentschanjeuchy."

This means, in effect, that the act of reading cannot simply proceed horizontally, as it is accustomed to do, but must involve itself almost at once in problems of exegesis. These problems, taken separately, are seldom insurmountable—it is relatively simple, for example, to connect the sacred books motif with the character of Finnegan. The motif comments on this character, whom the parodied Homeric epithet, "the Stuttering Hand," marks out as a epic hero, and who, we are told, antedates the "joshuan judges." This point takes us, of course, beyond the passage itself to the *Wake* as a whole, or at least to the fully amplified figure of Finnegan as an extension of those heroes from the mythic past who have risen from the dead and whose stories are recorded in sacred books. We are thus moved to remark upon the interplay between part and whole in *Finnegans Wake:* the motif of the sacred books depends upon the whole for the fulness of its significance, but at the same time it contributes to the whole, that is, to the amplification of Finnegan from a comic Dubliner into a mythic subject.

The act of reading, so to speak, is thus caught up in something like the hermeneutic circle: it cannot proceed except by constant movement from whole to part, and again from part to whole. For verbal motifs are not merely woven incidentally into the "texture" of Joyce's prose; it is rather that Joyce's prose is *constituted* by such patterns, and that all other functions of language have been subordinated to (and in some instances virtually replaced by) the construction of verbal motifs, whose vast and extraordinary interplay holds the book together (as Flaubert's "book about nothing" was to have been held together—by the strength of its style). Clive Hart, in his superb *Structure and Motif in "Finnegans Wake,"* has described the matter very well:

> Technically the *leitmotiv* is a highly self-conscious device. It functions primarily at the surface level, within the verbal texture. Clearly it does not commend itself to novelists who adopt a simple and self-effacing style, but it comes quite naturally from the pen of a Joyce. Thomas Mann, the most self-conscious of all exponents of the *leitmotiv* and the real architect of the fully developed literary motif, mixed it into a lucid, transparent, forward moving narrative style. We are, as a result, constantly impelled to shift our attention from the subject-matter seen through the words to the words themselves, and while this change of focus can often be stimulating in theory, some readers find it, in practice, extremely distracting. No such distraction lies in the way of the reader of *Finnegans Wake,* in which surface-texture has become all-important. Within it nothing is artificial because all is frankly artifice, nothing is superficial because all is surface. The more

clearly Joyce can focus our attention on the surface details of his style, the better we are able to appreciate his meaning. There is never any question of reading through the prose, which has virtually been engulfed by the *leitmotiv* technique. It is probably true to say that every paragraph in *Finnegans Wake* is both built up out of pieces drawn from elsewhere in the book and, conversely, capable of being broken down and related to all the diverse contexts from which those pieces came.[22]

It follows from this that to read the *Wake,* one must break down individual paragraphs into their constituent metaphoric combinations, and to relate each combination, each set of equivalences, to those other contexts in which it appears, as well as to those contexts in which it may not appear but to which it may be thematically similar.

This raises another, perhaps even more painful difficulty: What constitutes a "context" in *Finnegans Wake?* In ordinary speech contexts are built up syntagmatically, by the development of contiguous predications into a discourse. Similarly, in works of fiction context is a function of narrative, that is, the building up of contiguous relationships among characters and events. Although it is not impossible to "read through" many sections of the *Wake,* it nevertheless remains true that narrative is precisely what eludes us, synopses and plot reconstructions notwithstanding. Character and event are related metaphorically, not metonymically or contiguously. But the problem of context in the *Wake* derives not simply from the absence of a contiguous narrative but from the very nature of the Joycean utterance. How, for example, in the sentence from the passage quoted above—"he sternely struxk his tete in a tub for to watsch the future of his fates but ere he swiftly stook it out again"—are the references to Sterne, *Tale of a Tub,* and Swift related to the verbal chain in which they appear? The answer is, they are not related to the verbal chain at all, except by association with those similar words in which they are embedded: "sternely," "tete in a tub," "swiftly." These words, like the words which compose the sacred books motif, are so many "floating signifiers" (to borrow and only slightly abuse a term from Claude Lévi-Strauss): they are words which float freely above the syntagmatic relationships within which they are formed, thus to connect by processes of metaphor or equivalence with other floating signifiers, thereby creating contexts of an entirely different order from the kind that speech normally establishes. Joyce, that is to say, foregrounds his lexicon in large part by collapsing words into one another, and so brings to bear upon the syntagmatic order of his discourse a surplus of signifiers, whose effect is to break down one sort of context, the predicative, in order to create another, the substitutive or metaphorical.[23]

Precisely how this substitutive context functions is staggering to consider. For example, the table of cross-references compiled by Adaline Glasheen, aptly entitled, "Who is Who When Everybody is Somebody Else," tells us that for Humphrey Chimpden Earwicker at least sixty-three substitutions may be made, ranging from Tim Finnegan through diverse heroes from myth, Scripture, and literature, to Mr. Porter, which is another name for Earwicker, and which evidently connects him with the drunken porter in *Macbeth*. Included among these possible substitutions are Joyce himself, his father, Simon Dedalus, and Leopold Bloom.[24] This is to say, in effect, that Earwicker is not so much a character as he is a nexus of character equivalents—as are, indeed, Shem, Shaun, Issy, and Anna Livia Plurabelle, each of whom exists in something like a state of transformation, in which a single identity exfoliates into multiple identities, even as Joyce's lexicon is an exfoliation of words, each of which is not one word but many.

This collapsing of identities—this overcoming of differences among words and, beyond this, the overcoming of differences among characters and even events—brings up still another problem, that of determinacy of meaning. In a study entitled, *"Finnegans Wake* in Perspective," Clive Hart focuses upon the difficulties of interpretation which the reader of the *Wake* must face, and he poses what is perhaps the central question: How do we know when an exegesis of a given word or group of words is relevant to the context in which it appears? Hart's answer is that we really never know, but he adds that our ignorance is compensated by the fact that in any given case the relevance of word to context is likely to be virtually unlimited. The prehensive character of Joyce's lexicon is such that we are, Hart believes, compelled to interpret prehensively. For example, he observes of the opening line of Book II —"Every evening at lighting up o'clock sharp and until further notice in Feenicht's Playhouse" (p. 219)—that Joyce's "distortion" of some words implies the possibility of further distortions, so that "Every evening" could be interpreted (1) as an allusion to Eve ("else why speak twice about Eve?"); (2) as an allusion to the two Eves, Lilith and Mary; (3) as an allusion to the play, *Everyman;* (4) and even as an allusion to "a female counterpart of Everyman, which suggests in turn the idea of change-of-sex, or even of transvestism." [25] One hardly knows how to respond to such exuberance of interpretation, except to observe that it proceeds upon the assumption that nothing in the *Wake* is literal, that all is metaphor. The fact is that interpretation of the *Wake* cannot proceed except upon this assumption, and that accordingly the most innocent word must be suspect of containing within itself other words. Thus Adaline Glasheen believes that in the line "dame nature in all innocency had spontaneously and about the same hour of eventide sent them both" (p. 34), the word "eventide" functions as an allusion to Eve. The reasoning behind such an otherwise capricious or extravagant belief is that the *Wake* contains nearly a hundred allusions to Eve, that indeed a still closer investigation might discover a hundred more, and that under such circumstances any combination of lexical structures that includes or approximates the sequence "e-v-e" ought not to be regarded as an isolated event but as a part of a whole.[26]

The point is that substitutive contexts reverse, so to speak, the function of ordinary or predicative contexts. Consider that in ordinary speech context imposes limits upon and hence directs interpretation; but in the *Wake* these limits are exceeded by and indeed disappear beneath the superabundance of signifiers. That is to say, predicative contexts are determinate in their function: they provide boundaries which isolate or define the meaning of a word; substitutive contexts, by contrast, move toward a condition of indeterminacy, precisely because in such contexts the word does not function simply or even primarily as a unit of signification; it functions rather as a unit of equivalence. Thus, whereas in ordinary uses of language "eventide" could not mean "Eve" but only "evening," in *Finnegans Wake* the difference between "eventide" and "Eve" is not so secure; it is, on the contrary, an indeterminate difference.[27]

Elizabeth Sewell has observed that "one of the primary functions of language [is] to provide, in its words, small separate units for the mind to manipulate, convenient packets of experience which the mind can manage where it could not manage the chaotic multiplicity of total experience."[28] This is, if we excuse the metaphor which makes of words "convenient packets of experience," sound Saussurean doctrine. Language provides us with differences by means of which we may organize experience into comprehensible forms, according to which one thing cannot be anything but itself. Language, that is to say, differentiates experience because it is itself a system of differences, in which words derive their meanings from their opposition to one another. It appears to be in the nature of poetry to call this "primary function" of language into question, to the extent that poetic speech (as Coleridge believed, for example, or as Jakobson believes) executes an abolishment of differences—executes, that is, the formation of equivalences among separate identities. In what we might call conventional poetic uses of language, however, this formation of equivalences takes place within limits prescribed by language itself. For language, understood as a system of differences, allows this formation to proceed only so far, and on a determinate basis, so that metaphor, for example, is almost always at bottom a form of simile, in which A is (not B but) *like* B: the difference between terms is maintained. But Joyce carries this abolishment of differences into the system itself, for by collapsing words into one another and by subordinating predicative to substitutive contexts, he transforms the very function of language and makes of it a system of equivalences.

"It is possible," Clive Hart believes, "to prove . . . that *Finnegans Wake*, or any part of it, is about anything at all." [29] This is true, not in fact perhaps, but in principle, which is to say by virtue of the principle by which the *Wake* is designed. Rimbaud, Elizabeth Sewell says, sought "to create a poem-universe that should contain everything." [30] Such a poem-universe could only be approximated, she tells us.

> It [would] have to be a universe containing as many things as possible, and since, as we have seen, the actual number of things [would] inevitably be limited, each thing must connect with as many other things as possible. It [would] be a universe in which everything is related to everything else in every possible way, and everything in this universe must be included as significant and relevant, i.e. related into the whole. Ideally it would make one perfect system in which each thing was related wholly and perfectly to every other thing. The main characteristics of this universe, then, are that it is all-embracing and multiply interrelated.[31]

Joyce's "poem-universe" displays these "main characteristics," not in so many things but in so many words, for as a matter of *linguistic principle* everything in the *Wake* strives to connect and, indeed, identify with everything else. It is well to think of Coleridge in this connection, and his conception of "desynonymizing" as the process which a language undergoes during the course of its history. The abolishment of differences in Joyce's language, the movement to collapse all words into a synonym, suggests from the Coleridgean point of view at least an effort to press language back into time, thus to return to an original, undifferentiated utterance which contains within itself all that can be said—like Borges's Library of Babel, which supersedes all discourse because it contains all discourse. The problem is, of course, that this "poem-universe," which seeks to encompass all that is, destroys what it seeks in the very process by which its quest is conducted. For what is undifferentiated exceeds comprehension; indeed, it remains inaccessible to experience, quite as though it were nothing at all.

6

The Storyteller and the Problem of Language in Samuel Beckett's Fiction

The world of Samuel Beckett's fiction, it is now commonplace to observe, is governed at least in part by a Cartesian (or perhaps a Geulincxian) paradigm, according to which the minds of the several Beckett heroes gyrate, like so many closed systems, independently of the world. Murphy, a sort of prototype in this respect, understands his mind to be "hermetically closed to the universe without"; [1] he assumes *in actu* the incommensurability of mind and matter, and so chooses to live out the *cogito* of Descartes, transforming it from a first principle of thought into an ethical principle so rigorous in its demands that the premium which is thus placed upon the life of the mind virtually annihilates other reasons for being. In a similar way, the Unnamable entertains the possibility (he can do no more) that the void in which he finds himself is "perhaps merely the inside of my distant skull where once I wandered, now am fixed." [2]

Between Murphy and the Unnamable, however, there is this difference, that Murphy is able to discover in the depths of his mind a tranquility of spirit that is all but beyond the Unnamable's power to imagine: the Pyrrhonic silence of Murphy is a distant goal toward which the Unnamable, so immersed is he in his own stream of babble, can only vaguely incline. Clearly, part of the problem is that, unlike Murphy, the Unnamable is undone by a corollary which sooner or later must attach itself to the Cartesian dualism: namely, the incommensurability of words and things. Murphy, contemplative that he is, has no cause to be troubled by the problem of language, for if it is not given to man to know what transpires beyond the sphere of his mind, and if he finds this to be, as Murphy does, a splendid state of affairs, you cannot expect that he will want to speak. But if you make of this man a storyteller (which the Unnamable, in his residual way, appears to be), and if you demand of him that he practice his art, you will have placed him in the most difficult of circumstances, so that he will be forced to seek in human speech capacities of a kind which do not require for their fulfillment any sort of subject matter.

This immediately recalls Flaubert and his speculations concerning a "book about nothing." These speculations provide something of a context in which to place those curious dialogues between Beckett and Georges Duthuit:

> B.—The only thing disturbed by the revolutionaries Matisse and Tal Coat is a certain order on the plane of the feasible.
> D.—What other plane can there be for the maker?
> B.—Logically none. Yet I speak of an art turning from it in disgust, weary of its puny exploits, weary of pretending to be able, of being able, of doing a little better the same old thing, of going a little further along a dreary road.
> D.—And preferring what?
> B.—The expression that there is nothing to express, nothing with which to express, nothing from which to express, no power to express, no desire to express, together with the obligation to express.[3]

It has been recognized for some time that the problem enunciated here—the confrontation of the necessity of speech with its radical impossibility—helps to explain a good deal about the kind of fiction Beckett has been trying to write.[4] I should like to propose that this problem is in good measure what Beckett's fiction is finally about—that his fiction not only grows out of this problem but directs itself toward it, as though to make it a central theme. Several years ago Jacques Maritain described as "nocturnal" the kind of poet (he was thinking of St.-John Perse) whose concern is not "with the intellectual mystery of the significative and constructive power of the Word, but with the mysterious screen or obstacle that thwarts in every sign the function of signification." It is the drawing of this "mysterious screen" that Flaubert's "book about nothing" would have required for its realization. What makes this quotation worth remarking in connection with Beckett, however, is not only the fact that Beckett is so eminently "nocturnal" but that Maritain had specifically in mind a poetry which is conscious of itself *as poetry*—which is turned not toward the world but toward the "secret workings" of its language.[5] Beckett's fiction is deeply concerned with the "secret workings" of the speech by which it is actualized—but in this peculiar sense, that in each of the novels after *Murphy* there stands at the center a storyteller whose obligation to speak is thrown up against the conditions which make speech impossible, quite as though it were his burden to suffer as a problem of life what Beckett, judging from the dialogues with Duthuit, has chosen to suffer as a problem of art. What emerges, as we shall see, is precisely a problem of art, or more accurately a problem of the literary utterance compelled into being by language itself, which impinges upon the storyteller, thus to wrench from him an act of speech that is utterly without motive.

The essentials of this problem are already present in *Watt*, in Part Two of which an unidentified "I" appears to explain that he has taken down in a little notebook Watt's story of his days at Mr. Knott's house.[6] We are later to learn that this "I" is Sam, Watt's fellow inmate at the asylum to which Watt repairs following his term as Mr. Knott's servant. What compulsion drove Sam to record Watt's words we shall never know, but it must have been powerful. For when Watt's universe, following the incident of the Galls, father and son, begins to dissolve, so that he is no longer able to say of an event, "That is what happened then" (p. 73), Watt is not merely placed in the Cartesian condition of Murphy but is transformed into a kind of aphasiac:

> Looking at a pot, for example, or thinking of a pot, at one of Mr Knott's pots, of one of Mr Knott's pots, it was in vain that Watt said, Pot, pot. . . . For it was not a pot, the more he looked, the more he felt sure of that, that it was not a pot at all. It resembled a pot, it was almost a pot, but it was not a pot of which one could say, Pot, pot, and be comforted. [p. 81]

As a consequence of this dissociation of words and things, Watt's world, and indeed Watt himself, "become unspeakable" (p. 85), with the curious result that Watt is suddenly consumed by a need for words: "Not that Watt desired information, for he did not. But he desired words to be applied to his situation, to Mr Knott, to the house, to the grounds, to his duties, to the stairs, to his bedroom, to the kitchen, and in a general way to the conditions of being in which he found himself" (p. 81). Watt's is a primeval need for names in the face of namelessness, but Watt, no Orpheus he, cannot bring names to bear upon his world, and so aches "to hear Erskine's voice wrapping up safe in words the kitchen space, the extraordinary newel-lamp, the stairs that were never the same and of which even the number of steps seemed to vary" (p. 83).

Watt's only recourse is to verbal systems that contain their own principles of order, whatever the state of the world's affairs might be. The diverse hypotheses fabricated by Watt to deal with the question of Mr. Knott's dog—"By what means then were the dog and the food to be brought together . . . ?" (p. 93)—have as their proper function not the discovery of whatever laws might govern the Knott household, but protection against a state of being in which discoveries as such are impossible:

> [For] once Watt grasped, in its complexity, the mechanism of this arrangement, how the food came to be left, and the dog to be available, and the two to be united, then it interested him no more, and he enjoyed a comparative peace of mind, in this connexion. Not that for a moment Watt supposed that he had pene-

trated the forces at play, in this particular instance . . . or ob-
tained the least useful information concerning himself, or
Mr Knott, for he did not. But he had turned, little by little, a
disturbance into words, he had made a pillow of old words, for a
head. [p. 117]

Words, that is to say, have acquired for Watt a new function,
which is to stand in place of a world of things and activities,
not as a set of signs, but as a set of objects. They no longer
constitute a medium for signification; their purpose appears
rather to fill the void that Watt now finds extended before
him.

The Watt whom Sam encounters in the asylum is a Watt
dedicated to the transformation of disturbances into words,
which means quite simply that Watt's speech turns in upon
itself (thus to subsist, we may say, upon its own "secret work-
ings"). Never, Sam tells us, did Watt speak with anything but
a "scant regard for grammar, for syntax, for pronunciation,
for enunciation, and very likely, if the truth were known, for
spelling too, as these are generally received" (p. 156). As time
passes, however, Watt's utterances deviate even further from
the ordinary forms of discourse, becoming just so many formal
systems expelled roughly in Sam's vicinity. It is Watt's first
inclination, Sam discovers, to invert the word order of his
speech, but no sooner does Sam decode this manner of
speaking, than Watt inverts not the word order but the
letters of his words, thus to beget, for example, this improb-
able sequence: *"Ot bro, lap rulb, drad klub. Ot murd, wol
fup, wol fup. Ot niks, sorg sam, sorg sam. Ot lems, lats lems,
lats lems. Ot gnut, trat stews, trat stews"* (p. 165). Thanks,
presumably, to Sam, we are if nothing else able to behold
Watt's speech as it moves through its diverse metamorphoses,
finally to attain its apotheosis in a single periodic masterpiece:

Then he took it into his head to invert . . . now [the order] of
the words in the sentence, now that of the letters in the word,
now that of the sentences in the period, now simultaneously that
of the words in the sentence and that of the letters in the word,

now simultaneously that of the words in the sentence and that of the sentences in the period, now simultaneously that of the letters in the word and that of the sentences in the period, and now simultaneously that of the letters in the word and that of the words in the sentence and that of the sentences in the period. [p. 168]

Unfortunately, Sam failed to capture an example of this monumental utterance; but surely it was enough for him to have glimpsed the principle by which it was extended.

It has been shown that this principle glimpsed by Sam is mathematical in nature: Watt simply arranges and rearranges the counters of his speech until all possible moves have been exhausted.[7] At this point we could play Wittgenstein to Beckett's Watt and observe that Watt has done nothing more than substitute for the more commonplace rules of speech a set of procedures peculiarly his own, that there is nothing meaningless in the way Watt speaks, because, after all, his use of language appears to serve his needs quite well, and that, finally, it matters little whether Watt is able to speak of a world outside his mind, so long as Sam is able to determine the rules which govern Watt's language-game. It matters not at all, in short, whether Watt and Sam share the same world; it is only necessary that they exceed the limits of a private language, thus to share the same techniques of speech. By application of a mathematical method to the act of speech, Watt is able to speak in such a way that words accumulate as by a kind of inner necessity: the logic of external affairs is not required for their being. That Sam should have been able to gather from such speech the material for a story about Watt is implausible but not, theoretically, out of the question: "The meaning of a word is its use in the language," wrote Wittgenstein, and not its correspondence to a real object.[8] This perhaps helps to explain why Sam's narrative contains few hard facts (the traditional components of the novel); only conjectures, hypotheses, and other self-contained systems of discourse are required for the portrayal of the authentic Watt:

Here he stood. Here he sat. Here he knelt. Here he moved, to
and fro, from the door to the window, from the window to the
door; from the window to the door, from the door to the window;
from the fire to the bed, from the bed to the fire; from the bed
to the fire, from the fire to the bed, from the door to the fire,
from the fire to the door. [pp. 203–204]

And so on, until all possible moves within four distinct points
have been played out. The hard fact, it appears, is that Watt's
life is essentially a language-game, one which Sam (such are his
talents as a storyteller) is equipped to learn and to reproduce.

We might notice in passing that the application of mathe-
matical method to the act of speech is, in Watt's case, con-
ceivably a two-edged sword. For the question raises itself as to
whether the permutations which provide the dynamism of
Watt's utterances do not at the same time posit an end to
Watt, disappearance into the void perhaps, on the grounds
that once the permutations have run their course, and Watt is
left to stare into the metaphysical expanse that his powerless-
ness to know implies, it is all over for him. It would have been
better perhaps had Watt modeled his speech upon the square
root of minus two.

What in fact becomes of Watt we cannot say, for his mathe-
maticized speech and the postulate of his subsequent silence
and demise are circulated through Sam, whose chief concern
as narrator happens to be with Watt's days at Mr. Knott's
house, not with his disintegration (if that is what it is) at the
asylum. In short, Sam has a story to tell, beyond whose be-
ginning, middle, and end Watt's existence is of only marginal
importance. The point to mark, however, is that the problem
of language which afflicts Watt intervenes between Sam and
Watt's life and so afflicts Sam's narrative as well. For Sam has
at his disposal only the most general of facts concerning Watt,
and of these the most certain are those which must disrupt the
dynamics of narration: namely, that Watt's world during his
stay at Mr. Knott's house became "unspeakable," that Watt
nevertheless continued to speak, and that, by building up his
speech according to an analogy with a mathematical system,

he clothed this unspeakability in words. In defiance of these conditions, or perhaps because of them, Sam produced his story—one which, as a story about a discourse upon nothing, raises to a higher power the impossible dream of Flaubert:

> who may tell the tale
> of the old man?
> weigh absence in a scale?
> mete want with a span?
> the sum assess
> of the world's woes?
> nothingness
> in words enclose?
>
> [p. 247]

Sam's problems as narrator, such as we may suppose them to have been, suggest one way, perhaps the chief way, in which *Watt* constitutes a prelude to the trilogy of novels, *Molloy, Malone Dies,* and *The Unnamable.* For in the trilogy Beckett seems to have collapsed the figures of Watt and Sam into a type of storyteller whose art and life endure as one the incommensurability of words and things. Thus Molloy, as he struggles to tell the tale of his quest for his mother, digresses upon the peculiar difficulties of his craft:

> For to contrive a being, a place, I nearly said an hour, but I would not want to hurt anyone's feelings, and then to use them no more, that would be, how shall I say, I don't know. Not to want to say, not to know what you want to say, not to be able to say what you think you want to say, and never to stop saying, or hardly ever, that is the thing to keep in mind, even in the heat of composition. [p. 32]

We cannot fail to recognize here the master's voice, touching upon the "secret workings" of his fiction even as he places before us the problem that faces Molloy. Molloy's life, we may say, has become itself the impossible art. What this means is that, as in Watt's case, the world, the self, the past, are all of them unspeakable, and yet they must be bound together in the name of storytelling:

It's too difficult to say, for me. And even my sense of identity was
wrapped up in a namelessness often hard to penetrate. . . . And
so on for all the other things which made merry with my senses.
Yes, even then, when already all was fading, waves and particles,
there could be no things but nameless things, no names but
nameless names. I say that now, but after all what do I know
about then, now when the icy words hail down upon me, the icy
meanings, and the world dies too, foully named. All I know is
what the words know; and the dead things, and that makes a
handsome little sum, with a beginning, a middle and an end as
in the well-built phrase and the long sonata of the dead. [p. 37]

We ought not to be too surprised at the remarkable power of
Molloy's speech—it was the argument of Gorgias, after all,
that the namelessness of things need not diminish the elo-
quence of a discourse. Yet it is not clear that Molloy is com-
pelled to speak by the ideal of eloquence. Icy words rain in
upon him from an unknown source, so that finally, as he tells
us, "it little matters what I say, this, this or that or any other
thing. Saying is inventing. Wrong, very rightly wrong. You
invent nothing, you think you are inventing, you think you
are escaping, and all you do is stammer out your lesson, the
remnants of a pensum one day got by heart and long for-
gotten, life without tears, as it is wept. To hell with it any-
way. Where was I?" (p. 38).

This "pensum" to which Molloy refers may be regarded as
an outgrowth of Watt's need to turn disturbances into words
and Sam's compulsion to tell Watt's impossible story. But the
point is that the fundamental law of Molloy's universe (and of
the universe of the trilogy) is "the obligation to express";
speech is demanded of Molloy, and he complies—moved, it is
occasionally suggested, as by an indifferent muse:

I listen and the voice is of a world collapsing endlessly, a frozen
world, under a faint untroubled sky, enough to see by, yes, and
frozen too. And I hear it murmur that all wilts and yields, as if
loaded down. . . . And if I went on listening to that far whisper,
silent long since and which I still hear, I would learn still more,
about this. But I will listen no longer, for the time being, to that
far whisper, for I do not like it, I fear it. [pp. 49–50]

Molloy later explains that "every time I say, I said this, or I said that, or speak of a voice saying, far away inside me, Molloy, and then a fine phrase more or less clear and simple . . . I am merely complying with the convention that demands you either lie or hold your peace" (p. 116). But Molloy cannot hold his peace, nor can Moran, who, as he attains to the condition of Molloy, is every inch a man inspired: "I have spoken of a voice telling me things. I was getting to know it better now, to understand what it wanted. It did not use the words that Moran had been taught when he was little and that he in turn had taught to his little one. So that at first I did not know what it wanted. But in the end I understood this language. . . . It told me to write the report" (p. 240).

Even Malone, who seems on the face of it so much his own man (he explains away his storytelling, for example, by invoking the play-theory), does not really command the words he utters. "Words and images run riot in my head," he confesses at one point, "pursuing, flying, clashing, merging, endlessly" (p. 270), and some of these are such that he must guard against them: "I know those little phrases that seem so innocuous and, once you let them in, pollute the whole of speech. *Nothing is more real than nothing.* They rise up out of the pit and know no rest until they drag you down into its dark" (p. 262). Given this response of Malone to his utterances, we should not be surprised at his report, not long after, that "a strange desire has come over me, the desire to know what I am doing, and why" (p. 264).

The Unnamable's case is easily the most severe "I who am here," he says, announcing once more the impossible aesthetic, "who cannot speak, cannot think, and who must speak, and therefore perhaps think a little" (p. 416). He is convinced (for the most part) that this unfortunate condition has been imposed upon him by a "college of tyrants":

> What I speak of, what I speak with, all comes from them. It's all the same to me, but it's no good, there's no end to it. It's of me now I must speak, even if I have to do it with their language, it will be a start, a step towards silence and the end of madness, the madness of having to speak and not being able to,

except of things that don't concern me, that don't count, that I
don't believe, that they have crammed me full of to prevent me
from saying who I am, where I am, and from doing what I
have to do in the only way that can put an end to it. . . . It's a
poor trick that consists in ramming a set of words down your
gullet on the principle that you can't bring them up without
being branded as belonging to their breed. But I'll fix their gib-
berish for them. [pp. 448–449]

The Unnamable is, in effect, a victim of language—of words
not his own, which transform him from whatever he may have
been (he has occasional glimpses of a more tolerable past) into
a subject in which the pensum to speak abides as a kind of
alien principle of identity. Indeed, the icy rain of words that
Molloy endures becomes the Unnamable's whole universe,
even his very self: "The words are everywhere, inside me, out-
side me, well well, a minute ago I had no thickness, I hear
them, no need of a head, impossible to stop them, impossible
to stop, I'm in words, made of words, others' words, what
others, the place too, the air, the walls, the floors, the ceiling,
all words" (p. 537).[9]

We might notice parenthetically that such a universe is of a
piece with the universe of Watt, but with this difference, that
Watt made a dwelling-place in words—his compulsion to
speak was sufficiently his own to bring him satisfactions of a
kind, "a pillow of old words, for a head," or protection per-
haps against a want of things; whereas the Unnamable finds
himself surrounded and penetrated by words against which he
needs protection—the protection of silence. Watt was faced, at
least on theoretical grounds, with the possibility that, once his
speech touched those fixed number of points within a closed
system, silence would follow. But the form of the Unnamable's
discourse is open, not closed: mathematics plays no part in this
world of words, and so the Unnamable finds it impossible to
stop speaking.

The Unnamable could, on this basis, be described as the
Cartesian spirit run to seed, its universe a purely a priori
cosmos in which words alone exist, as though awaiting the act

of deduction that, like Godot, never comes ("this dust of words, with no ground for their settling" [p. 537]). Or, again, the Unnamable is the fictional character conscious of himself as such ("I'm in words, made of words")—a fictional character, say, who is bereft of the forms and ingredients of a novel the way Watt is bereft of a world of things and persons, events and activities, and so on. In any case, there remains for the Unnamable only a discourse—"affirmations and negations invalidated as uttered, or sooner or later" (p. 401)—whose principle of composition is such that predications batter against the limits of context:

> What can they be hatching anyhow, at this eleventh hour? Can it be they are resolved at last to seize me by the horns? Looks like it. In that case tableau any minute. Oyez, oyez, I was like them, before being like me, oh the swine, that's one that won't get over in a hurry, no matter, no matter, the charge is sounded, present arms, corpse, to your guns, spermatozoon. I too, weary of pleading an incomprehensible cause, at six and eight the thousand flowers of rhetoric, let myself drop among the contumacious, nice image that, telescoping space, it must be the Pulitzer Prize, they want to bore me to sleep. . . . [pp. 526–527]

We see in this passage the shadow of a fictional situation—the accused, or perhaps his advocate (or perhaps both), awaiting the return of the jury—but it remains a shadow only, not simply because the situation is disrupted by alien material, but because it is itself only a momentary and uncertain burst of storytelling, whose locutions are awash with other, merely insinuated contexts. We have here something like a fictional equivalent of the art of diffusion that characterizes (as we have seen) the poetry of Mallarmé and Valéry. As applied by the storyteller, however, diffusion as a principle of composition is devastating in a way that it can hardly be for the poet, because what is finally diffused is a discourse of enormous bulk: so alien are the parts, one to another, that they disallow the formation of any whole—disallow, that is to say, not only the formation of the conventional structures of fiction (plot, character, and so on), but indeed the formation of any extended structure of meaning. Words fly apart at the very instant of speech, for there is no stable and enduring center around which they may be organized; on the contrary, the center of the Unnamable's discourse exists at the given moment in which any one of his utterances is expelled. Or, again, to borrow Jakobson's formulation, the parts of the Unnamable's discourse are contiguous spatially, by virtue of a pure act of writing, but they are almost entirely without that semantic contiguity which transforms random predications into authentic contexts.

Similarly, Molloy's discourse flows without benefit of a controlling center: words accumulate digressively—"And as to saying what became of me, and where I went, in the months and perhaps the years that followed, no. For I weary of these inventions and others beckon me. But in order to blacken a few more pages may I say I spent time at the seaside, without incident" (p. 89). Just so, the blackening of pages becomes at last the motive of Moran's report: "I had to admit it must once have been a good bicycle. I would gladly describe it, I would gladly write four thousand words on it alone" (p. 211). Malone, characteristically, sets out with a great display of organization—"So first of all my stories and then, last of all, if all goes well, my inventory. And I shall begin, that they may plague me no more, with the man and the woman" (p. 247)—but his several stories dissipate in the telling, precisely because the act of writing cannot be held fast to a single locus:

> A mere local phenomenon is something I would not have noticed, having been nothing but a series or rather a succession of local phenomena all my life, without any result. But my fingers too write in other latitudes and the air that breathes through my pages and turns them without my knowing, when I doze off, so that the subject falls far from the verb and the object lands somewhere in the void, is not the air of this second-last abode, and a mercy it is. [p. 312]

Moreover, as death approaches, Malone's utterances grow even more unlocalized, dwindling finally into so many spasms of words. As for the Unnamable, of course, he may be talking still:

> Perhaps it's done already, perhaps they have said me already, perhaps they have carried me to the threshold of my story, before the door that opens on my story, that would surprise me, if it opens, it will be I, it will be the silence, where I am, I don't know, I'll never know, in the silence you don't know, you must go on, I can't go on. I'll go on. [p. 577]

It is, as the voice in *Texts for Nothing* says, "for ever the same murmur, flowing unbroken, like a single endless word and therefore meaningless, for it's the end gives the meaning to words." [10] The simile of the "single endless word" describes very well the language of Beckett's trilogy: it suggests a kind of *Ur-word*, wholly undifferentiated and without boundary—an uninterrupted verbal extension into time (or, being written, into space)—whose indeterminacy disintegrates the act of intelligence that would give it a meaning. It is this *Ur-word* which the storytellers are obliged to utter. More than this, the *Ur-word* forces itself through the speakers in the trilogy, and as it does so it dissolves those differences which would specify their identities. Thus Moran, as he begins to speak, grows more and more like Molloy, and thus the Unnamable can define himself only as a flow of words, because the very difference between word and speaker is itself abolished. Ordinarily, language takes on form and meaning during the act of speech, because the speaker is a locus of differences; but in *The Unnamable* (which in this respect brings the movement of the trilogy to a kind of resolution) language destroys this locus, transforming the speaker into a wholly transparent medium through which it may proceed without sacrifice to its aboriginal character.

This notion of an *Ur-word*, which takes possession of a speaker and imposes upon him an incomprehensible obligation to speak, may be further applied to *How It Is*—despite the fact that in this book Beckett seems to work toward the restoration of certain conventional patterns of storytelling:

"how it was I quote before Pim with Pim after Pim how it is three parts I say it as I hear it" [11]—three parts, beginning, middle, and end, spoken as heard, quite in the posture of Hesiod. Indeed, in the journey which takes the speaker (or amanuensis) to and from Pim, we have what must be the activity of a mimetic spirit, concretizing into shape and movement a virtual world: "vast tracts of time" and a sea of mud, into which at any moment persons, objects, and events may be introduced. Yet the forms and ingredients of recognizable experience cast only a discontinuous shadow, for the field thus enclosed within this rudimentary narrative form displays the principle of diffusion with easily as much rigor as in the trilogy:

> abject abject ages each heroic seen from the next when will the last come when was my golden every rat has its heyday I say it as I hear it
>
> knees drawn up back bent in a hoop I clasp the sack to my belly I see me now on my side I clutch it the sack we're talking of the sack with one hand behind my back I slip it under my head without letting go
>
> something wrong there [p. 10]

It is easy to see what is wrong: the operations of syntax by which words form semantically contiguous utterances can now manage only "bits and scraps" of speech—speech issued as received, as though on ticker tape: "an image too of this voice ten words fifteen words long silence ten words fifteen words long silence long solitude" (p. 126). No longer a continuous flow of words, discourse must now leap, like a Mallarmean poem, across scattered silences. From the accumulation of such leaps of discourse it is possible (as I have tried to show elsewhere) to deduce a tale of tormentors and victims, travelers and abandoned lovers, all organized systematically into a muddy network of encounters and departures.[12] But such a tale is in fact merely adumbrated: the order and continuity which it implies are illusions finally beyond the speaker's power to achieve. The unity of his discourse tends at best to be thematic in character—the consequence of a preoccupation with a finite set of subjects: the mud, the dark, his sack, his tins, Pim, the anatomy, a set of proper names to which a set of persons do not consistently correspond: Bem, Bom, Krim, Kram, and (or so the speaker conjectures) "999997 others journeying alone rotting alone martyring and being martyred oh moderately listlessly" (p. 127).

There are moments, particularly in Part One of the novel, when the spasmodic character of the speaker's discourse seems to transcend its peculiar defects. For among the subjects to which he has access is the past, either his own or (what is more likely) one invented for him as part of his assigned quotation. And on such occasions as memory, or whatever, permits the evocation of this past, his utterances approach the condition of the lyric:

> On the muddy belly I saw one blessed day saving the grace of Heraclitus the Obscure at the pitch of heaven's azure towering between its great black still spread wings the snowy body of I know not what frigate-bird the screaming albatross of the southern seas the history I knew my God the natural good moments I had. [p. 34]

One senses here the ghostly figures of Yeats and Coleridge. The utterance suggests, in any case, the sensibility not simply of the storyteller but of the poet, perhaps even the visionary ("ah these sudden blazes in the head as empty and dark as the heart can desire then suddenly like a handful of shavings aflame the spectacle then" [p. 35]), one whose faith in what he once saw has long been lost but whose hope for its renewal mysteriously lingers: "A moment of the tender years the lamb black with the world's sins the world cleansed the three persons yes I assure you and that belief the feeling since ten eleven that belief said to have been mine the feeling since then the vast stretch of time that I'd find it again the blue cloak the pigeon the miracles he understood" (p. 70). Poignant, this, the more so as the speaker joins to his burst of personal history the bits and scraps of what once may have filled an educated mind:

> mad or worse transformed a la Haeckel born in Potsdam where Klopstock too among others lived a space and laboured though buried in Altona the shadow he casts

> at evening with his face to the huge sun or his back I forget it's not said the great shadow he casts towards his native east the humanities I had my God the flashes of geography

> not much more but in the tail the venom I've lost my latin one must be vigilant so a good moment in a daze on my belly then begin I can't believe it to listen

> to listen as though having set out the previous evening from Nova Zembla I had just come back to my senses in a subtropical subprefecture that's how I was had become always was it's one or the other the geography I had. [p. 42]

Storyteller, lyricist, desultory polymath—a man of parts in any case, fixed by some incredible curse to murmur his life away in the mud.

The curse is incredible, outrageous, but there is no doubt as to it origin, for beneath the new trappings that bedeck *How It Is*—its fund of details, its lyric impulse, its illusions of structure—there lies the old aesthetic, impossible as ever: "in the dark mud hearing nothing saying nothing capable of nothing nothing" (p. 61). Indeed, if, from time to time, we should hear the resonance of the Unnamable, we ought not to be surprised:

> it comes the word we're talking of words I have some still it would seem at my disposal at this period one is enough aha signifying mamma impossible. [p. 26]

> the voice time the voice it is not mine the silence time the silence that might help me I'll see do something something good God. [p. 40]

> can't go on we're talking of me no Pim Pim is finished he has finished me now part three not Pim my voice not his saying this these words can't go on. [pp. 86–87]

In such passages as these *How It Is* displays openly its fundamental character: it is a story ("all the same like the rest a little darker" [p. 109]) uttered at the far reaches of disintegration by a storyteller who cannot speak, who finds himself nevertheless pressed into speech by mysterious infusions of words, and who therefore speaks—or, in the case of *How It Is,* who quotes from an unknown discourse, evidently as surrogate to that "anonymous voice self-styled quaqua the voice of us all" (p. 139), which becomes in Part Three a principal if uncertain point of interest. The typical Beckett crux, however, is that the speaker in *How It Is* proceeds, as does the Unnamable, by "affirmations and negations invalidated as uttered, or sooner or later": "Pim never was and Bom whose coming I await to finish be finished have finished me too that Bom will never be no Pim no Bom and this voice quaqua of us all never was only one voice my voice never any other" (p. 87). The speaker speaks only to disavow his speech, thus to place all within the empty space of indeterminacy.

This disavowal of a transcendent voice—the voice "of someone in another world yes whose kind of dream I am" (p. 145) —parodies in a rather obvious way the theory of impersonality which brackets the artist, making of him a god who dwells, in the now famous words, "within or behind or beyond or above his handiwork, invisible, refined out of existence, paring his fingernails." The parody, in effect, calls the artist back into existence—for to Beckett belongs, after all, the ultimate voice—the voice "of him who God knows who could blame him must sometimes wonder if to these perpetual revictuallings narrations and auditions he might not put an end" (p. 139). What is important, however, is not the identity of this voice but its function, which is to execute that "obligation to express" which drives Beckett's storytellers to tell their tales, such as they are. In his more recent, shorter fiction, however, Beckett has, in a sense, called himself into question. In *Lessness,* for example, the illusion of voice, so strong in the trilogy and in *How It Is,* is disavowed not by any hapless creature but by the very nature of the discourse created:

Ruins true refuge long last towards which so many false time
out of mind. All sides endlessness earth sky as one no sound no
stir. Grey face two pale blue little body heart beating only up-
right. Blacked out fallen open four walls over backwards true
refuge issueless.

Scattered ruins same grey as the sand ash grey true refuge. Four
square all light sheer white blank planes all gone from mind. Never
was but grey air timeless no sound figment the passing light. No
sound no stir ash grey sky mirrored earth mirrored sky. Never but
this changelessness dream the passing hour.[13]

In *How It Is,* utterances took of form of sentences truncated
by interventions of silence—but they were sentences, however
shadowy, to the extent that substantive groped after verb and
verb after object. Semantic contiguity was pursued, though
imperfectly attained. The utterance, "I have journeyed lost
Pim found Pim it's over that life those periods of that life"
(p. 20), suggests an act of speech struggling to complete itself:
it is alive, though "moderately, listlessly," with syntactic
energy. In *Lessness,* by contrast, words couple and are enclosed
within periods, but what is absent is precisely the illusion of
a speaker groping for connections. Words are fixed in physical
proximity to one another on the page, but there is no move-
ment in which they are caught up and by means of which they
might interact. When sentences do occur, they immediately
disintegrate: "He will curse God again as in the blessed days
face to the open sky the passing deluge. Little body grey face
features crack and little holes two pale blue. Blank planes
sheer white eye calm long last all gone from mind" (p. 8).

Yet it is not even true to say that sentences disintegrate, for
disintegration is itself an activity, a dramatic application of
force, whether from within or without, that impels an object
toward some altered condition. *Lessness* is Beckett's singularly
undramatic work: it is a composition in which language and
speech face one another across an impasse:

In four split asunder over backwards true refuge issueless
scattered ruins. He will live again the space of a step it will be

day and night again over him the endlessness. Face to white
calm touch close eye calm long last all gone from mind. Grey face
two pale blue little body heart beating only upright. He will go
on his back face to the sky open again over him the ruins the
sand the endlessness. Earth sand same grey as the air sky ruins
body fine ash grey sand. Blank planes touch close sheer white all
gone from mind. [pp. 16–17]

It is the act of speech which draws discrete words from the
lexicon of a language and organizes them into predications. In
Lessness, however, words are drawn out of a lexicon—a nar-
rowly circumscribed lexicon, hence the torturous repetition—
but they remain discrete and isolated particles, as though
they were so many subordinate locutions without a larger
structure in which to function. One can, as in *How It Is,*
extrapolate a narrative—a man reposes among ruins, his true
refuge; his little body is prostrate, but his still beating heart
remains upright; his two pale blue eyes confront an endless
sky, which is grey like the ashen earth; the man dreams (evi-
dently) "of days and nights made of dreams of other nights
and better days" (p. 17), and that as in those better days he
will once more curse God, as a consequence of which "un-
happiness will reign again" (p. 18); fortunately or unfor-
tunately, as the case may be, such dreams are dispelled by "the
dawn dispeller of figments" (p. 21). Character, setting, even the
possibility of incident—the materials for a narrative exist, but
the repetition of a mere handful of details suggests inertia, an
inability to move details forward, as though the lexicon itself
were a narrative from which bits and pieces of a fiction might
be extracted, but extracted only, and not reconstituted as a
narration.

Narrative without narration: *langue* without *parole*—it is
toward this radical formula that the whole of Beckett's fiction
tends. The opposition between language and the act of speech
is already present in the condition which forces Beckett's
storytellers to utter words that are not their own. It derives
from the opposition between the pensum to speak and the
impossibility of speech imposed by the dissociation of words

and things, and even more from the increasing inability of these storytellers to establish among words relationships of a kind that will generate determinate discourse. Language imposes itself, that is to say, upon situations in which it becomes progressively more difficult for it to function, until at last in *Lessness* it seems hardly to function at all, except insofar as it exists on the page as a relic of a discourse once performed but never to be performed again.

A final point to mark is that this problem of the function of language is not so much literary as it is, in the strict sense, linguistic. It is, indeed, a problem of literary language, insofar as it derives from the way Beckett manuevers language into the foreground of his fiction. Moreover, this act of foregrounding involves (as it did for Joyce) a radical modification of conventional narrative structures. At the same time, however, it is an act which proceeds on the basis of a use of language that deviates not from ordinary discourse but rather from successful discourse. Beckett does not foreground language by amplifying the devices of style; one cannot properly speak in Beckett's case of a "literary" use of language, for he does not in any particularly noteworthy way organize language into systems of verbal equivalences. He disrupts the very operations of language, just as Mallarmé and Joyce did, but he does so purely and simply, without recourse to style as a way of filling the empty foreground left by an indeterminate meaning. Instead, he chooses to dramatize this disruption: what the discourse of his fiction enacts is precisely a breakdown in the operations of language. We can put the matter another way by considering that the basic fictional unit for Beckett is the moment of speech. It is a moment, however, in which our expectations are confounded by the failure of the act of speech to generate functioning linguistic relationships. Thus in *Watt* words repeatedly form mathematical rather than grammatical combinations; in the trilogy sentences fail to cohere properly into contexts; in *How It Is,* and again in Beckett's latest fiction, the very process by which sentences are formed staggers to a halt.

What is the reason for this failure of speech? Beckett criticism has with occasional exceptions tended to regard the theme of failure in his work from points of view that are variously literary and moral, according to which the failure of human activity becomes an instance of comedy and a judgment concerning the state of human affairs. There remains, however, the point of view of language itself. In connection with the trilogy we speculated briefly upon a hypothetical *Ur-word*, a perpetual and undifferentiated utterance that is implied in the way language imposes itself upon a series of wretched storytellers. We might recall this notion here as a way of suggesting that it is language itself which destroys the act of speech, in order to recover and maintain in being the moment before speech, in which it can exist freely in an unstructured form, thus to be wholly and utterly itself, untouched by the designs of human intention. It is impossible, perhaps, to imagine this moment that precedes speech, because the very effort to imagine involves us in processes that begin the shaping of an utterance. Yet Beckett has sought to imagine this moment—to imagine language in the freedom of its own world—by dramatizing acts of speech that never quite escape the uncertain void from which, in our ordinary experience, utterances routinely depart, leaving trails of meaning as they move.

PART THREE

*The Language of Poetry and
the Being of the World*

7

Negative Discourse and the Moment before Speech: A Metaphysics of Literary Language

In chapter 3 I quoted Michel Foucault's remark that, during the nineteenth century, literature ceased to exist simply as a form of signification and became instead "a manifestation of a language which had no other law than that of affirming—in opposition to all other forms of discourse—its own precipitous existence." The purpose of this chapter is to inquire further into the existence of language, and particularly into the metaphysical or ontological status of that form of discourse which affirms this existence—which establishes, that is to say, the being of language as its content or meaning. Notions of metaphysics or ontology are prodigious by their very nature and need to be conjured with great care; but they are also important, to the extent that any inquiry into the ontological status of literary language becomes at the same time an inquiry into its value. What is the value, after all, of a form of discourse that is characterized by the foregrounding of language itself, and which on this account reduces meaning to a problematic and even indeterminate condition? The value of such a discourse is doubtless formal or aesthetic—or at least it is in some cases, though evidently not in all—but it will be our purpose here to ask whether matters of form and beauty do not in their turn disclose a value of a more fundamental nature, such as that which obtains in the relationship between the being of language and the being of the world.

Let us return once more to Foucault's *Les Mots et les choses:*

> In its original form, when it was given to men by God himself, language was an absolutely certain and transparent sign for things, because it resembled them. The names of things were lodged in the things they designated, just as strength is written in the body of the lion, regality in the eye of the eagle, just as the influence of the planets is marked upon the brows of men: by the form of similitude. This transparency was destroyed at Babel as a punishment for men. Languages became separated and incompatible with one another only in so far as they had previously lost this original resemblance to the things that had been the prime reason for the existence of language. All the languages known to us are now spoken only against the background of this lost similitude, and in the space that it left vacant.[1]

It is perhaps impossible to speak of language without at some point invoking the myth of a primordial sign, which is to say the myth of an ideal unity of word and being. And in turn it is perhaps impossible to speak of this myth without taking up sooner or later the story of Babel, which duplicates typologically the story of man's fall from the harmony of his original paradise by dramatizing the fall of the word from its original harmony with the world. The story of Babel, after all, is not simply the story of the proliferation of tongues, but of the proliferation of words and their disproportionate abundance in relation to the world of things. The fall of the word, that is to say, is its dissociation from the world and its isolation among other words in "a space left vacant" by the world's disappearance.

One way to regard the writers that we have just examined is to see in their use of language an effort to reenact this fall of the word. Recall, for example, Mallarmé's question in "Crise du vers": "Why should we perform the miracle by which a natural object is almost made to disappear beneath the magic waving wand of the written word, if not to divorce that object from the direct and the palpable, and so to conjure up the pure idea?" We may say that Mallarmé invokes here the mythical unity of word and being, but he does so only to reverse it or to turn it inside out: the power of language is no longer to call up the presence of an object but rather to return it to its original absence. The very act of speech is thus an act of dissociation, whereby the word is split off from the world and isolated in vacant space.

The origin of this way of thinking about words and things appears to lie in Hegel's conception of speech as a dialectic of negation and signification. In one of the Jena Lectures of 1803–1804, Hegel wrote: "The first act by which Adam made himself master of the animals was to impose a name on them; that is, he annihilated them in their existence as beings." [2] This dissociation of word and thing is perhaps a fall from paradise, but it is a fortunate fall in the sense that man is by this means abstracted from the life of the senses and situated in a world of meanings. Adam, by his speech, annihilated the immediate presence of the world and in its place established a mediating or ideal presence—the word. Alexandre Kojève, in his *Introduction to the Reading of Hegel*, explains this notion as follows: "The being which negates the given real dialectically also preserves it as negated—that is, as unreal or 'ideal': it preserves what is negated as the 'meaning' of the discourse by which it reveals it. Hence it is 'conscious' of what it negates." [3] That is to say, the activity of speech annihilates the world of things in the very process of signification; in speech the world of things is displaced by the world of the spirit.

What is interesting, however, is that in Mallarmé's conception of the poetic utterance we discover only the purely negative side of this Hegelian process: "When I say: 'a flower!' then from that forgetfulness to which my voice consigns all floral form, something different from the usual calyces arises, something all music, essence, and softness: the flower which is absent from all bouquets." Mallarmé places a premium not upon the ideal presence or meaning of the object but upon the condition of its absence: he speaks in order to conjure not the idea as a locus of intelligibility but "the pure idea," which,

like Hegel's pure abstractions of Being and Nothing, is utterly
without content. Hence Mallarmé's remark, "My work was
created only by elimination. . . . Destruction was my Bea-
trice." [4] For it was Mallarmé's conviction, as we have seen,
that the contemplation of "the pure idea"—the contempla-
tion of *le Néant*—is an aesthetic experience. In the condition
of absence, which is to say in the void between the world of
existents and the universe of meaning, the essence of beauty is
to be found.

Such an understanding of beauty is not as altogether eso-
teric as it may seem. In an essay entitled "The Aesthetic
Experience and the Aesthetic Object," Roman Ingarden makes
the interesting point that the experience of beauty involves a
displacement of our natural attitude toward the world, insofar
as there "occurs a distinct *narrowing* of the field of conscious-
ness with reference to this world, and though we do not lose
an unconscious sensation of its presence and existence, though
we continue feeling in the world, the conviction of the exis-
tence of the real world, which constantly colors all our actu-
ality, withdraws somehow into shade, loses its importance and
strength. In the later phases of an intensive aesthetic experi-
ence there may occur—and how well-known to us—the
phenomenon of a quasi oblivion of the real world." [5] One
might describe Mallarmé's poetry as an effort to actualize the
essence of beauty by engaging the negative resources of lan-
guage, thus to amplify this sense of the world's oblivion. De-
struction, the Beatrice of Mallarmé, thus becomes a positive
principle—a way of overcoming the opposition between the
experience of beauty and the experience of being in the
world.

The idea that beauty comes into being at the expense of
the world brings to mind once more Flaubert's dream:
"What seems beautiful to me, what I should like to write, is a
book about nothing. . . ." The point to mark about the
dream of such a book, or about Mallarmé's ideal of an ab-
solute purity of discourse, is that it implies a form of literature
that feeds upon its own impossibility: it implies an almost

violently paradoxical form of literature, one which requires for its creation the failure of language. An entry in Valéry's *Analects* fleshes out this point: " 'The Beautiful' implies effects of unsayability, indescribability, ineffability. And the word itself says *nothing*. It has no definition; for a true definition must be constructive." This is, to be sure, an ancient theme: language as a finite system is inadequate to the transcendence of beauty. What turns over in Valéry's mind, however, is precisely the idea of the negativity of beauty, together with the possibility that, by virtue of this negativity, the very inadequacy of language becomes a resource. "Ineffability: 'words fail us' "—and yet literature seeks to establish itself upon this failure. As Valéry puts it, "Literature tries to create with words this state of wordlessness," for the poet is driven by a "thirst caused by that which finds expression in this impotence [of language]." "Beauty is negative," and only the negative of discourse can express it.[6]

It was Hegel who phophesied the death of art, on the grounds that "when the idea of Beauty seizes itself as absolute or infinite Spirit, it also at the same time discovers itself to be no longer completely realized in the forms of the external world"; that is, it can no longer find expression in such finite elements as objects, images, and words.[7] But if beauty thus departs from the world and so transcends the finite elements of expression, we should not be surprised if the artist feels compelled to follow—to pursue what no longer exists within the world he was accustomed to portray. "I really identified myself with this Being, this Being that has ceased to exist," writes Antonin Artaud in "The New Revelations of Being." "And this Being revealed to me all things. I knew it, but could not say it, and if I can start to say it now, it is because I have left reality behind." [8] Being, as it ceases to exist, induces a state of wordlessness; it makes speech impossible, and so perhaps fixes the writer in the condition of Sartre's Roquentin: "Things are divorced from their names. They are there, grotesque, headstrong, gigantic, and it seems ridiculous to call them seats or say anything about them at all: I am in the midst of things, nameless things. Alone, without words, defenceless." [9] Roquentin, of course, tells us that he confronts existence itself—the bare, unmediated or uninterpreted being of things from which language had protected him but protects him no longer. The "being" of Artaud is more mysterious, less philosophical, and certainly less an enemy of the spirit than Sartre's: it is simply a nameless Other which has departed from the world of experience, and which beckons to Artaud, who quits the world in turn, choosing to dwell among words instead of things—and thereby renewing, as he says, the efficacy of his language. But how can this be so? How can the act of speech be predicated upon the condition of nameless-ness which makes speech impossible? The answer (which is the answer of Flaubert, Mallarmé, Valéry) lies in the negative unity which Artaud, by his departure from reality, thus establishes between word and being: the fall of language into namelessness coincides with "this Being that has ceased to exist" sufficiently to provide a new condition for the possibility of discourse.

We need, however, to define this negative discourse more precisely, and to inquire on a more systematic basis into its historical significance. Negative discourse, let us say, is a form of speech which attempts to isolate the act of signification from its results, that is, from the formation of a signified. But what need does such a form of speech fulfill? What are the conditions which disclose its necessity or, indeed, its value? The example of Artaud, who nowhere identifies his mysterious "Being" with beauty, suggests that we are confronted here with a phenomenon which is not reducible to the tradition of aesthetic formalism.

One critic who has tried to deal with this issue is Roland Barthes, whose *Le Degré zéro de l'écriture* turns upon the argument that negative discourse is the distinguishing feature of modern poetry. According to Barthes, classical or tradi-tional literary language conforms to the basic structures of ordinary speech insofar as its activity of signification is syn-tagmatic or relational, "which means that in it words are abstracted as much as possible in the interests of relationships. In it, no word has a density by itself, it is hardly the sign of a thing, but rather the means of conveying a connection. [The word extends], as soon as it is uttered, towards other words, so as to form a superficial chain of intentions." The classical literary utterance, that is to say, is so constructed as to dissolve its signifiers in the very process of forming a signified. In modern literary uses of language, by contrast, we find the attempt "to eliminate the intention to establish relationships and to produce instead an explosion of words. For modern poetry . . . destroys the functional nature of language. It retains only the outward shape of relationships [the interplay of signifiers], their music, but not their reality [the signified]. The Word shines forth above a line of relationships emptied of their content, grammar is bereft of its purpose, it becomes prosody and is no longer anything but an inflexion which lasts only to present the word." [10] We have here perhaps a polemical as well as a critical and historical judgment: what Barthes is saying is that modern poetry is not simply "poetic discourse" and therefore merely a different kind of discourse from prose or conversation. Modern poetry is nondiscourse: the modern poetic act is not intentional; it is a refusal to mean.

Immediately, of course, we can think of any number of modern literary works which are intentional in nature, which *do* mean. For Ezra Pound (to take perhaps the most obvious example) language remains a way of getting things into a poem, even to the extent of transforming the poem into an encyclopedia on the model of the ancient epic. But the example of Pound only points up the fact that Barthes is using the term "modern" in a normative rather than a merely chronological sense. For him the typically modern poet is Mallarmé, in whose view words were so many precious objects to be strewn like dice across the white space of a book's page—in whose view, indeed, typography was to replace syntax as a way of establishing relationships among words. Between Mallarmé and Barthes, however, there is this important difference: the negative discourse of Mallarmé was motivated in large measure by the negativity of beauty. To isolate the word in the void between things and meanings is to establish it as a transcendent reality; but it is at the same time to situate it in the realm where beauty is to be discovered. But Barthes is careful to separate the formalist use of language from the aestheticism with which it is normally associated. "The field of the writer is nothing but writing itself," Barthes argues, "not as the pure 'form' conceived by an aesthetic of art for art's sake, but, much more radically, as the only area [*espace*] for the one who writes"—the only area, that is to say, in which language manifests itself as a being which appropriates literature, thus to establish itself over and against the world of things as the principle of motivation, the new "mythical alibi," for the creative act. In *Creative Intuition in Art and Poetry,* Jacques Maritain made roughly the same point: "Modern poetry cannot be judged and understood in the perspective of classical aesthetics and mere literature," because modern poetry has abolished beauty as the reason for its being and concerns itself with its own "secret workings," with those obscure linguistic processes by which it is created.[11]

The problem is, of course, that the language of virtually any poem, modern or otherwise, seeks to preserve itself throughout the process of signification. Sigurd Burckhardt, in an essay entitled "The Poet as Fool and Priest," has observed that "the nature and primary function of the most important poetic devices—especially rhyme, meter, and metaphor—is to release words in some measure from their bondage to meaning, their purely referential role, and to give or restore to them the corporeality which a true medium needs."[12] After all, language for a poet is rarely or never a purely transitive medium—a medium acted upon solely for the purposes of signification. Gerard Manley Hopkins once said, in his essay "Rhythm and the Other Structural Parts of Rhetoric—Verse," that "we may think of words as heavy bodies, as indoor and out of door objects of nature and man's art"; and he went on to observe that, like natural bodies, words possess centers of gravity and

centers of illumination. The function of a word in a rhythmic
structure is to be found in the relationship or interplay be-
tween these two centers, which determine, respectively, its
stress and pitch.[13] Hopkins thus continues the tradition of
ancient rhetoric, according to which language is understood
to be corporeal in character, a substantial medium that is
not to be effaced by the formation of meaning. And to the
extent that the poet amplifies the corporeality of his language,
he actively pursues the dissociation of words and things: he
constructs a negative discourse, in which language itself moves
to become the subject or purpose of the act of speech.[14]

What are we to think, however, when the devices which the
writer employs to liberate his words from their function are
not merely the traditional figures of rhetoric and poetic but
are rather such uses of language as are implied in Flaubert's
dream of "a book about nothing" or in Barthes's conception
of modern poetic language? What are we to think of uses of
language which displace signification in a radical and almost
absolute way? Tradition, indeed, pales before the accomplish-
ment of *Finnegans Wake:* "in the Nichtian glossary which pur-
veys aprioric roots for aposteriorious tongues that is nat
language in any sinse of the world and one might fairly go
kish his sprogues as fail to certify whether the wartrophy
eluded at some lives earlier was that somethink like a jug, to
what, a coctable." [15] Here is language apotheosized by its fall
—language at play within what Hugh Kenner called "a uni-
verse of independent words obeying their chemical affinities
with no restraint from things." [16] The point is that the
"Nichtian glossary" amplifies and, in a sense, fully liberates
the natural inclination of literary speech toward negative
discourse, for this glossary is composed of words that resolutely
refuse to be contained within those linguistic relationships the
formation of which ordinarily drives forward the act of
speech. The Joycean word, as we have seen, becomes a "float-
ing signifier" that (to quote Barthes again) "shines forth above
a line of relationships emptied of their content." Indeed, there
is in *Le Degré zéro de l'écriture* a passage in which Barthes

seems to have *Finnegans Wake* precisely in mind: "Each poetic word is . . . an unexpected object, a Pandora's box from which fly out all the potentialities of language; it is [a word] produced and consumed with a peculiar curiosity, a kind of sacred relish. This Hunger of the Word, common to the whole of modern poetry, makes poetic speech terrible and inhuman. It initiates a discourse full of gaps and full of lights, filled with absences and over-nourishing signs." [17] Speech becomes, that is to say, a discontinuous utterance, in which the word, as an "over-nourished" manifold of signs, becomes a weight too great for the verbal chain to bear, for the act of speech in the *Wake* turns everywhere upon a violent incongruity between word and voice, as though the illusion of speech had been created only to be called into question by a language that is perhaps impossible for man to utter.

Incongruity between word and voice is, of course, the central theme of Samuel Beckett's fiction, which dramatizes the terrible movement of the human voice as it is propelled by words not its own toward empty space, there finally to disappear (as in *Lessness*), leaving behind only the free play of words, which is to say their unaccountable appearance within a field of writing that is defined hardly at all by sentence and context. Just so does Beckett actualize the modern theme of negative discourse, or what he calls "the expression that there is nothing to express, nothing with which to express, nothing from which to express, no power to express, no desire to express, together with the obligation to express." This dialectic, in which the compulsion to speak is set against the impossibility of expression—and which so neatly parodies Flaubert's agony during the writing of *Madame Bovary* or Mallarmé's impotence before the blank page—focuses upon the moment before speech. It implies an act of speech that is forced back upon itself, thus to establish in the foreground a language that refuses to submit to speech—that refuses to be used as a system of signifiers to conjure a signified—in order to maintain itself in being against the annihilation of words that acts of speech ordinarily perform.

The question, however, remains: What is the value of a language thus liberated from its function? What claims can be made upon our attention by a language which appropriates the poet's act of speech in order to proclaim its own transcendence? What is to be gained by a return to the moment before speech? Neither Joyce nor Beckett provides us means by which to answer these questions. On the contrary, modern critics have been inclined to value these writers to the extent that models of signification can be reconstructed from the transformations which constitute the texts of *Finnegans Wake* and *How It Is*. But we need to face the problem of value from the standpoint of language itself in order finally to come to terms with it.

One writer who has done precisely this is Maurice Blanchot, whose fiction (*Thomas L'Obscur,* for example) is as powerful an exaltation of the negative resources of language as can be found anywhere in modern literature. In "La Littérature et la droit à la mort," Blanchot moves by a sequence of paradoxes toward the idea that the negative is the true and proper subject of literary art. The most critical of these paradoxes is the idea of the annihilating word:

> I say: "this woman," and immediately I dispose of her. . . . No doubt, my language kills no one. However, when I say "this woman," actual death is announced and is already present in my language; my language says that this person, who is there, now, can be detached from herself, subtracted from her existence and her presence and plunged suddenly into a nothingness of existence and presence; my language signifies essentially the possibility of this destruction; it is, at every moment, a resolute allusion to such an event. My language kills no one. But, if that woman were not really capable of death, if she were not at every moment of her life menaced by death, bound and united to it by a tie of essence, I could not accomplish this ideal negation, this deferred assassination that is my language.[18]

Here the Hegelian and Mallarmean idea of speech is heightened by Heidegger's figure of man as a *Sein zum Tode,* a "being toward death." Speech is an ideal negation; it is an ideal act of murder which prefigures an actual annihilation. For the void which speech creates and within which meaning seeks to establish itself as an ideal presence over and against the world of things and persons, is primordial in character. It is the abyss of nothingness whence man comes and toward which his being carries him. "Language begins only with the void," Blanchot says, "plenitude and certitude do not speak." [19] Man, possessed as he is of the capacity for signification, is a creature of the void. His very will to meaning removes him, like Hegel's Adam, from the world in which he exists. His very act of consciousness, understood as a conferring or discovery of meaning, is an act of destruction.

But notice what power is here attributed to man! It is the negative of the power of Orpheus to call the world into being. Man may annihilate the world at will; but what interests Blanchot is that man may also maintain the world in being. For by his silence man may return himself to the world of things, establish himself once more (in Heidegger's formula) as a "being-in-the-world," which is to say that through his silence he may once more establish himself in the immediate presence of the world. It is for this reason that Blanchot writes: "The ideal of literature could be this: say nothing, speak and say nothing." [20] For Blanchot, however, this negative discourse is not (as it is for Barthes) accomplished solely for the sake of language. To be sure, for Blanchot as well as for Barthes language is understood to appropriate the poetic act and to speak through that act nothing but itself; but Blanchot pushes Barthes's "mythical alibi" for the act of speech onto wholly different ground. He seeks to return the poet to that original time before the world seemed to man to be a privileged signified to be grasped in an act of representation. "Language," Blanchot says, "perceives that it owes its meaning, not to what exists, but to its recoil before existence." Ordinary speech is just such a recoil—a withdrawal of language away from things into a world of signifieds, in which language itself exists only as a transparent and transitive medium. And yet there remains the primitive impulse of language not to speak *of* things but *to speak things themselves.* Language in ordinary speech is the purveyor of meanings, not of things; accordingly, as Blanchot puts it, "If one speaks of things only by saying of them that by which they are nothing, then, indeed, the only hope of saying everything is to say nothing." [21]

What Blanchot means is that to speak and yet to say nothing is a way of allowing language to maintain the *plenum;* and this is to say that a literary use of language, as it approaches the condition of negative discourse—a discourse which disrupts or reverses the act of signification—is a way of holding the world in being against the annihilation that takes place in man's ordinary utterances. Understood in this way, the poet does indeed become a kind of Orpheus, a poet of the earth, whose song shields the world against the void into which ordinary speech seeks to cast it. So Hegel, indeed, predicted the death of art, for in such a view as Blanchot's, poetry in the traditional sense, as a form of signification or representation, is destroyed. Paradoxically, however, this death (rather like the death of Orpheus) moves suddenly to become a rebirth. "The language of literature," Blanchot says, "is the search for the moment which precedes it"—the moment before speech, or the moment of existence.[22] In this quest, "all that is physical [in language] plays a premier role: the rhythm, the weight, the mass, the figure, then [in the manner of Mallarmé] the paper on which one writes, the trace of the ink, the book." [23] For when the poet, by building up what Blanchot calls "the materiality of language," makes us aware of the "irreality" or nothingness of his speech, it is then that he is most creative. His negative discourse preserves language in its unspoken condition, which is the condition in which things exist as beings, not as signifieds.[24]

Blanchot's thought here converges upon several key themes in Heidegger's later writings on language. Indeed, these writings constitute the most complete inquiry into the problem of value posed by what Heidegger calls "the poetic experience with language," that is, the experience of language itself as it discloses itself through poetry.[25] In poetry, Heidegger says, we encounter not the language of signs but the being of language —language as an immediate or uninterpreted presence, which surrounds and penetrates us and makes us a part of itself. But Heidegger does not, like Barthes, think of the being of language in isolation; it is for him a term in an equation which reads, "the being of language: the language of being"—"Two phrases held apart by a colon, each the inversion of the other" (p. 94). This equation, according to Heidegger, is the "guideword" to the essence of language. "The essential being of language," we are told, "is Saying as Showing [disclosure]. Its showing character is not based on signs of any kind" but upon its very existence as the language of being—that language by which being discloses itself to us (p. 123). The being of things (*das Sein dem Seienden*) is disclosed, that is to say, not through the formation of meaning but through the very being of language—through language itself, as it exists in the moment before speech:

> Speaking is known as the articulated vocalization of thought by means of the organs of speech. But speaking is at the same time also listening. It is the custom to put speaking and listening in opposition: one man speaks, the other listens. But listening accompanies and surrounds not only speaking such as takes place in conversation. The simultaneousness of speaking and listening has a larger meaning. Speaking itself is a listening. Speaking is a listening to the language which we speak. Thus, it is a listening not *while* but *before* we are speaking. This listening to language also comes before all other kinds of listening that we know, in a most inconspicuous manner. We do not merely speak *the* language—we have already listened to the language. What do we hear? We hear language speaking. [pp. 123–124]

The importance of this moment before speech is that it harbors the unity of word and being: it is the moment "in which the being of language speaks as the language of being," and so discloses the being of things—the very presence of the world (pp. 79–80).

We shall inquire in the next chapter into Heidegger's conception of poetry as a kind of primordial speech by which the world is for the first time placed before man and maintained in being thereafter as his dwelling-place. For now, however, we ought to consider the relationship between the speech of language and human speech. It is the unity of word and being which originally makes human speech possible and to which man customarily appeals for the validation of his utterances; but too often man presumes to speak on his own, without listening to language and indeed regarding language as a mere tool or instrument by which to arrange his intentions before his listeners as so many signs to be deciphered. The whole of Heidegger's discussion of language, from *Sein und Zeit* through the later essays, is a persistent complaint against such speech and the conception of language as a mere instrument of signification. His own discourse is itself a calculated affront to such speech, and even more it is an affront to the tradition of philosophical utterance, particularly as that tradition seeks the being of things as a signified tossed up by a language of signs. For Heidegger is a philosopher who makes us aware of the presence of language. His speech is never transparent; it never proceeds according to the decorum of clarity that distinguishes logical discourse. Indeed, in at least one respect the character of his language may be said to resemble Joyce's, for Heidegger habitually collapses words into a single term, thus to fashion a lexicon of manifold or prehensive signs: "being-in-the-world," "being-toward-death," "being-concerned-with-the-world-of-one's-care."

One hesitates to call such language poetic: to do so is in some measure to explain it away. Like the poet, however, Heidegger is concerned to transform language in a way that releases it from or opposes it to conventional usage. At the end of "On the Way to Language," as a kind of peroration, Heidegger quotes Wilhelm von Humboldt's remark that, at a given point in their history, "a people could . . . impart so different a form to the language handed down to them that it would thereby turn into a wholly other, wholly new language." [26] The value of such "a wholly other, wholly new language," is that it restores man to that original, primitive condition in which he first encountered the word and discovered in that encounter the proximity of being. But this encounter with the word is not, for Heidegger, an encounter with any sort of object; it is not the discovery of a sign that betokens some distant or unforeseen reality. On the contrary, it is, at least in the later essays, understood to be an entry into the realm of language itself:

> In order to be who we are, we human beings remain committed to and within the being of language, and can never step out of it and look at it from somewhere else. Thus we always see the nature of language only to the extent to which language itself has us in view, has appropriated us to itself. That we cannot know the nature of language—know it according to the traditional concept of knowledge defined in terms of cognition as representation —is not a defect, however, but rather an advantage by which we are favored with a special realm, that realm where we, who are needed and used to speak language, dwell as *mortals*. [p. 134]

This passage recalls Humboldt's idea that "each language draws a circle around a people to whom it adheres which it is possible for the individual to escape only by stepping into a different one." It recalls the idea of language as a circle whose center is everywhere and whose circumference is nowhere—or, again, the idea of language as a being that appropriates the act of speech and discloses itself through it. Language in this sense is not reducible to the sign. Indeed, human speech, as it is appropriated by language, becomes a speech that transcends or precedes the discourse of signs to the extent that it is able to disclose what can never be grasped through a sign: namely, being itself. "Saying will not let itself be captured in any statement," Heidegger says. "It demands of us that we achieve by silence the appropriating, initiating movement within the being of language—and do so without talking about silence" (pp. 134–135). We arrive here at Heidegger's version of the idea of negative discourse: "Every primal and proper Naming states something unspoken, and states it so that it remains unspoken." [27] Only by returning to that primitive condition before speech, in which man first enters into the realm of language, is he able to disclose the unspeakable—not by speaking *about* it, not by trying to enclose it within a system of signs, but by allowing language to speak through him and to disclose through him its very being, which is at the same time the being of the world.

The importance of poetry for Heidegger is that it reproduces this original moment before speech: it is a transformed discourse which conducts us not into a universe of signs but into the realm of language. It is negative discourse, which reveals the unspoken that ordinary speech conceals beneath its wealth of meanings. Heidegger thus establishes for literary language a metaphysical ground—a metaphysical reason for its being. And he makes clear, what is more, what our own response to literary language ought to be—not an act of interpretation but a listening to the language of the poem. In an essay on Georg Trakl's poetry, "Language in the Poem," Heidegger observes that "the dialogue of thinking with poetry aims to call forth the *nature* of language, so that mortals may learn again to live within language." As in the case of Trakl's work, the language in the poem "is essentially ambiguous." It is not the expression of determinate significations; it is not reducible to a language of signs. Accordingly, "we shall hear nothing of what the poem says so long as we bring to it only this or that dull sense of unambiguous meaning." [28] The language in the poem is an opening into the realm of language, and only by listening to this language in the poem can we return to our origins, thus to locate ourselves in the very being of the world.

8

Poetry as Reality: The Orpheus Myth and Its Modern Counterparts

In this chapter I want to consider once more the idea that poetry is not simply a form of signification but an activity which goes beyond meaning to engage the world itself. Instead of regarding it, however, as a negative discourse which returns us to a world of existents by abolishing the world of signifieds, I want to turn it to positive account and to inquire into the idea of poetic speech as an activity which brings the world into being for the first time and which maintains it there as the ground of all signification. "This activity," as Albert Hofstadter describes it in connection with Croce, "is genuinely creative, for in it man's world and self are originated and maintained, not found already finished." [1] For the origin of this idea we may look to the Orpheus myth, and specifically to the power of Orpheus to summon things into his presence. In Book x of Ovid's *Metamorphoses*, for example, we find this account: "A hill there was, and on the hill a wide-extending plain, green with luxuriant grass; but the place was devoid of shade. When here the heaven-descended bard sat down and smote his sounding lyre, shade came to the place. There came the Chaonian oak, the grove of the Heliades, the oak with its deep foliage, the soft linden, the beech . . ." [2]—and so on, until each tree in the traditional catalogue has made its appearance. This power of Orpheus over nature prompted

Bacon to adopt him as a model for the scientist; before Bacon, the alchemists had placed Orpheus among their patrons, Zoroaster, Hermes Trismegistus, Linus, and Musaeus.[3] It is hard to tell who had the better claim to the singer's blessings —the alchemists, perhaps, since they were, in their way, responsible for preserving and transmitting the tradition of magic. But the alchemist, after all, is a cultural residue, whose dubious power rests with a few secret utterances; whereas, by contrast, Orpheus is preeminently the poet-magus, whose power displays, in Ernst Cassirer's words, that "characteristic 'wholeness' of the mythical picture of the world, in which all the differentiations of things are dissolved into a mythical-magical chain of causality." [4] The power of Orpheus extends beyond the creation of song to the building up of a world, because the sphere of his activity is governed by an identity of word and being. "Gesang ist Dasein," wrote Rilke in the third of his *Sonette an Orpheus* (1922): [5] song is being—the world is poetry, for it is only upon the ground of the poetic word that the world can take on meaning and reality.

The alchemist, for his part, may be regarded as a fragment tossed up by the historical dismemberment of Orpheus, by which I mean that process of demythologization that marked the gradual dissociation of word and being. In this process the world emerged as a structure of parts and relations, a substance steadfast in existence, to which the mind was more or less adequate in its power to know. *Magikē*, accordingly, gave way to the *Logos* as the principle of the world's intelligibility, and as it did so the figure of the poet-magus lost its reason for being. In place of the identity of poetry and reality that gave life to Orpheus, poetic theory instituted the doctrine of *mimesis*, which established the poet over and against the world as a mere onlooker. The magic of poetry, in turn, came to be understood in terms of a psychology of rhetoric: by skilled imitation, or perhaps by imagining a more perfect world, the poet could persuade his audience to follow nature in conduct and in thought; but no longer could his song build up the world.[6]

It was not until the eighteenth century, and the advent of what Roman Ingarden has called "the controversy over the existence of the world," [7] that the idea of the poet-magus could once more be called into play. For in this controversy the idea of existence suffered the criticism leveled against the so-called copy-theory of knowledge (upon which the doctrine of *mimesis* was based). It was one of Locke's fundamental principles, for example, that the mind knows not things as they exist but only the phenomenal world that is given in experience; and this principle opened up the possibility, fully exploited by Hume, that the world customarily said to be apprehended in experience does not correspond to what is given in fact. Hume argued that, so far from being unified and intelligible—so far from being an apprehension of things and events, activities and relationships—experience shows itself upon analysis to be no more than a flow of discrete impressions. By this argument, however, Hume set the terms for Kant's "Copernican Revolution," according to which the world is regarded as a structure built up within experience by imagination and understanding and not as a ready-made object that reproduces copies of itself in the mind. The mind, that is, arranges the undifferentiated flow of sensations into an ideal temporal and spatial field and reconstitutes it there as a world of object and relationships. Such a world, to be sure, remains purely phenomenal: "The domain that lies out beyond the sphere of appearances is for us empty." [8] Yet this phenomenal world does not depend for its intelligibility upon its correspondence to a world of existents, for it is the product of an objectifying synthesis, whereby what is formless and unknowable takes on form and, therefore, the possibility of meaning.

It will not do, of course, to claim for Kant's description of the mind's power of synthesis an Orphic significance. Kant's critical idealism and the myth of Orpheus belong to radically opposed worlds, and only by violence to the one or the other can they be brought to share a mutual intelligibility. Yet history, in its way, appears to have wrought such a violence, for Kant's "Copernican Revolution," so far from remaining a purely philosophical idea with its own place and purpose within a strictly epistemological field, took on life as a kind of cultural phenomenon, thus to appear in diverse contexts and to serve ends which Kant never would have allowed.[9] I have in mind particularly that effort on the part of a number of German romantic poets and thinkers to "poetize philosophy," which in part meant the transformation of Kant's account of mental activity into a theory of poetic activity. The mediating figure in this effort was Schelling, in whose *System des Transzendentalen Idealismus* (1805) the critical idealism of Kant gives way to an aesthetic idealism which holds that "the ideal world of art and the real world of objects are products of one and the same activity." [10] Schelling's chief concern, of course, is with the ideal world of art, that is, with those works of genius by whose mediation we may transcend the world of objects—transcend, indeed, all forms of opposition, whether between subject and object, real and ideal, finite and infinite —and attain to a consciousness of the Absolute. Here let us simply mark the idea that "the objective world is only the primitive, as yet unconscious poetry of the Spirit," [11] for here poetry and the world merge once more, not, to be sure, in a mythic union, but in one made possible by Kant's description of how the mind forms an object for itself by synthesizing the chaos of sensation. Under the aegis of Schelling, the identity of poetry and reality became the central principle of Novalis's so-called magical idealism: "Poetry is what is absolutely and genuinely real." [12] This is so, because "we know something only insofar as we express it—that is, make it," [13] and insofar as our expression is poetic in character, that which we know becomes, like the world which Orpheus calls into his presence, a kind of ultimate poem. To be sure, Novalis's development of this idea is only fragmentary, and, like Schelling, he subordinates it to a theory of "transcendental poetry," whose orientation is not toward the world but toward the sphere of the infinite.[14] Yet the Orphic theme remains an explicit part of his thought: "We are on a mission," he wrote of himself and his fellow poets, "our calling is to fashion the earth." [15]

Adumbrations of this idea are to be found in a number of

English romanticists—in Coleridge, obviously, since his fa-
mous definition of imagination reproduces Schelling's idea
that the world of objects and the world of art are grounded
upon the same activity. In Book III of the *Prelude,* as a way
of announcing the theme of solitude, Wordsworth twice takes
up this idea:

> Unknown, unthought of, yet I was most rich—
> I had a world about me—'twas my own;
> I made it, for it only lived to me.[16]

Or, again:

> Hitherto I had stood
> In my own mind remote from social life,
> (At least from what we commonly so name),
> Like a lone shepherd on a promontory
> Who lacking occupation looks forth
> Into the boundless sea, and rather makes
> Than finds what he beholds.
>
> [III, 513–519]

The shepherd's activity is a prototype of the poet's—although,
as "Lines Composed a Few Miles above Tintern Abbey" sug-
gests, the poet engages the world on perhaps a more reciprocal
basis, creating what he sees out of impressions generated by
nature. Even so, such creation is a solitary experience, and it
stands in sharp contrast to the activity of Shelley's universal
mind. In Act III of *Prometheus Unbound* Prometheus speaks
of

> lovely apparitions, dim at first,
> Then radiant—as the mind, arising bright
> From the embrace of Beauty (whence the forms
> Of which these are the phantoms) casts on them
> The gathered rays which are reality.[17]

Earl Wasserman finds in these lines evidence of Shelley's
"ontological idealism," an utterly eclectic system that blends
traditional Neoplatonic formulas with ideas that derive from
the diffuse climate of the post-Kantian world.[18] Thus in this

passage art and reality merge in the unity of mind, which casts
the light of being upon the phenomena of experience. Nor are
these phenomena merely the shadows of the natural world;
they are, as Prometheus goes on to say, "the progeny immortal
/ Of Painting, Sculpture, and rapt Poesie" (iii, iii, 54–55). Of
somewhat greater interest, however, is the speech we examined
in chapter 2, in which the Earth announces the transformation
of human language into the language of the gods:

> Language is a perpetual Orphic song,
> Which rules with Daedal harmony a throng
> Of thoughts and forms, which else senseless and
>   shapeless were.
>
>   [IV, 415–417]

Here Shelley touches directly upon the Orpheus myth; yet
notice that he does so with a Kantian gesture. For the Orphic
character of language is made to consist in its power of
synthesis—in its ability to build up into form and idea that
which is undifferentiated. Language, that is to say, is not a
complex of words and structures that breaks down a given
reality into its diverse grammatical identities; it is not, to
borrow Wilhelm von Humboldt's distinction, an *ergon* or
product but an *energeia* or formative activity that mediates
between a constructive mind and "senseless and shapeless"
material.

This notion of language as a formative process is central to
Edgar Allan Poe's "The Power of Words," an obscure little
dialogue between two angels, Agathos and Oinos, in which it
is proposed that in the beginning God may well have created
the heavens and the earth, but he created "in the beginning
only"; [19] the universe as it is now constituted owes its presence
to "the host of Angelic Intelligences." As Agathos explains it,
air (or ether) is "the great medium of *creation*," whence it
must follow that "all motion, of whatever nature, creates."
This is so because "as a true philosophy has long taught . . . ,
the source of all motion is thought": through "the *physical
power of words*" thought generates impulses upon the ether,

thus to shape particles of matter into an ordered cosmos (IV, p. 143). Now what is of interest here is that, as everywhere in Poe, the angels are finally not angels at all but poets, and accordingly the process of creation which Agathos describes becomes less a theory of occult dynamics than an idea of poetry that conforms to the Orphic model. For as the two angels hover above a particularly beautiful star, Agathos recalls that "it is now three centuries since, with clasped hands, and streaming eyes, at the feet of my beloved—I spoke it [this star]—with a few passionate sentences—into birth" (IV, p. 144). What is more, the star which Agathos claims to have created belongs to the universe of *Eureka,* which, as Poe tells us, is patterned after the "cosmos" of the German naturalist Alexander von Humboldt (XVI, pp. 186–187). It is a universe of pure extension—a diversity of atoms (in Poe's variation, atoms of a spiritual as well as material character) diffused throughout Newtonian space. The atoms are fragments of an original unity to which Poe ascribes the name God, which God created in the beginning (but in the beginning only) by breaking down into a chaos. In "The Power of Words" Poe makes it the business of the angels, or poets, to utter this chaos into form: through the power of their speech the "Angelic Intelligences" are able to build up the particles of a broken divinity into a cosmos. Those "few passionate sentences" of Agathos constitute an activity of synthesis by which an undifferentiated mass takes on form and identity as a world—and not as a world only but as a kind of apotheosized lyric, an Orphic song generated into being by an overflow of powerful feelings.

And so Agathos emerges as an authentic poet-magus, whose power of magic takes on somewhat greater clarity and definition in the wake of Kant's "Copernican Revolution." There remains, however, an important and fundamental difference between Agathos and the Orpheus of myth. For Orpheus surrounds himself with his poem: he creates an environing world. By contrast, Agathos is the poet in space, whose creation is a kind of pure poem, like Flaubert's "book about nothing," which hangs "like the earth, suspended in the void." Agathos's star has only its beauty to recommend it, and perhaps its pathos as a relic of a lost love; but the world of Orpheus is a place to dwell.

This distinction between Agathos and Orpheus is worth remarking because it provides a way of distinguishing between romantic and modern versions of the Orpheus myth. It may be said that in our own century the myth has been rescued from dreams of transcendence and restored to its true earthly character. This is so even in the aesthetic idealism of Benedetto Croce. In the manner of Vico, Croce identifies poetry and language, but he does so on the basis of Wilhelm von Humboldt's thesis that "man lives with his objects mainly . . . as language turns them over to him." Humboldt had made it clear, in Croce's view, that "language is not a thing rising out of the need of external communication; on the contrary, it springs from the wholly internal thirst for knowledge and the struggle to reach an intuition of things." [20] Hence the Crocean formula: "Intuitive knowledge is expressive knowledge." Language is an expressive movement which objectifies a world, but this process of objectification is at the same time an intuition of the world. And because this expressive movement is essentially aesthetic in character, our encounter with the world is nothing less than a poetic event. "It has sometimes been thought," Croce writes, "that art is not a simple intuition, but an intuition of an intuition. . . . Thus man would attain to art by objectifying, not his sensations, as happens with ordinary intuition, but intuition itself. But this process of raising to a second power does not exist" (p. 12). Art does not reproduce an already given world; it is itself the giving of a world: it functions, as Hofstadter puts it, "in the primal constitution of human reality." [21] Between the work of art as such and the world in which man lives there is no essential difference, even as there is finally no difference in kind between the so-called genius and ordinary men: "It were better to change *poeta nascitur* into *homo nascitur poeta:* some men are born great poets, some small" (p. 14). But the point to mark is that this world which we objectify—this aesthetically given world—encloses us: we cannot, like Agathos, "leap into the transcendent such as it is easy to proclaim with empty words, but impossible for thought to execute—thought which is entirely a thinking in terms of life and the world." [22]

We can put this another way, that the activity of the human spirit has meaning only in relation to its life in the world, that man cannot come to be what he is except as he secures for himself a world in which to be. This is a typically modern notion—an expression of the modern impulse to place a premium, after so long a time, upon the world of our natural attitude. What distinguishes Croce from Schelling, for example, is that Croce is an aesthetic idealist of the critical mold, for whom "the very term Metaphysic . . . expresses a vain attempt to rise from a world of objects to a world of being, of supreme objects which are not objects—inviting and pushing one along the path of the Transcendent from which the critical spirit ever turns away, scenting the nearness of a crash into the void." [23] Croce's aesthetic idealism is oriented (like the spirit of Orpheus) toward the earth, which is to say toward that world within whose horizons human life and history run their course.

A similar notion forms a central theme in the work of Martin Heidegger. For Heidegger, man is preeminently a being-in-the-world for whom existence takes on meaning and reality only as he opens himself up to the being of his finite situation. Here we will be concerned with the so-called middle period of Heidegger's career, during which time he began in earnest his inquiry into the nature of language and, in turn, into the nature of poetry as a way of describing man's historic relation to his world and to being.[24] A good point of departure here is provided by one of Heidegger's famous enigmas: "Language is the house of being." [25] This metaphor belongs to Heidegger's interpretation of the Heraclitean *Logos*, according to which word and being are said to enjoy a luminescent communion made possible by man's entry into the world. In an essay on Rilke (whose *Sonette an Orpheus* have exerted considerable influence upon Heidegger),[26] he writes: "If we go to a spring or through the forest, we are already passing through the word 'spring' and through the word 'forest,' even though we do not speak these words or think of anything linguistic." [27] Language here appears to have been returned to a mythic universe in which the word supports, by virtue of its own reality, the world of things. For it is Heidegger's argument that the relationship in which man and world confront one another is both essentially and historically linguistic in character, which is to say that it is authentic human speech which opens up a world before man and, at the same time, opens man to the world and to the being of the world. What is important to notice, however, is that it is the speech of the poet (and the poet-thinker) that constitutes authentic speech. Indeed, if, as we walk through the world, we find ourselves as though in a colloquy of words and things, it is because our world is a field disclosed by the poet—a field, that is, which the poet has established in being.

"Only where there is language," Heidegger writes, "is there a world." [28] "Without the retaining word, the whole of things, the 'world,' sinks away into darkness, together with the 'I'." [29] It is this conception of language which underlies, and indeed prompts, the premium which Heidegger places upon poetry. In the essay "Hölderlin and the Essence of Poetry" (1935), Heidegger remarks, along the general lines of Humboldt's distinction between language as *ergon* and language as *energeia,* that the true function of language consists not in the transmission of information but in conversation (*das Gespräch*). On the basis of a passage from one of Hölderlin's drafts for the hymn "Freidensfeier"—

> Much man has learnt.
> Many of the heavenly ones has he named,
> Since we have been a conversation
> And have been able to hear from one another

—Heidegger writes: "We—mankind—are a conversation. The being of man is founded in language. But this only becomes actual in conversation" (p. 277). Language here is not merely a set of words but an activity—a kind of Orphic activity. For the being of man is actualized in his speech: conversation gathers a people into communal existence, which is at the same time existence among a world of things which conversation holds up out of the darkness. Beyond this, however, conversation is a gathering together in time: it is a historical activity. Characteristically, Heidegger lays special emphasis upon the past tense of Hölderlin's lines: it suggests to him that "we have been a single conversation since the time when it 'is time.' Ever since time arose we have *existed* historically" (p. 279). And this historical dimension leads Heidegger upon a quest for beginnings: if conversation holds man and his world in being, "how does this conversation, which we are, begin?" (p. 280). The answer is, in the primordial speech of the poet. "The poet names the gods, and names all things in that which they are," Heidegger says, and he goes on to make a (by now) familiar point: "This naming does not consist merely in something already known being supplied with a name; it is rather that when the poet speaks the essential word, the existent [*das Seiende*] is by this naming nominated as what it is. So it becomes known as existent. Poetry is the establishing of being by means of the word" (p. 281). The poet does not simply identify an already existing, already apprehended reality; his naming is, for Heidegger, a disclosure of the world—an utterance by virtue of which "things for the first time shine out" (p. 281).

The poet, that is to say, calls the world into man's presence: he opens up a field for conversation. The epistemological ground of this process is to be found not in Kant but in the phenomenology of Edmund Husserl. From the phenomenological standpoint, the phenomenal world is to be understood, not in the Kantian sense of a world of "mere" appearances that implies an unseen and unknowable noumenal reality, but in the purely descriptive sense of a world that comes into appearance before man—a world which is present to human consciousness and which consciousness cannot escape except by adopting attitudes (like the Cartesian doubt) which orient it away from the world. It is Heidegger's view, though by no means Husserl's, that this coming-into-appearance, this "shin-ing-out," constitutes the being of things, or what Heidegger calls *das Sein dem Seienden,* "the being of beings." Being, in this sense, is never a transcendent substance nor a substance of any kind: "Being is never an existent. But, because being and the essence of things can never be calculated and derived from what is present [that is, can never be deduced], they must be freely created, laid down and given. Such a free act of giving is establishment" (p. 281). And such a creation, such "a free act of giving," is performed by the poet: by the power of speech he establishes the being of things and so provides man with a world, which is to say that, as he calls the world into being, he establishes man *in the world.* "The speech of the poet is the establishment not only in the sense of the free act of giving but at the same time in the sense of the firm basing of human existence on its foundation" (pp. 281–282).

At this point, for the sake of clarification, we may ask: Where does the poet get this power, and what precisely is its nature? In his later essays, as we saw in the previous chapter, Heidegger locates the source in the being of language itself, which speaks through the poet as the language of being and thereby discloses the presence of the world. In "Hölderlin and the Essence of Poetry," however, Heidegger appears at first to explain this power by an appeal to Hölderlin's mythol-ogy. "The poetic word only acquires its power of naming," we are told, "when the gods themselves bring us to language" (p. 287). The poet is he who "has been cast out—out into that *Between,* between gods and men" (p. 288), rather like Orpheus, the "heaven-descended bard" who is both god and man. The poet receives his language from the gods and passes it to the people, and in the process he opens up a world before the people and gathers the people into conversation, that is, into a communal existence: "Only and for the first time in this Between is it decided, who man is and where he is settling his existence" (pp. 288–289). And so, Heidegger adds, borrowing once more a line from Hölderlin, " 'Poetically, dwells man on this earth' " (p. 289).

For Heidegger, however, the gods who bring, through the mediation of the poet, language to the people, are not merely the figures of Hölderlin's imagination; they are, rather, historical figures, in the sense that they are the gods of ancient Greece—specifically the Greece of Heraclitus and Parmenides, those poet-thinkers for whom divinity was understood in terms of the power of the *Logos*. In his *Introduction to Metaphysics* (first published in 1953 but composed for a lecture course in 1935), Heidegger examines the concept of the *Logos*, and he subjects it to a radical interpretation. For Heidegger rejects the traditional concept of the *Logos* as Reason, particularly as it implies the use of method and the process of analysis; he wants to know how the *Logos* was understood in the beginning, that is, by Heraclitus and Parmenides. And in the beginning, Heidegger argues, the *Logos* did not mean rational discourse; quite the contrary, it meant "gathering"—that act of gathering the flux into unity and permanence by virtue of which the world first emerged into the light of being.[30] The key notion here is that of emergence. For "gathering" is not simply a synthesis in the Kantian sense; rather, "this gathering has a fundamental character of opening, of making manifest" (p. 170). It is an act of disclosure, and as such it is for Heidegger a poetic act. The *Logos*, that is to say, is interpreted by Heidegger not as reason but as poetry: the *Logos* is the . poetic act which makes manifest the world, which calls the world into what Heidegger terms the "unconcealment" of being (p. 170).

Thus the Heraclitean unity of *Logos* and being becomes at bottom a unity of poetry and being. Heidegger is quite explicit on this point. In order to elucidate his idea that "the essence of language is found in the act of gathering within the togetherness of being" (p. 173), Heidegger takes up the question of the origin of language—a question, he says, which has remained unanswered "not because men have not been clever enough," but because "the origin of language is in essence mysterious. And this means that language can only have arisen from the overpowering, the strange and the terrible, through man's departure into being. In this departure language was being, embodied in the word: poetry. Language is the primordial poetry in which a people speak being" (p. 171). We cannot fail to recognize here the Orphic theme. Heidegger, in his quest for beginnings, has returned to the threshold of myth, in which word and being, poetry and the world, form a unity which reason was subsequently to analyze into its several parts. Indeed, what is essentially the myth of Orpheus provides Heidegger with the means by which the historical meaning of being may be articulated. In the beginning all was darkness, until man departed into being—that is, until man himself came into the "unconcealment" of being. But man's departure into being requires at the same time the correlative appearance of the world. The mediating figure in this event—the figure upon which the possibility of this event is grounded—is the poet, or more precisely the poet-magus, who utters that primordial word which at once establishes the world in being and situates man as a being who dwells in the world. The poet-magus derives his power from the fundamental unity of word and being: it is by the presence of the word that the aboriginal darkness is displaced by the light of being, in which light the world and man are originated and maintained by the word's continuing presence.

It is worth emphasizing, in this connection, that Heidegger's poet, like Orpheus, is the poet of earth. "Upon the earth, and in it, historical man grounds his dwelling in the world," writes Heidegger in "The Origin of the Work of Art" (also from 1935, but unpublished until 1950).[31] The earth here is a metaphorical ground, an extension of the phenomenological metaphor of horizon. The earth marks man's temporal and spatial finitude, but more than this it testifies to the fundamental limitations of both man and his world. For in contrast to the world, which is called up by the poet into the openness of being, the earth remains that undisclosed field which, as

Heidegger says, "sets to naught every attempt to penetrate into it. . . . The earth appears openly illuminated as itself only when it is perceived and preserved as that which is essentially undisclosable, that which recedes before every disclosure and constantly keeps itself closed up" (p. 673). The earth, that is, constitutes the very horizon of being within which man and the world stand unconcealed, and as such it constitutes the horizon of the poet's activity: the word of the poet, in effect, establishes an opening upon and within the earth. Here the being of things is made manifest; here man finds his environment, his dwelling-place.

Heidegger's conception of the earth and how it circumscribes the world which the poet establishes for man becomes the more interesting when we place beside it Wallace Stevens's conception of the nature and limitations of imaginative activity. At the core of Stevens's thought, as it is now commonplace to observe, lies the bare and familiar concept:

> The magnificent cause of being,
> The imagination, the one reality
> In this imagined world.[32]

We have here, of course, the romantic doctrine of imagination stated in its boldest and simplest terms. The extent to which Stevens committed himself to this doctrine has never been made entirely clear and doubtless will remain matter for dispute.[33] It seems to have been Steven's purpose not merely to reaffirm this doctrine but instead to reevaluate it—perhaps even to deliver, in his own eclectic way, a critique of the doctrine—by defining the nature and function of imagination within the limitations which govern what he calls "the corporeal world, the familiar world of the commonplace, in short, our world." "The corporeal world," Stevens says, enigmatically as always, "exists as the common denominator of the incorporeal worlds of its inhabitants." [34] That is to say, each man dwells in a reality of the mind, an incorporeal world, of which (paradoxically) the corporeal world is a dimension which he shares with other men. It is this paradox into which Stevens inquires in his poetry and which he struggles to preserve, on the grounds that, if indeed the imagination is "the magnificent cause of being," it nevertheless remains true that the world in which we live presents itself not as imagined but as real, not as a mere reflection of the mind but as a concrete world of persons and places, objects and sequences, problems and purposes. "The greatest poverty," runs one of Stevens's most famous lines, "is not to live / In a physical world"; it is the greatest poverty, for example, to aspire to transcendence—to the paradise of a "non-physical people," for whom "the green corn gleaming" can only be a barely remembered or merely illusory experience (p. 325).

We saw earlier that what distinguishes the Orpheus of myth from Poe's Agathos is that Orpheus creates an environment, whereas Poe's poet-angel is a transcendent figure situated in the void. In "Angel Surrounded by Paysans" Stevens presents us with his own poet-angel, one whose sphere of activity, however, is not empty space; on the contrary, he describes himself as "the angel of reality":

> I have neither ashen wing nor wear of ore
> And live without a tepid aureole,
>
> Or stars that follow me, not to attend,
> But, of my being and its knowing, part.
>
> I am one of you and being one of you
> Is being and knowing what I am and know.
>
> Yet I am the necessary angel of earth,
> Since, in my sight, you see the earth again.
>
> [p. 496]

Perhaps the first thing to notice about Stevens's angel is that he appears without the traditional angelic trappings ("ashen wing," "wear of ore," "aureole"): he is, like Wordsworth's poet or Croce's artist, indistinguishable from ordinary men ("I am one of you")—or he would appear so, except that he is at the same time, like Orpheus, a mythic figure, "A figure half-seen, or seen for a moment, a man / Of the mind" (p. 497).

Stevens appears to regard him as a possibility—a possibility of a kind once actualized in the world of myth but now simply a possibility, even as the subject of a poem can doubtless never be more than a possibility. For the "angel of earth" is characterized by the ideal unity of being and knowing (what he knows is said to be an extension of his being), and this unity is of the same order and kind as the unity of word and being that underlies what Stevens, in "Description without Place," calls "The thesis of the plentifullest John": namely, "the theory of the word for those / For whom the word is the making of the world" (p. 345). It is Stevens's conviction, however, that this unity of being and knowing, word and being, can only be of theoretical value. For the world alone is actual: it is here, before and around us. We can do no more than establish the conditions of its possibility, which means that as soon as we try to account for the presence of our world we step beyond it into the domain of the possible—into philosophy, or myth, or (what is the case with Stevens himself) into the writing of poems about poetry. From this standpoint the figure of Orpheus is a possibility, just as Johannine Word is a possibility, but both were possibilities once actualized by belief. Stevens proposes neither a myth nor a religion but simply a fiction—a supreme possibility, in whose truth it is perhaps impossible to believe, though no more so than it is impossible to believe in those diverse abstractions that constitute a poem.

These considerations lead, it is evident, to "Asides on the Oboe," wherein we are told that our "final belief / Must be in a fiction" (p. 250). There is a contradiction here (fictions, after all, tend to assuage but not to survive disbelief), which the body of the poem seeks to emphasize rather than to overcome. For the poem proposes, as an object for belief, neither a god nor even a man but

> The impossible possible philosopher's man,
> The man who has had the time to think enough,
> The central man, the human globe, responsive
> As a mirror with a voice, the man of glass,
> Who in a million diamonds sums us up.

[p. 250]

In the context of the poem this "impossible possible philosopher's man" is offered first as the source of consolation in time of war ("in his poems we find peace"), but to the extent that consolation is impossible he becomes the supreme singer of the dirge "for those buried in their blood" (p. 251). For our purposes, however, it is sufficient to notice that he is the Orphic figure who "dewily cries, / 'Thou art not August unless I make thee so'" (p. 251). He is the man of imagination as such, an abstraction which subsumes all men. In "Primitive like an Orb" he is appropriately tagged "the giant of nothingness"—a figure to whom no real existence and no absolute identity are attributed. The giant is the author of the "essential poem," an ultimate abstraction that defines the possibility of the world—"As if the central poem became the world, / And the world the central poem" (p. 441). For this "essential poem" is "something seen and known in lesser poems" (p. 440): it is "the miraculous multiplex of lesser poems" (p. 442). And just so does the giant himself depend upon lesser acts of imagination for his significance:

> That's it. The lover writes, the believer hears,
> The poet mumbles and the painter sees,
> Each one, his fated eccentricity,
> As a part, but part, but tenacious particle,
> Of the skeleton of the ether, the total
> Of letters, prophecies, perceptions, clods
> Of color, the giant of nothingness, each one
> And the giant ever changing, living in change.
>
> [p. 443]

The giant is a possibility adumbrated in the actual: he is transcendental only as a hypothesis brought to bear upon diverse and particular acts of the mind. He is, so to speak, an interpretation, a possible meaning displayed by events that take place in the world.

This is to say that imaginative activity takes on meaning for Stevens only as an event in the world. Thus, for example, the woman who sings by the sea in "The Idea of Order at Key West" is unmistakably in the world ("The ever-hooded, tragic-gestured sea / Was merely a place by which she walked to sing" [p. 129]). What is more, she clearly shares this world with the two travelers who observe her. At the same time, however, she is said to be

> the single artificer of the world
> In which she sang. And when she sang, the sea,
> Whatever self it had, became the self
> That was her song, for she was the maker. Then we,
> As we beheld her striding there alone,
> Knew that there never was a world for her
> Except the one she sang and, singing, made.
>
> [pp. 129–130]

In a similar way, the somewhat more generalized man with the blue guitar affirms that "I am a native in this world / And think in it as a native thinks," yet in this world "things are as I think they are / And say they are on the blue guitar" (p. 180). In "Description without Place" we are told that "to seem—it is to be, / As the sun is something seeming and it is." And so it may be said, of a queen, that

> Her green mind made the world around her green.
> The queen is an example . . . The green queen
>
> In the seeming of the summer of her sun
> By her own seeming made the summer change.
>
> [p. 339]

The queen provides an example of that act of the mind which, like the song of Orpheus, makes possible an environing world. Stevens points in the instances cited here not toward the imagination purely and simply as the one reality in a created world but toward a process within which the world appears as a correlative of an imaginative act—a correlative apart from which that act cannot take place.[35] There never was a world for the woman at Key West, except the one she fashioned by the power of her utterance; yet hers is not a private world but the world which is always there and which she, by her singing, establishes as the horizon of her being. Except for her singing, she would be a worldless being, a being closed to the world;

except for her singing, she perhaps would not be at all. As Stevens says of the two travelers in "Holiday in Reality," "they knew that to be real each had / To find for himself his earth, his sky, his sea" (p. 312).

We can put this another way: philosophers distinguish between the transcendental and the empirical ego—between a pure ego which stands as a self-contained structure independent of any act or content of consciousness and a phenomenal ego that is immersed in its own contents, that is, in a stream of phenomena.[36] A roughly similar distinction might be brought to bear upon Stevens's conception of imagination.[37] For Stevens, anything like a transcendental ego can only be a fiction, an abstraction pleasing and perhaps paradigmatic but still an abstraction. For if the mind makes possible a world, it must suffer at the same time the limitations of that world. There is, for one thing, the question of time. Stevens almost always describes imaginative activity in terms of the natural cycle: the imagination composes out of the nothingness of winter a springtime world that grows into summer; but quite as inevitably summer disintegrates into autumn, finally to return once more to the primitive condition of winter.[38] And man, Stevens makes clear, is situated within this cycle:

> Now it is September and the web is woven.
> The web is woven and you have to wear it.
>
> The winter web is made and you have to bear it,
> The winter web, the winter woven, wind and wind . . .
>
> [p. 208]

There is, however, a more fundamental limitation than time. In his later poetry Stevens comes increasingly to underscore the fact of human finitude by an appeal to the image of the rock, which appears not, perhaps, as a metaphysical ground, as Roy Harvey Pearce suggests, but as a ground similar to Heidegger's earth: it is a kind of ultimate horizon.[39] In the poem entitled "The Rock," it is identified as "the habitation of the whole," a phrase whose meaning Stevens goes on to elucidate in the following way:

> It is the rock where tranquil must adduce
> Its tranquil self, the main of things, the mind,
>
> The starting point of the human and the end,
> That in which space itself is contained, the gate
> To the enclosure, day, the things illumined. . . .
>
> [p. 528]

For Frank Doggett the rock here "is the content of the mind, the object that is nothing without the subject, that, by its inclusion in the mind or subject, becomes the unity of the world." [40] Doubtless the rock is the content of the mind, but if the rock is "the habitation of the whole," then it is also the mind's habitation. For upon the rock both the world, "the main of things," and the mind are "adduced," that is brought forward, as though into the light. Such a reading appears to underlie Joseph Riddel's definition of the rock—as succinct a definition as perhaps the image will bear: "The rock is that in which man must dwell, the inclusive world of thing and idea which harbors the self, and paradoxically, which the self harbors." [41]

This we recognize to be the central paradox of Stevens's thought. What we want to observe, however, is that this paradox states the Orphic theme. In "An Ordinary Evening in New Haven," for example, Stevens dilates in a sequence of thirty-one lyrics upon the relation of man's mind to his being-in-the-world. What is New Haven, Stevens asks at the outset, if not "A recent imagining of reality" (p. 465)? The supposition is (and it has never been more than a supposition) that "these houses are composed of ourselves," thus to constitute

> an impalpable town, full of
> Impalpable bells, transparencies of sound,
>
> Sounding in transparent dwellings of the self,
> Impalpable habitations that seem to move
> In the movement of the colors of the mind. . . .
>
> [p. 466]

The mind dwells in an impalpable habitation of its own making—an impalpable habitation, not because it is not really

there, but because "Reality [is] a thing seen by the mind, /
Not that which is but that which is apprehended" (p. 468).
The existence of the world is subordinate to the fact of its
presence, and it is the presence of the world that concerns
Stevens. "We seek," he writes at one point,

> The poem of pure reality, untouched
> By trope or deviation, straight to the word,
> Straight to the transfixing object, to the object
>
> At the exactest point at which it is itself,
> Transfixing by being purely what it is,
> A view of New Haven, say, through a certain eye,
>
> The eye made clear of uncertainty, with the sight
> Of simple seeing, without reflection. We seek
> Nothing but reality.
>
> [p. 471]

"The poem of pure reality": New Haven is perhaps such a
poem, precisely as it comes to be what it is (a commonplace
world, the habitation of the self) in the diverse perceptions
of its citizens. It is "the common denominator of the incor-
poreal worlds of its inhabitants"—a world whose possibility is
explained by recourse to the fiction of the ultimate poem, that
"multiplex of lesser poems."

"The poem of pure reality" thus becomes a world in which
not only human imagination is at play but also man's "instinct
for earth" (p. 476). Professor Eucalyptus, for example, seeks
nothing beyond reality; he seeks God "In New Haven with an
eye that does not look / Beyond the object" (p. 475). For his
"instinct for heaven"—his impulse toward transcendence—is
counterbalanced (and, in a way, fulfilled) by

> The instinct for earth, for New Haven, for his room,
> The gay tournamonde as of a single world
>
> In which he is and as and is are one.
>
> [p. 476]

It is this Orphic instinct for earth that distinguishes that act of
the mind by which the world is actualized as a dwelling-place.
Accordingly,

If it should be true that reality exists
In the mind: the tin plate, the loaf of bread on it
The long-bladed knife, the little to drink and her

Misericordia, it follows that
Real and unreal are two in one: New Haven
Before and after one arrives, or, say,

Bergamo on a postcard, Rome after dark,
Sweden described, Salzburg with shaded eyes
Or Paris in conversation at a cafe.

[pp. 485–486]

The point here seems quite carefully made: it is possible that reality exists in the mind, but if so, it exists as a reality of places and situations—a reality viewed from within, at several distances and from diverse points of view, as by one who dwells there. A line from Husserl's *Paris Lectures*, not too far removed from its context, provides us with a suitable paraphrase: "I am the ego in whose stream of consciousness the world itself—including myself as an object in it, a man who exists in the world—first acquires meaning and reality." [42]

It has been remarked of Stevens that, for him, "poetry must be expressive of a continuing dialogue between mind and reality." [43] We have seen in what sense this is true for Heidegger: at the word of the poet both man and world enter into the light of being and are maintained there in concrete, historical existence. The word, by virtue of its unity with being, belongs not only to man but to the world, so that man, when he walks through the world, finds himself in a world of words as well as of things. The terms of Stevens's inquiry into this possibility are, of course, of a different order from Heidegger's:

The world lives as you live,
Speaks as you speak, a creature that
Repeats its vital words, yet balances
The syllable of a syllable.

[p. 268]

Similarly, in "Things of August," Stevens speaks of a poetry whose "solemn sentences, / Like interior intonations," become at the same time

> The speech of truth in its true solitude,
> A nature that is created in what it says.
>
> [p. 490]

An elaboration of this notion is to be found in "The Discovery of Thought." As one of the "Adagia" tells us, "It is not every day that the world arranges itself in a poem," [44] and, just so, Stevens here imagines a condition without poetry:

> At the antipodes of poetry, dark winter,
> When the trees glitter with that which dispoils them,
> Daylight evaporates, like a sound one hears in sickness.

Nevertheless, it is "always at this antipodes," in this dark world of dissolution and silence, that

> One thinks that it could be that the first word spoken,
> The desire for speech and meaning gallantly fulfilled,
>
> The gathering of the imbecile against his motes
> And the wry antipodes whirled round the world away—
> One thinks, when the houses of New England catch the
>   first sun,
>
> The first word would be of the susceptible being arrived,
> The immaculate disclosure of the secret no more obscured.
> The sprawling of winter might suddenly stand erect,
>
> Pronouncing its new life and ours, not autumn's prodigal
>   returned,
> But an antipodal, far-fetched creature, worthy of birth,
> The true tone of the metal of winter in what it says.[45]

The poet speculates upon an original utterance by virtue of which "the wry antipodes [are] whirled round the world away." This is the moment of poetry, and it is at the same time a disclosure of being—but notice that it is the world that speaks: "The sprawling of winter might suddenly stand erect, / Pronouncing its new life and ours." The world, we may say, is an event of poetry, but poetry is an event in the world, in which nature itself begins to speak.

In other contexts, however, poetry and reality are reciprocal in more complicated ways. In "The Idea of Order at Key West," for example, the inhuman cry of nature is an undifferentiated utterance set over and against the woman's measured song, which is "uttered word by word" (p. 128). Yet what motivates the woman's song, we learn, is "The maker's rage to order words of the sea" (p. 130)—to differentiate "The grinding water and the gasping wind" (p. 129), thus to enable nature to speak a human language and finally to exist as a human world. "Autumn Refrain" takes up this same theme, but from a different point of view, according to which the speech of nature becomes an integral and necessary part of the process by which the poetic utterance is actualized. Unlike the woman in "The Idea of Order at Key West," the poet in this poem is not singing but, like Heidegger's poet perhaps, listening, as though situated in the moment before speech. He has heard the desolate "skreak and skritter" of grackles give way to the silence of a "yellow moon of words about the nightingale," which is a "nameless air" that he has never heard and, indeed, will never hear, except insofar as some form of synthesis can be achieved between silence and sound, or between the nightingale of poetry and the grackles of reality. As it happens, in the midst of the silence "Some skreaking and skrittering residuum" lingers, and as this residuum of sound "grates these evasions of the nightingale," the silence becomes charged with a kind of music:

> And the stillness is in the key, all of it is,
> The stillness is all in the key of that desolate
>   sound.
>
>   [p. 160]

Poetry, we may say, is the speech of the world made articulate by human language; or, again, poetry is human language made real by its articulation within the world. Both propositions are true, but true only in relation to each other. For

Stevens, that is to say, man's world is predicated upon a mutual dependency of word and being; or, better, it is predicated upon a dialogue, in which the identity of poetry and reality

> makes music seem
> To be a nature, a place in which itself
>
> Is that which produces everything else.

[p. 287]

Conclusion: The Orphic and Hermetic Dimensions of Meaning

This book has attempted to isolate and examine two aspects of poetic speech: its formal character, by which it creates a work of language, and its ontological character, by which it originates and maintains a human world. The poetic act may seek to disrupt the processes of signification, thus to make language itself its subject by isolating the word in a purely synchronic and worldless order, but at the same time it has the power to make signification possible by bringing both the world and man to language within a diachronic order or an order of presence. Little has been said directly, however, about the act of speech in its ordinary character as an utterance which generates a meaning that can be recovered by interpretation. Indeed, it may appear that this study has systematically diminished the concept of meaning by diminishing the speech of ordinary men in favor of the radical discourse of Orphic and hermetic poets. Heidegger and Mallarmé, for example, who take up the idea of language from diametrically opposed points of view, are nevertheless alike in placing a value upon the act of speech precisely to the extent that it frees itself from the discourse of everyday life. Both oppose language to the formation of "mere" meaning, and in their own utterances both have done violence to their respective traditions of discourse by bringing language to the edge of an unspeakable kingdom.

It is possible, however, to speak in a more positive way about the relation of Orphic and hermetic modes of speech to the problem of meaning, for both Heidegger and Mallarmé enunciate theories of language whose purpose it is to modify our sense of how human speech may be interpreted. It is Heidegger's intention, for example, to enlarge the domain of meaning beyond the limits of the sign, and to formulate the problem of hermeneutics not in terms of what texts mean but in terms of what utterances can disclose concerning their relation to the being of the world.[1] Human understanding, for Heidegger, finds its resolution in the recovery of the ground of intelligibility and not simply in the recovery of isolated meanings. By contrast, the formalist or structuralist tradition that is informed by Mallarmé's spirit seeks to contract the domain of meaning, at least insofar as it substitutes for traditional hermeneutics a hermeneutics of form that transposes the aim of interpretation from the question of what a work means to the question of how it is made. Human understanding, in this sense, looks toward the disclosure of a structural intelligibility as the fundamental property of human discourse, and accordingly it is able to think of meaning in terms of designs and relations rather than simply in terms of contents.[2]

There is, it seems to me, considerable virtue in speculating upon the problem of meaning from the standpoint of this opposition between Mallarmé and Heidegger, or between structuralism and the phenomenology of language. This is so, particularly if we take as our point of departure the problem of the Janus-like character of the linguistic sign. The sign appears to derive its power of signification from the formal principles that determine its relative position within a semiotic system; at the same time, however, it claims for itself its ancient power to transcend the system and to announce a meaning on the basis of its unity with a world of things. From the structuralist point of view, the sign is a negative entity: its being lies in what it is not, that is, in the systematic way in which it signifies its opposition to other words in the language. Removed from the system, it ceases to be anything at all. For Heidegger, however, the sign must escape its bondage

to system, for it is a mediation in a discourse whose subject is
a presence that can never be reduced to the status of a signi-
fied. If speech is to possess hermeneutic value, if it is to be
more than mere "talk," it must allow itself to be governed by
what Heidegger calls "a different rule of the word"—the rule
of being, and not the rule of form:

> The word's rule springs to light as that which makes the thing
> be a thing. The word begins to shine as the gathering which first
> brings what presences to presence.
> The oldest word for the rule of the word thus thought, for
> Saying, is *logos:* Saying which, in showing, lets things appear in
> their "it is."
> The same word, however, the word for Saying, is also the word
> for *Being*, that is, for the presencing of beings. Saying and Being,
> word and thing, belong to each other in a veiled way, a way
> which has hardly been thought and is not to be thought out to
> the end.
> All essential Saying hearkens back to this veiled belonging of
> Saying and Being, word and thing. Both poetry and thinking are
> distinctive Saying in that they remain delivered over to the mys-
> tery of the word as that which is most worthy of their thinking,
> and thus ever structured in their kinship.[3]

Clearly, the word as Heidegger conceives it is hardly a sign at
all—hardly a signifier which designates a signified. Hans-Georg
Gadamer, who has developed Heidegger's thinking on this
matter into a radical critique of the concept of the sign, formu-
lates the phenomenological position as follows: "The lin-
guistic word is not a sign which one grasps, not a sign which
one makes or gives to others, not an existent thing which one
takes up and burdens with the ideality of meaning in order to
make an other existent visible. . . . Rather, the ideality of
meaning lies in the word itself. It is always already meaning-
ful." [4] The word is already meaningful, because it is always
"present-at-hand," already a part of man's world as the speech
of being, the *Logos*. Whereas, for the structuralists, the value
of the word lies in the relationships which it forms with other

words, for Heidegger its value lies in its identity with being. For the structuralists, the sign is a closed, empty form. The signified which it makes possible is never a transcendent referent, nor is it any sort of content; it is always a differentiation within a realm circumscribed by language. For Heidegger, however, the sign is open—or, rather, it is an opening through which the world of things is allowed to make its appearance.

It is this openness of the sign which helps to explain why the speech of Orpheus cannot be understood in terms of a work: it is always a poetry which exceeds the enclosure of the poem, because its meaning lies in the world which it brings into being, quite as though the intelligibility of words were always to disappear before the superior intelligibility of things. Thus Heidegger, as we saw at the end of chapter 7, proposes that our response to a poem ought to take the form of "a dialogue between thinking and poetry"—a dialogue, however, whose aim is not to recover a "poetic statement" but "to call forth the nature of language, so that mortals may learn again to live within language," which for Heidegger means to live within the horizon of a world which language has power to disclose. But hermetic poetry is intelligible only in terms of the work: it is not a "saying," not a predication or reference or disclosure; it is primarily a "making"—the making of a closed structure of relationships among the components of a language.

One could go on to elaborate further the specific differences between structuralism and Heidegger's phenomenology of language. The point is that they stand in firm opposition to one another and illuminate one another superbly as a consequence. A more striking point, however, is that both the structuralists and Heidegger are preoccupied with essentially the same question, one that leads them to go beyond traditional hermeneutics in quest of a prior ground: namely, What are the conditions which make meaning (and therefore hermeneutics) possible? Structuralism, Roland Barthes tells us, "is a mode of thought (or a 'poetics') which seeks less to assign completed meanings to the objects it discovers than to know how meaning is possible, at what cost and by what means. Ultimately, one might say that the object of structuralism is not man endowed with meanings but man fabricating meanings, as if it could not be the content of meanings which exhausted the semantic goals of humanity, but only the act by which these meanings, historical and contingent variables, are produced." [5] Thus structuralism concerns itself with the invariant in all human discourse, that is, with the a priori laws which govern the functioning of language in any act of speech. Heidegger, too, seeks an a priori foundation upon which to raise what he calls, in *Being and Time,* "the doctrine of signification." Like Barthes, he believes that "we must inquire into the basic forms in which it is possible to articulate anything understandable." But for Heidegger this inquiry must proceed upon an ontological rather than a logical basis. Indeed, in *Being and Time* he placed before himself a task which appears to have directed the whole of his later writings on language: "the task of *liberating* grammar from logic." This is a task, he continues, which "requires *beforehand a positive* understanding of the basic a priori structure of discourse in general as an *existentiale"*—that is, as one of the ways in which man is constituted not as a fabricator of meanings but as a being-in-the-world. The ground of meaning can never be disclosed merely by speaking *about* language. It will not do, for example, simply to construct a Universal Grammar on the basis of "a comprehensive comparison of as many languages as possible, and those the most exotic." Instead, we must inquire into the being of language: "In the last resort, philosophical research must resolve to ask what kind of Being goes with language in general. Is it a kind of equipment ready-to-hand within-the-world, or has it Dasein's kind of Being, or is it neither of these? What kind of Being does language have, if there can be such a thing as a 'dead' language? What do the 'rise' and 'decline' of a language mean ontologically?" —and so on.[6] Clearly, questions of this kind are in quest of an a priori event, not an a priori form, as the condition of meaning's possibility.

But if structuralism and the phenomenology of language thus converge upon a common problem—the problem of meaning—we need to ask whether this convergence is merely an accident of history, in which two ways of thinking about language remain contemporaneous but mutually exclusive, or whether they do not at the same time enter into a reciprocal relationship, thus to disclose their fundamental interdependence. Here it will be useful to inquire briefly into Edmund Husserl's writings on language. For Husserl, as for Heidegger, language exists as an event in man's lived experience of his world, or what Husserl came to call the "Life-World." In this world, Husserl writes in "The Origin of Geometry" (1936), "Everything has its name, or is namable in the broadest sense, i.e., linguistically expressible." It is a world, in short, which presupposes language, or, more precisely,

> its objective being presupposes men, understood as men with a common language. Language, for its part, as function and exercised capacity, is related correlatively to the world, the universe of objects which is linguistically expressible in its being and its being-such. Thus men as men, fellow men, world—the world of which men, of which we, always talk and can talk—and, on the other hand, language, are inseparably intertwined; and one is always certain of their inseparable relational unity, though usually only implicitly, in the manner of a horizon.[7]

The community of men is established within the reciprocity of word and thing and is inseparable from it. In our Life-World, we are always conscious of this reciprocity as the horizon of the speakable, yet we seldom direct our attention to it as such. We do not inquire, for example, how it comes to pass that language and world are correlatives of one another, or that we always speak of the world and can speak of it with ease and certainty. The possibility of meaning exists as a fact of our life in the world, quite as though we possessed hard evidence for a case that requires no solution.

To raise questions about our Life-World, however, is at once to step out of it; it is to enclose the world in "brackets," thus to reduce it to so many themes for investigation. Just so, to direct our attention to language is to lift it out of the world: it is to bracket "its existence in the real world grounded in utterance and documentation" and to examine instead its "ideal existence." [8] In the *Formal and Transcendental Logic* (1929), Husserl defines "the ideality of language" as an "ideal unity," such that "the word itself, the sentence itself, is an ideal unity, which is not multiplied by its thousandfold reproductions" in daily acts of speech.[9] The "ideality of language" thus corresponds roughly to the Saussurean concept of *langue*—roughly, because this ideality is for Husserl composed of several strata, extending from the level of phonetic structures to the level of "*a priori* meaning-forms," that is, "the basic forms of propositions, the categorical proposition with its many particular patterns and forms of members, the primitive types of propositionally complex propositions, e.g., the conjunctive, disjunctive and hypothetical propositional unities, the differences of universality and particularity, on the one hand, and of singularity on the other, the syntactical forms of plurality, negation, the modalities, etc." These meaning-forms, Husserl says, are "rooted in the ideal essence of meaning as such" and "resemble an absolutely fixed ideal framework" against which any empirical language can be (and ought to be) investigated. Accordingly, it becomes possible to ask: "How does German, Latin, Chinese, etc., express 'the' antecedent of a hypothetical, 'the' plural, 'the' modalities of possibility and probability, 'the' negative, etc.?" [10]

In short, it becomes possible to speak once more of a "pure logical grammar," that is, of an a priori system of forms which makes possible the utterance of an intelligible statement. Husserl came to understand, however, that this logically prior system of forms is only that: it is only prior in the logical sense. Granted that "no speech is conceivable that is not in part essentially determined by this *a priori*," it is nevertheless the case that these forms are "empty" and must be fulfilled by an intentional experience.[11] The act of speech is, in this view, a fulfillment of language, for "in speaking we are continuously performing an internal act of meaning which fuses with the words and, as it were, animates them. The effect of this animation is that words and the entire locution, as it were, embody in themselves a meaning, and bear it embodied in them as their sense." [12] Indeed, it is only because of speech—only because we do speak of the world in our daily engagement with it—that it becomes possible to speak of language at all. *Nihil est in lingua quod non prius fuerit in oratione.* Accordingly, it appears that one must be prepared to acknowledge an ontological as well as a formal or logical a priori condition for the possibility of meaning. One should be prepared, that is, to examine the problem of meaning along two distinct fronts: from the standpoint of man's life of speech within the horizon of the speakable, as well as from the standpoint of how language is made and how its formal elements are organized in the formation of an utterance or in the development of a discourse.

But how is such a twofold examination to proceed coherently and without contradiction? We know from the example of Ernst Cassirer in *The Philosophy of Symbolic Forms* that it could proceed systematically according to a method designed to resolve contradictions by synthesizing opposites into a unified theory. Thus Cassirer remarks upon the inadequacy of both empiricism and idealism in dealing with the problem of the sign by observing that "one posits a concept of the given particular but fails to recognize that any such concept must always, inplicitly or explicitly, encompass the *defining* attributes of some universal; the other asserts the necessity and validity of these attributes but fails to designate the medium through which they can be represented in the given psychological world of consciousness." Cassirer then lays down his own postulate—the postulate of critical idealism—upon which to construct a concept of the sign as symbol, or symbolic form, that is, as a structure which possesses the integrity of a formal a priori, but which at the same time is constitutive of a world of things. "If," he says, "we start not with abstract postulates but from the concrete basic form of spiritual life, this dualistic antithesis is resolved. The illusion of an original division between the intelligible and the sensuous, between 'idea' and 'phenomenon,' vanishes."

It is the case, however, that Cassirer achieves this unity at the expense of the world, which is incorporated into the philosophy of symbolic forms as a world *in intellectu,* not a world *in re.* "True," Cassirer says, "we still remain in a world of 'images'—but these are not images which reproduce a self-subsistent world of 'things'; they are image-worlds whose principle and origin are to be sought in an autonomous creation of the spirit." In the face of such activity of the spirit, the very notion of ontology loses its meaning and requires to be abandoned: "the question of what, apart from these spiritual functions, constitutes absolute reality, remains unanswered, except that more and more we learn to recognize it as a fallacy in formulation, an intellectual phantasm. The true concept of reality cannot be squeezed into the form of mere abstract being." [13] But what is from the point of view of critical idealism a naive realism is from the phenomenological point of view not a metaphysics of any sort but our natural attitude, and however naive philosophically this attitude might be, however much it might stand in the way of systematic thought, it is the distinctive attitude of our spiritual life—the attitude, what is more, which informs our very life of speech. And it is the argument of Heidegger's phenomenology of language that this life of speech repeatedly discloses to systematic thought an irreducible Other whose habit it is, like a Shakespearean ghost, to trouble an otherwise orderly kingdom.

We should be mistaken, of course, to suppose that the claims of systematic thought against this ghostly Other, this phantasm of being, can easily be dismissed; but it is possible to place over and against a method which seeks to resolve oppositions systematically a habit of mind which confronts oppositions as they are and seeks, not to overcome them or to dissolve them into one another, but simply to understand their meaning and the form of their incompatibility. In confronting the opposition between Bentham and Coleridge, for example, John Stuart Mill observed that, "By Bentham, beyond all others, men have been led to ask themselves, in regard to any ancient or received opinion, Is it true? and by Coleridge, What is the meaning of it?" The difference between these two questions is grounded upon a difference between two kinds of rational inquiry. The one is critical and evaluative, the other historical and interpretive. In Mill's words, Bentham "took his stand outside the received opinion and surveyed it as an entire stranger to it," whereas Coleridge "looked at it from within, and endeavoured to see it with the eyes of a believer in it; to discover by what apparent facts it was at first suggested, and by what appearances it has ever since been rendered continually credible—has seemed, to a succession of persons, to be a faithful interpretation of their experience." The one translated the speech of others into his own language and judged its validity on the basis of a synchronic method of empirical analysis and verification. The other translated himself into the speech of others, not in order to test the truth of distinct and isolatable conceptions, but to recover the act of thinking by which these conceptions were originally formed. He did so, Mill says, because "the fact that any doctrine had been believed by thoughtful men, and received by whole nations or generations of mankind, was part of the problem to be solved, was one of the phenomena to be accounted for." [14]

It is according to this point of view—the point of view of a historical and interpretive habit of mind—that it becomes possible to regard the problem of meaning not simply as a theoretical problem of the Janus-like character of the sign, but as a historical problem of understanding the ways in which, in our own day, men have tried to deal with the nature of language and meaning. In this sense, structuralism and the phenomenology of language are no longer merely isolated, mutually exclusive versions of how the question of meaning may be treated; on the contrary, they disclose, by virtue of the nature of their opposition, the very nature of the problem— indeed, they become "part of the problem to be solved." The value of the historical standpoint is that it makes it possible to hold this opposition squarely in view, and to understand the meaning of each term in the opposition not as a stranger to it but from within, as "with the eyes of a believer in it." From the position of either structuralism or phenomenology considered by itself, this historical attitude can only seem contradictory; but in fact it is by thinking through the speech of others—by thinking through the respective positions of structuralism and phenomenology—that the contradictory claims of logic and ontology can be made a basis for the understanding of language itself.

Instead, therefore, of taking up the problem of meaning by constructing a new system in the manner of Cassirer, we may proceed historically in the manner of Paul Ricoeur, in whose writings on language we find something like a play of voices among a diversity of thinkers who have taken language for their theme: Heidegger, Husserl, the structural and transformational linguists, Wittgenstein, and even Sigmund Freud. These thinkers provide Ricoeur with a context in which the opposition between the formal or logical and the ontological dimensions of language becomes the foundation for a distinction between two dimensions of meaning: the semiotic or diacritical meaning of signs within the system of language, and the semantic or intentional meaning of sentences in the act of speech. In *Freud and Philosophy* (1965), Ricoeur defines the relationship between these two dimensions as a dialectic of absence and presence, according to which "man's adoption of language is in general a way of making him absent to things by intending them with 'empty' intentions, and, correlatively, of making things present through the very emptiness of signs." By his adoption of language, man turns from the world (in the manner of Hegel's Adam) and situates himself within a system of purely formal or "empty" relations. To utilize Frege's distinction between *Sinn* and *Bedeutung,* he situates himself in a world of meaning without significance, of sense without reference—and there he would remain, were he, like Mallarmé, a creature of the void, and were language entirely a transcendent reality that required nothing from man for its existence. But man, for Ricoeur as for Heidegger, remains throughout a being-in-the-world, and his language comes fully into being only in the reality of his speech. "Language has its own way of being dialectical," Ricoeur says. Thus "each sign intends something of reality only by reason of its position in the ensemble of signs; no sign signifies through a one-to-one relation with a corresponding thing; each sign is defined by its difference from all others." But this basic Saussurean principle is incomplete by itself. The paradigmatic relations among signs constitute a semiotic system, but the meanings which inhere in this system will remain merely virtual or empty significations until they are combined in an intentional act of speech. Following Husserl, Ricoeur insists that only in speech is man able to "fulfill" these purely formal relations among signs; only in speech is he able to fill the emptiness of language with the presence of the world. As Ricoeur says, "it is by combining together the phonemic and the lexical differences, hence by setting into play the double articulation of phonemes and morphemes, that we speak the world." [15] For it is in the act of speech that the sign is actualized as part of man's life in the world. The act of speech does not take place in a void of purely formal relations: it is not a hermetic act but an event in the world—an Orphic utterance in which world and word are brought forward as in a single presence.

In order to explain how this is so, Ricoeur says, "It is necessary to balance the [structuralist] axiom of the closure of the universe of signs by attention to the primary function of language which [according to Heidegger] is to say. In contrast to the closure of the universe of signs, this function constitutes its openness or opening." [16] The act of speech is the opening up of language to the world, but it is at the same time an opening up of the world to language. It is only by virtue of the hermetic nature of language that meaning is possible, insofar as words mean only because they signify their differences from other words in the system; but it is the function of this negative verbal meaning to make possible man's positive intention of things. If, as Ricoeur says, "the constitution of the sign as sign presupposes a break with life, activity, and nature," it is necessary to add that the "use of meanings," their "combination in sentences in a given situation," presupposes a return to the world—a return not merely to "lived experience" but to experience alive with intelligibility.[17]

It is worth noticing that Ricoeur speaks of a "balance" between structuralist and phenomenological axioms, not of their synthesis into a holistic theory of meaning. For Ricoeur, "a theory of meaning requires two dimensions, not one": it requires a semantics as well as a semiotics, even as a theory of language requires the two dimensions of *langue* and *parole*.[18] But if the relationship between these two dimensions of meaning is that of a dialectic of absence and presence, of departure and return, we need to understand in greater detail the dynamics of "saying" in order to understand precisely how this dialectic works. In a sense, the phenomenological dialectic of absence and presence needs to be balanced by a linguistic account of the relationship between the semiotic and the semantic. Ricoeur himself appears to have recognized that this is so, and in an essay entitled "Structure, Word, Event," he looks to Noam Chomsky's generative-transformational grammar for a linguistics of the sentence that will complete the structuralist's linguistics of the sign.

Precisely how Chomsky's grammar can be accommodated to Ricoeur's thinking is at this point clear only in broad outline. Chomsky, for his part, looks forward to the formulation of a theory that will "define a certain infinite correlation of sound and meaning," and so constitute "a first step toward explaining how a person can understand an arbitrary sentence of his language." [19] For what is remarkable about language, in Chomsky's view, is that it contains within itself not only an inventory of signs but systems of rules which enable a speaker to generate and interpret an infinite variety of original sentences. As a first step toward explaining this fact of linguistic competence, Chomsky has applied to the act of speech the mathematical concept of transformation, according to which an invariant or deep semantic structure may be transformed into any number of variants or phonological surface structures. This concept of transformation may be applied to any utterance in any language, and thus it constitutes the foundation for a potential universal grammar. It is Chomsky's conviction that the grammar of any language can be shown to consist "of a syntactical component that specifies an infinite set of paired deep and surface structures and expresses the transformational relationship between these paired elements, a phonological component that assigns a phonetic representation to the surface structure, and a semantic component that assigns a semantic representation to the deep structure." [20] Syntax is thus not a single set of rules for the combination of words into sentences; rather, it comprises a double system of rules—"a *base* system that generates deep structures, and a *transformational* system that maps these onto surface structures." [21]

The point for speculation is whether the "base system" in this syntactical model can in any way be correlated with Ricoeur's dialectic of the semiotic and the semantic. Chomsky, as it happens, rarely speaks of the problem of meaning except with the most guarded skepticism, and in keeping with this skepticism he has tried to construct a grammatical theory that is essentially formalist in character.[22] Nevertheless, Chomsky is fully aware that the issue of how syntax and meaning are related lies at the heart of his inquiry, and he foresees the necessity of formulating a universal semantics that will complement his universal grammar, thus perhaps to explain more rigorously than has thus far been possible how the generation of deep structures constitutes at the same time the generation of meaning.[23]

One point to consider in this context is Chomsky's conception of the sign and its relation to the base system of syntactical rules. In *Aspects of a Theory of Syntax* (1965), he analyzes in some detail the structure of the base system, and he finds that it consists of two components: a lexicon or set of "lexical entries," and a set of categorical and functional "notions" according to which any sentence may be rewritten to reveal one or more "embedded" structures of predication—to reveal, for example, a noun phrase that functions as the subject of a predicate, a verb phrase that functions as the predicate, and a noun phrase that functions as the object of the predicate. The full description of a deep structure will disclose a more complex set of relations than those which constitute a predication, but it is clear that the distinctive feature of the deep structure is the predicate. On this point, it is interesting to notice, Chomsky is in fundamental accord with his avowed but benign adversaries, the structural linguists. It is the position of Emile Benveniste, for example, that "the distinctive characteristic, distinctive beyond all others and inherent in the sentence [is the] predicate. All the other characteristics which we can recognize in the sentence come second with respect to this one." [24] The hard question for both Chomsky and Benveniste, however, concerns the process by which the sign is integrated into this structure of predication. How, after all, are the two components of the base system, the lexicon and the set of categorical and functional notions, related? Put simply, Chomsky's argument is that they are related by rules which invest the sign with a grammatical meaning. This is perhaps why Chomsky chooses not to speak of "signs" but rather of "lexical entries," because the sign is more than simply a phonological difference (a "lexical formative") that determines a difference in conceptual value. For Chomsky, the "lexical entry" is a complex structure that "contains information that is required by the phonological and semantic components of the grammar and by the transformational part of the grammar, as well as information that determines the proper placement of the lexical entries in sentences." [25] Specifically, Chomsky improves upon the structuralist concept of the sign by defining it as an organization of "features" that specify the grammatical contexts in which it may be used: category features, strict subcategorization features, and selectional features—each set of which functions as a system of controls that invest a speaker's use of language with a logical coherence.[26]

It is Chomsky's effort to disclose the logic of speech that places him in the tradition of Aristotle, the medieval logicians, the Port Royalist Grammarians (with whom he explicitly identifies himself), and Husserl. The central theme which informs this tradition is that man is characterized as a linguistic being, not because he is able to attach names to things, but because he is able to organize the meanings of his language into logical forms. Thus Husserl tells us that, "As regards the field of meaning, the briefest consideration will show up our unfreedom in binding meanings to meanings, so that we cannot juggle at will with the elements of a significantly given, connected unity. Meanings will fit together only in antecedently given ways, while other possibilities of combination are excluded by laws, and yield only a heap of meanings, never a single meaning." [27] These laws of combination apply, however, "not to what is singular in the meanings to be combined, but to the essential *kinds, the semantic categories,* that they fall under." The meaning of a sentence is thus not simply a function of the separate meanings of its component signs, that is, of words conceived as semiotic units; it is also, and perhaps more fundamentally, a function of the relationships that can be established among words conceived as *generic* units, that is, as nominal, verbal, or relational forms:

> To consider an example: The expression "This tree is green" has a unified meaning. If we formalize this meaning (the independent logical proposition) and proceed to the corresponding pure form of meaning, we obtain "This S is P," an ideal form whose range of values consists solely of independent (propositional) meanings. It is now plain that what we may call the "materialization" of this form, its specification in definite propositions [or what Chomsky calls its transformation into surface structures], is possible in infinitely many ways, but that we are not completely free in such specification, but work confined within definite limits.

> We cannot substitute any meanings we like for the variables "*S*"
> and "*P*". . . . Where nominal material stands, any nominal ma-
> terial can stand, but not adjectival, nor relational, nor completed
> propositional material.[28]

Chomsky's generative-transformational theory of syntax is
essentially a detailed, linguistic explanation of this idea of
the pure grammatical forms of meaning. The point is that
signs are organized not only according to the principle of
opposition but according to categorical principles which
specify their combinational features. The rules which govern
these features determine the relations of signs to "the pure
forms of meaning"—to ideal propositional structures which
are logically prior to the sentence and whose transformation
into a phonological surface structure makes it possible for the
sentence to be interpreted as a single unit of meaning, that is,
as a single act of predication.

It is the generation and transformation of deep or ideal
propositional structures that mediates between sign and sen-
tence. In phenomenological terms, it is the function of the
generative-transformational system to mediate between the
closed universe of signs and the openness of "saying," be-
tween sense and reference, or (as Ricoeur sometimes says)
between difference and reference.[29] Ricoeur's dialectic of the
semiotic and the semantic, then, is nothing less than a philo-
sophical description of the linguistic process by which we
organize discrete meanings into logically coherent wholes—
into statements which, in principle at least, intend something
of reality. I say, "in principle," because in fact predications
may be logically coherent and yet remain "unfulfilled" in the
sense in which Husserl and Ricoeur use this term. Philos-
ophers in the tradition of Rudolf Carnap and Max Black re-
currently trouble themselves over such sentences as "The
theory of relativity is blue" and "Socrates is a prime number,"
which serve to illustrate the meaninglessness of which natural
languages (as against artificial languages designed by a mathe-
matical logic) are capable.[30] Among such examples (which

anyone can compose, it being within the province of linguistic competence to play with language) are Chomsky's "Colorless green ideas sleep furiously" and "The boy may frighten sincerity." Neither sentence violates the logic of phrase structures by which propositions are generated; but they do violate "selectional rules" that proscribe such semantic incongruities as "colorless green" ("This green is colorless"), which, like many poetic locutions, asserts an equivalence whose meaning remains entirely within the enclosure of language. The problem here, we should notice, runs deeper than the positivist's distinction between nonsense and reference; it is a problem of intentionality. What is crucial about a sentence like "The boy may frighten sincerity," for example, is that it suffers from semantic indeterminacy: it discloses a formally coherent structure but not an intention. As Coleridge would say, it does not contain within itself the reason why it is so and not otherwise. We can, of course, make a guess as to how its meaning is to be understood, and a student of literature is likely to take for granted that it is meant to be interpreted allegorically—but notice that such an assumption implies a very important point: namely, that "The boy may frighten sincerity" does not exist by itself but presupposes a larger order of meaning of which it forms a part or an instance. The assumption implies that when we read the sentence allegorically, we implicitly extrapolate a context or discourse that specifies an intention by determining a sense in which "The boy may frighten sincerity" can be used.[31]

Another way to put this would be to say that only within or by means of discourse can a field of reference be established that will "fulfill" the properly formal character of a given predication. This field of reference, moreover, is twofold: it consists of an intentional object and an intending speaker. Beyond this, we should understand that to assert the primacy of discourse in this way is not to deny that the proposition is structurally the basic unit of speech; rather, it is to question whether problems of linguistic meaning can be adjudicated purely and simply by recourse to a concept of "grammaticalness." [32] Specifically, it is to argue that the dialectic of the semiotic and the semantic cannot adequately be understood in terms of the random or isolated sentence but must take into account the larger structure of discourse itself, on the grounds that it is only at the level of discourse that world and speaker become fully present in speech as determinants of meaning. Human speech is propositional, but it is not axiomatic. And even if it were stipulated that wholly "context-free" or "self-evident" propositions—sentences which are not merely "automatized" expressions whose meanings have been fixed by frequency of occurrence—can by themselves break the closure of language, such propositions cannot be made exemplars in an adequate theory of meaning, because it is more often the case that even the meaning of a well-made sentence will remain merely virtual until it is anchored within a larger order of meaning established by other predications. This is certainly true of pronomial utterances ("He is dead") as well as of fanciful utterances ("I am dead"), but more importantly it is true of instances in which intentionality is distributed along a plane of propositions, such that no one sentence is comprehensible by itself—as in poetry, scientific and philosophic discourse, and even in linguistics itself, whose propositions are bizarre when isolated from the carefully organized contexts in which they are meant to be understood.

Linguists are now beginning to deal with this problem of formally correct but indeterminate sentences by seeking alternatives to Chomsky's theory of a "presupposition-free syntax," in which semantic interpretation is made to rest purely and simply upon the restraints of syntactical rules.[33] As it happens, however, the problem which truly vexes this line of thinking about sentence and context is as much historical as theoretical: we are confronted by a conflict between two ideas of discourse. On the one hand, phenomenologists of language—Heidegger, Ricoeur, Gadamer, Merleau-Ponty—define discourse variously in terms of the Diltheyan concept of "living speech": the instance of speech as an event in the world, an exchange between speakers or speaker and listener within a horizon already formed by language. On the other hand, in linguistics and particularly among the structuralists, discourse is conceived as an integrated system of propositions, that is, as a *written text* isolated from the consciousness that originally composed it.

The opposition here is once more between the logical and the ontological dimensions of human speech. We have already encountered Husserl's description of the linguistic nature of man's world: "Men as men, fellow men, world—the world of which men, of which we, always talk and can talk—and, on the other hand, language, are inseparably intertwined; and one is always certain of their inseparable unity, though usually only implicitly, in the manner of a horizon." Human speech is, in this sense, an event which takes place within a determining field of reference formed by the mutual presence of man and world, and it cannot be conceived except in terms of such a field. Language as speech, as "saying," is worldly (and therefore referential) by the very nature of its being. For Heidegger and Gadamer, who oppose any distinction between *langue* and *parole,* man's being in the world presupposes his discourse, which is grounded upon a unity of word and being that logical thought about language cannot comprehend. Ricoeur, for his part, formulates the phenomenological position as follows:

> In speech the function of reference is linked to the role of the *situation of discourse* within the exchange of language itself: in exchanging speech, the speakers are present to each other, but also to the circumstantial setting of discourse, not only the perceptual surroundings, but also the cultural background known by both speakers. It is in relation to this situation that discourse is fully meaningful; the reference to reality is in the last analysis reference to that reality which can be pointed out "around" the speakers, "around," so to speak, the instance of discourse itself. Language is, moreover, well equipped to insure this anchorage; the demonstrative articles, the spatial and temporal adverbs, the personal pronouns, the tenses of the verb, and in general all the ostensive indicators of language serve to anchor discourse in the

circumstantial reality which surrounds the instance of discourse. Thus, in living speech, the *ideal* meaning of what one says bends toward a *real* reference, namely, to that "about which" one speaks; at its limit this real reference tends to get confused with an ostensive designation wherein speech [as Merleau-Ponty argues] joins up with the indicative gesture, that of pointing out.

A text, for Ricoeur, is an obliteration of this worldliness of discourse. Writing is "not without reference," but this reference remains merely virtual until it is actualized by reading or interpretation. And insofar as "reference is deferred, in the sense that it is postponed, a text is somehow 'in the air,' outside of the world or without a world; by means of this obliteration of all relation to the world, every text is free to enter into relation with all the other texts which come to take the place of the circumstantial reality shown by living speech." [34]

It is the worldless text, however, that linguistics, structuralism, and traditional hermeneutics take for their object of study. In this instance, man is not a being-in-the-world but a fabricator of utterances whose meanings must be accounted for by recourse to rules of form. This means that a fully adequate theory of meaning—or even an adequate theory of linguistic descriptions which regards the problem of meaning simply as a component of the general problem of linguistic form—must eventually go beyond the syntax of propositions to describe the rules which govern the composition or generation of texts. What is needed, in other words, is a "grammar of discourse" that will specify the kinds of relations that are possible among propositions or that are necessary for propositions to be fully determinate. Until recently, such a grammar had been unthinkable, not only because what is required is a *universal* grammar of discourse, but because it had been supposed that linguistic analysis could not be extended beyond the level of the sentence. Benveniste, for example, has written that "the proposition cannot enter as part into a totality of a higher rank. A statement can only precede or follow another statement in a consecutive relationship. A group of propositions does not constitute a unit of an order superior to the proposition. There is no linguistic level above the categoremic level." To be sure, sentences do form discourses: "It is even by discourse that it can be defined: the sentence is the unit of discourse." It is so, however, only "insofar as it is a segment of discourse and not as it could be distinctive with respect to other units of the same level," which means that the sentence does not bear the same relation to discourse as the phoneme and morpheme do to the sentence.[35] Essentially the same point is made from the side of transformational grammar by Jerrold Katz and Jerry Fodor in their important essay, "The Structure of a Semantic Theory": namely, that discourse is simply a quantitative extension of the sentence and therefore irrelevant to the problem of meaning.[36]

Nevertheless, ever since Vladimir Propp's study of the morphology of the Russian folktale in 1928, it has been recognized that narrative discourse could be rigorously analyzed as a structure of integrated relations in which a *qualitative* difference obtains between part and whole.[37] And in "The Structural Study of Myth" (1955), Claude Lévi-Strauss argued that mythic narratives are not merely congeries of fantasy but are expressions which reflect the fundamentally logical nature of mythic thought. His "working hypothesis," as he calls it, is that myth is a kind of secondary linguistic system whose constituent units, or "mythemes," are comparable to phonemes and morphemes, except that they are organized on a level above the sentence. A mytheme is, in effect, a complex semiotic unit, insofar as it takes on meaning by virtue of its relative position within a network of mythemes whose relationships are defined by principles of equivalence and opposition. A myth may therefore be analyzed according to a method analogous to Troubetzkoy's structural analysis of phonemes.[38] In the Oedipus myth, for example, the marriage of Oedipus to his mother and Antigone's burial of Polynices are equivalent mythemes, since both events disclose an overvaluation of kinship relations; similarly, both the fateful parricide and the murder of Polynices represent an undervaluation of kinship relations. Both sets of equivalents thus face one another diacritically. Specifically, they are maintained in an opposition which focuses upon the problem of kinship and ultimately upon the central issue which the myth tries to resolve: (as Lévi-Strauss reads it) the contradiction between a belief in the autochthonous origin of man and the inescapable experience that his origin is progenitive.[39]

This leaves open, however, the question of how myth as a system of signs is related to myth as *récit*. We can perhaps define mythic narrative as a discourse which develops systematically along a double plane of metaphor and metonymy: it possesses both a diachronic order of events and a synchronic order of mutually determining (and therefore necessary) relations—an order of mythemes which function as signifiers to transform events into meanings.[40] According to Lévi-Strauss, however, no single narrative version of a myth can fully disclose this order of signifiers. Structural analysis alone is equipped to accomplish this task, and it does so by collating as many variants of the myth as anthropology is able to recover, superimposing them one upon the other, thus to reconstruct an order of combinations that can never be fully actualized, no more than any act of speech can fully exhaust the totality of signs that constitute a natural language. Thus the Oedipus myth, Lévi-Strauss says, consists of all its versions: the Homeric, the Sophoclean, and even the Freudian—an implausible assertion, unless one understands that myth is not a structure of contents but a system of formal relations. Mythic discourse is thus not a revelation but a *use* of myth analogous to the use of language in the act of speech.

Understood in this way, the concept of myth as a secondary linguistic system implies in turn the concept of a secondary grammar—a narrative grammar, for example, which generates structures that may be transformed .into any number of coherent sequences of events. In recent years the concept of secondary grammars, or of grammars which function above the level of the sentence, has been the subject of considerable speculation. In *Grammaire du Décaméron,* for example, Tzvetan Todorov develops a theory of narrative grammar based on an analogy between the categories of traditional grammar (clause, modality, and so on) and the categories of plot.[41] Similarly, in "Éléments d'une grammaire narrative," Algirdas Greimas distinguishes between a "base grammar" (*grammaire fondamentale*), which is essentially logical in its function, and a "surface grammar" (*grammaire superficielle*), which is either figurative, as in poetry, or "anthropomorphic," as in narrative. Greimas defines the relationship between these "levels of grammar" in terms of an analogy between the syntactic "operations" of the base grammar by which linguistic units are integrated into sentences, and the syntactic "techniques" of the surface grammar, by which poetic or narrative units (*énoncés*) are integrated into texts.[42] This analogy between operation and technique corresponds to the analogy which the British linguist Michael A. K. Halliday draws between grammatical structure and grammatical function, according to which the structure of a clause can be described in terms of its "ideational function," or function of signification, its "interpersonal function," or modality, and its "textual function":

> language has to provide for making links with itself and with features of the situation in which it is used. We may call this the *textual* function, since this is what enables the speaker or writer to construct "texts," or connected passages in a discourse that is situationally relevant; and enables the listener or reader to distinguish a text from a random set of sentences. One aspect of the textual function is the establishment of cohesive relations from one sentence to another in a discourse.[43]

This postulate of a "textual function" of language is of considerable interest, because it implies a distinction between structure and event, or between the logic and the ontology of speech. The basic unit of speech in the formal or structural sense is, as we have seen, the sentence; but in the ontological sense, or from the standpoint of what Halliday calls "language in use," the sentence is superseded by the "textual component," which Halliday defines as "a set of options [Greimas would say 'techniques'] by means of which a speaker or writer is enabled . . . to use language in a way that is relevant to context." [44] It is the textual component which makes it possible for an individual to speak coherently upon a single theme or to respond to the speech of another in a dialogue that forms a unified order of utterances.

The key notion here, however, is that of the "coherence" or "cohesion" of texts. What are the formal, linguistic conditions which will account for our sense that a poem or an essay is a unified structure of meanings and not merely a set of random sentences? Or, better, by what system of linguistic rules may we account for our intuition that a poem by Mallarmé, or a work like Samuel Beckett's *The Unnamable,* is composed as though according to a principle of diffusion? At present, such questions cannot be answered from a strictly linguistic point of view. There is currently under way, however, a "Project for Textual Linguistics" at the University of Konstanz, the aim of which is to develop models for the construction of a text-grammar.[45] A number of preliminary studies indicate that these models will rely heavily on Chomsky's theories, according to which, for example, the coherence of texts could be explained by the postulate of a "textual deep structure," that is, a deep semantic structure that is mapped onto the text itself by means of a complex system of transformation rules.[46] In "Outlines of a Model for a Grammar of Discourse," Werner Kummer proposes a text-grammar constructed on the basis of a logical calculus, or by recourse to a mathematical logic which characterizes relations between sentences according to the categories of consequence, presupposition, synonymy, hyponymy, and so on.[47] Whatever the case, a grammar of texts will necessarily be extremely abstract, and it may be that such a grammar can be constructed only in concert with a typology of texts, or in terms of such secondary grammars as a "generative poetics" or a "generative narrativics." [48]

What is clear, however, is that linguistic research at the level of the text coincides with Harold Weinrich's observation that the concept of linguistics as "a science of small units which pass gradually into larger units, finding its limit at the level of the sentence," can no longer be maintained. For the units of language are not simply "given":

> On the contrary, the linguist has to gather them by a process of segmentation and analysis. But what are his preliminary "givens"? If nothing is given, he must necessarily start from speculative principles, and surely he will find it difficult ever to get beyond speculation. But certainly he can permit himself *one* donnée as a basis for concrete research, namely the text, either oral or written, exchanged between speaker and listener (or author and reader) in the communicational act. All linguistics—even the generative-transformational version—is obliged to start from texts which it first segments into higher and then into lower units. The "elements" [phonemes, morphemes, lexical and syntactic categories, words and sentences] do not find their proper place at the beginning but at the end of the analysis, always allowing for the possibility of reversing the process, that is, starting from the elements obtained and proceeding synthetically and "generatively" to the text. If Descartes was right in considering analysis and synthesis as two aspects of the same method, texts must be the alpha and omega of the linguistic method.[49]

The implication here, as in Halliday's theory of grammatical functions, is that our life of speech cannot be contained within "the magic border of the sentence," but rather is characterized by our capacity to organize meanings into coherent wholes on a number of different linguistic levels. We should understand that our linguistic competence ranges across a hierarchy of levels—sign, sentence, text—and that it is only by examining the interplay of these levels that the dynamics of language, or rather the dynamics of its *use,* can be fully understood.

The implication of what Weinrich says, however, extends even further. For the real problem which linguistics faces is not whether it will be able to construct a grammar of texts, but whether in accomplishing this and other tasks it will be able to keep in mind the fundamental worldliness of human speech. It is this worldliness of speech which has moved a number of linguists to concern themselves with questions of linguistic function and to consider the problem of meaning from the standpoint of relationships between utterance and context, or between the act of speech and its situation.[50] Thus Jerzy Pelc, for example, warns against the dangers inherent in applying to natural languages the norms and concepts that pertain to artificial languages found in mathematical logic and cybernetics. Analogies between natural and artificial languages, as it happens, are what make contemporary linguistics possible, and perhaps without a model provided by a logical calculus the construction of a text-grammar will remain out of the question. As Pelc says, however, what must be kept in the foreground of such research is the recognition that the language which we use in our life of speech is "occasional" by its very nature. Unlike the expressions of a propositional calculus, the expressions of a natural language cannot be understood in terms of their systematic performance alone, but must be accounted for in terms of a dialectic of meaning and use, of structure and event. They "are not supposed to play their representative, communicative, expressive and emotive role alone. They can do so only in a group, together with their linguistic environment and . . . extralinguistic situation." [51]

The phenomenologists of language would, as we have seen, enforce this point even more rigorously than someone like Pelc. Thus Ricoeur proclaims the worldlessness of texts on the basis of an opposition between speaking and writing. This distinction (which linguists tend to undervalue or ignore) lies at the heart of the opposition between structuralism and the phenomenology of language, even as it informs the opposition between Orphic and hermetic poetries: witness the contrast between Mallarmé's typographical efforts to escape the lyricism of the human voice, or Barthes's concept of "the pure act of writing," and Wallace Stevens's conception of "speaking humanly":

> To say more than human things with human voice,
> That cannot be; to say human things with more
> Than human voice, that, also, cannot be;
> To speak humanly from the height or from the depth
> Of human things, that is acutest speech.[52]

It is this contrast between typography and voice which a theory of linguistic descriptions and above all a theory of meaning must take into account. And on this point, it is striking to notice, both the structuralists and the phenomenologists are agreed. Thus Roland Barthes proposes "two autonomous linguistics: a linguistics of the syntagma and a linguistics of the sentence, a linguistics of the spoken word and a linguistics of the written," on the grounds that speaking and writing belong to two entirely different orders of linguistic competence. The goal of writing, in Barthes's view, is the perfection of form. Writing is, in a sense, a fulfillment of linguistic form—a fulfillment which is repeatedly celebrated in literature and in which literature in turn finds the reason for its being.[53] The paradox is that in our encounter with written texts, and particularly (as philosophers seem always to be insisting) in our encounter with literature, we are frequently made witness to an apparent failure of language. For in the written text meaning no longer appears simply in its theoretical form as an intention to be understood; on the contrary, it manifests itself first as a problem, as a difficulty to be overcome, requiring the application of those techniques of reading and analysis that have been institutionalized in hermeneutics and literary criticism.

In the case of spoken utterances, however, this paradox is reversed. "Listen to a conversation," Barthes tells us: "note how many sentences have an incomplete or ambiguous structure, how many clauses are subordinated without reason or without being assigned to clear antecedents, how many subjects lack predicates, how many correlatives lack a partner, and so on, to the extent that it may be wrong to continue calling some of these 'sentences,' even 'incomplete' or 'ill-formed' ones." [54] What Barthes is asking us to do, of course, is to treat an instance of discourse as if it were an instance of writing. Transcriptions of speech into writing are always remarkable for what they disclose about spoken utterances: the failure of grammar and even more sharply the abrogation of style appear to entail incredible failures of signfication—incredible, because these failures are for the most part unremembered by those who witnessed the original instance of speaking. Actually, it is more often than not the transcription which fails: that is, it fails to preserve the meaning of what was said —a meaning which can only be partially restored by an editor's reconstruction of what was meant.

For Walter Ong, this example of what happens to meaning in transcription is only one among many testimonies to the ontological priority of sound over sight, of the domain of the spoken word over the domain of the written. "Sound," he says, "is more real or existential than other sense objects, despite the fact that it is also more evanescent. Sound itself is related to present actuality rather than to past or future. It must emanate from a source here and now discernibly active, with the result that involvement with sound is involvement with the present, with here-and-now existence and activity." [55] For its part, the spoken word, the word as sound, involves us not only with present time but with *presence* in the phenomenological sense, that is, the mutually determining presence of person and world. It is this involvement with presence that is muted or (as Ricoeur says) interrupted by writing, for writing isolates speech from sound, person, and actuality: it creates its own world—a textual universe which compensates for absence by seeking the perfection of form. In effect, writing embodies the act of speaking in its own special closure of sentence and context, of mutually determining propositions, of systems of conjunction and disjunction, progression and recurrence. One might even say that writing transforms meaning into a problem in order to preserve it: it reduces meaning to a closure of relations that awaits to be broken by activities of analysis and interpretation. [56]

The question is: How are speaking and writing related to

one another? They are two modes of linguistic performance, each requiring a different order of skills, but both grounded finally upon the fact of man's linguistic competence. More importantly, they emphasize the doubleness of language. Speaking magnifies the ontological dimension of language, together with the worldliness that makes linguistic meaning possible; writing, by contrast, magnifies the formal dimension of language and the logical requisites of intelligibility. Speaking testifies to the priority of being, writing to the priority of form, but language encompasses this double priority and finds its fulfillment in their dialectical relationship. Man speaks or writes only by breaking with life, by withdrawing from a natural intimacy with the world into language. But his language is not merely a dwelling-place made of words; rather, it is a dwelling-place made worldly by his utterance. The doubleness of language is manifested on the plane of speaking or writing as the double articulation of word and world, as the speech of language and the speech of being. As Mikel Dufrenne says, it is language which makes possible the transition from "a condition of mere living to one of thinking"—to meaning as a transitive activity. "It is language which introduces the requisite distance between the signifying and the signified. It is by the mediation of language that the interval is created where thought can come into play. Nevertheless . . . the mediation is one that separates and unites at the same time. If language digs a trench between the world and me, it also throws a bridge across it." The actual presence of the world is abolished, but only to be created once more as an intelligible presence—a presence that is not only actual but speakable.[57]

It is, however, poetry, even more than ordinary speaking or writing, which asserts this doubleness of language. What we have called the Orphic and hermetic modes of poetic speech disclose the two essential movements of any poetic act—a withdrawal from the world into a universe of language, which is a movement whose immediate end is to celebrate the transcendence of language, its being as such; and a return (as though from the moment before speech) to earth, which is a movement that brings word and world together, thus to establish the unity in which, as Heidegger says, "the being of language speaks as the language of being." It is this dialectical movement which we glimpsed at the outset of this study in Pierre Emmanuel's image of the poet who is both destructive and creative, who speaks the annihilating word of language in order to speak in turn the creative word of being —that divine word by which man and world are originated and maintained in one another's presence. What we see now, however, is that the speech of the poets is not opposed to the speech of ordinary men but is homologous to it, for the dialectic of Orphic and hermetic poetries is nothing less than a poetics informed by the dialectic of the semiotic and the semantic, of departure and return, that makes possible the expression of meaning in everyday life.

For, indeed, even as the theory of meaning must take into account the ontology as well as the logic of texts, so too must poetics seek not only to explain how poetry is made but also how its design is fulfilled by the presence of the world. Poetics, in this sense, must be a structuralism which defines the poem in relation to itself as a system of internal dependencies; but it must also be a phenomenology which defines the poem in relation to its situation, that is, in terms of its historical existence. The poem must be understood both as structure and as event—as a text which possesses its own harmony of relations, but which at the same time can only come into being within a network of other texts, or within literary history, and beyond this within the human life-world. The poem is both object and utterance, both a thing made and a thing spoken, which discloses itself within the horizon of the speakable, and which at the same time discloses that very horizon, thus to account for (as the ancient myths of poetry have always proposed to account for) the very possibility of human speech itself.

Notes

Introduction

1 *Selected Letters of Gustave Flaubert,* trans. Francis Steegmuller (New York, 1953), pp. 127–128.
2 Pierre Emmanuel, "Sache te taire," in *Chansons du dé à coudre* (Paris, 1947), p. 55.
3 "The Nature of Language," in *On the Way to Language* (New York, 1971), p. 59.
4 *Man and Language,* trans. Stanley Godman (Chicago, 1963), p. 36.
5 Ibid., p. 44.
6 Gottfried Benn, *Gessämelte Werke* (Limes, 1956), I, p. 208.
7 *On the Way to Language,* p. 82.
8 *Language and Philosophy,* trans. Henry B. Veatch (Bloomington, Ind., 1963), p. 98.
9 *Writing Degree Zero,* trans. Annette Lavers and Colin Smith (New York, 1968), p. 46.
10 *The Collected Poems of Wallace Stevens* (New York, 1964), p. 473.
11 *Poesie raison ardente* (Paris, 1948), pp. 73–74: "Le poète, d'instinct, abolit l'objet, et rend la chose à son silence, qui est l'antique respiration du tout. Il rétablit ainsi dans le monde une innocence et un néant: innocence, puisque le monde se retrouve antérieur à la parole, et néant, puisque la parole (ne fût-ce que temporairement) en est exclue. Ce faisant, le poète abîme, avec une hardiesse étonnante le fossé qui séparait l'homme du monde. Homme, il ne peut inverser le sens du temps; et de la contradiction entre l'acte originel, l'acte *seul* qu'il vient

d'accomplir, en rendant la matière aux eaux primordiales, et sa nature coupable, limitée, accablée d'histoire, naît l'orgueilleuse nostalgie du pur néant, volonté d'être le Dieu créateur, qui sur les eaux retient le Verbe prêt à fondre."

12 *Opus Posthumous,* ed. Samuel French Morse (New York, 1969), p. 176. For the reference to Heidegger, see *On the Way to Language,* p. 94.

13 Ibid., p. 168.

Chapter 1

1 *The Philosophy of Ernst Cassirer,* ed. Paul Arthur Schilpp, trans. Robert Walter Bretall and Paul Arthur Schilpp (Evanston, Ill., 1949), p. 878. The essay first appeared as " 'Geist' und 'Leben' in der Philosophie der Gegenwart," in *Die Neue Rundschau,* 1 (1930), 244–264.

2 *Essay on Criticism,* II, 309–10, *The Poems of Alexander Pope,* ed. John Butt (New Haven, 1963), p. 153.

3 From the introduction to *A Treatise Concerning the Principles of Human Knowledge,* in *The Works of George Berkeley, Bishop of Cloyne,* ed. T. E. Jessop (London, 1949), p. 40.

4 *The Philosophy of Symbolic Forms,* trans. Ralph Manheim (New Haven, 1953), I, p. 94.

5 "Poetry and Abstract Thought," in *The Art of Poetry,* trans. Denise Folliot (New York, 1958), p. 65.

6 "The Poet's Rights Over Language," ibid., p. 171.

7 For the concept of deviation as it is applied to poetic language, see Samuel R. Levin, "Deviation—Statistical and Determinate—in Poetic Language," *Lingua,* 12 (1963), 276–290. See also G. N. Leech, "Linguistics and the Figures of Rhetoric," in *Essays on Style and Language,* ed. Roger Fowler (London, 1966), pp. 135–156.

8 The key work here, of course, is Ferdinand de Saussure's *Cours de linguistique générale* (1916). For the concept of generative-transformational grammar, see Noam Chomsky, *Syntactic Structures* (The Hague, 1957).

9 The notion that words are units of a mechanical system is usually associated with such Neo-Grammarians as Karl Brugmann and Hermann Osthoff, in their *Morphologische Untersuchungen* (1878); the application of the organic analogy to lan-

guage is a nineteenth-century commonplace, but an important work in this connection is August Schleicher's *Die Darwinische Theorie und die Sprachwissenschaft* (1863); the approach to language from the standpoint of a "mathematical psychology," in which the contents of the mind are regarded as discrete and isolatable units, was taken by H. Steinhal, in *Einleitung in die Philosophie der Sprachwissenschaft* (1871). See Cassirer's essay, '"Structuralism in Modern Linguistics," *Word*, 1 (1945), 99–120.

10 *The Dialogues of Plato*, trans. B. Jowett (Oxford, 1953), 189e–190a.

11 *Plato's Epistles*, trans. Glenn R. Morrow (New York, 1962), 342a–342b.

12 *Preface to Plato* (Cambridge, Mass., 1963), pp. 36–86.

13 Ibid., p. x.

14 The conflict among cultural ideals during Plato's time is discussed by Werner Jaeger in *Paideia: The Ideals of Greek Culture* (Oxford, 1947), esp. II, pp. 46–70.

15 "Against the Logicians," trans. R. G. Bury (Cambridge, Mass.: Loeb Classical Library, 1933), I, 65.

16 Ibid., I, 84.

17 *Ancilla to the Pre-Socratic Philosophers*, trans. Kathleen Freeman (Oxford, 1948), p. 132.

18 Trans. G. L. Hendrickson and H. M. Hubbel (Cambridge, Mass.: Loeb Classical Library, 1937), XIX, 61.

19 Trans. A. T. Murray (Cambridge, Mass.: Loeb Classical Library, 1924), III, 210–225.

20 See, for example, *Ramus, Method, and the Decay of Dialogue* (Cambridge, Mass., 1958), pp. 270–292, and *The Presence of the Word: Some Prolegomena for Cultural and Religious History* (New Haven, 1967), pp. 17–87.

21 Trans. W. Rhys Roberts (London, 1910), pp. 211–212. See Larue Van Hook, *The Metaphorical Terminology of Greek Rhetoric and Literary Criticism* (Chicago, 1905), pp. 35–44.

22 *On Literary Composition*, p. 235.

23 (London, 1593), p. A. iij.

24 See the anecdote in Plutarch, "De Gloria Atheniensium," in the *Moralia*, trans. Frank Cole Babbitt (Cambridge, Mass.: Loeb Classical Library, 1927), IV, 347E–348F: "When Pindar was still young, and prided himself on his felicitous use of words, Corinna warned him that his writing lacked refinement, since he

did not introduce myths, which are the proper business of poetry, but used as a foundation for his work unusual and obsolete words, extensions of meaning, paraphrases, lyrics, and rhythms, which are mere embellishments of the subject matter."

25 Ed. Gladys Doidge Willcock and Alice Walker (Cambridge, 1936), p. 154.

26 Migne, *Patrologia* (Paris, 1900), 199, p. 969B, 186.

27 *La Poetica di Bernardino Daniello* (Vinegia, 1536), p. 22: "Niuno e de suoi Dialoghi . . . nel quale egli non pur sotto fauoloso uelame et misterio (nella guisa che i Poeti soglion fare) ma con chiarissimi & risplendenti lumi di parole, et con grandissimi numerii suoi concetti non esprima."

28 (Basileae, 1564), pp. 17–18: "Verba orationem conflant, res ipsae sententias. Hae sine oratione, hoc est sine uerbis esse non possunt: at uerba sine sententijs possunt."

29 *Elizabethan and Metaphysical Imagery* (Chicago, 1947), esp. pp. 61–78.

30 I, 163–181. Ed. Dámaso Alonso (Madrid, 1935), pp. 69–70. The following is from Edward Meyer Wilson's English translation, *The Solitudes of Don Luis de Góngora* (Cambridge, 1965), pp. 15–16:

> Then the soft skins upon the cork-bed laid
> Invited him to take more gentle rest,
> Than to the prince between his Holland sheets
> Purple of Tyre or Milanese brocade.
> No Sisyphus, by fuming wines oppressed,
> Climbing Ambition's hillside till he greets
> The summit of his ponderous vanity,
> The jest of Fortune when awake, was he . . .
> He slept to wake at last when birds serene—
> And sweet bells in sonorous feathers clad
> —Gave the Dawn's tidings glad
> To Phoebus, who from his pavilion hoar
> Of foam arose, then from his car to pour
> Rays on the Cottage, obelisk of green.

31 Austral Edition (Espasa-Calpe, Argentina, 1942), p. 19: "Es un acto del entendimiento que exprime la correspondencia que sa halla entre los objetos. La misma consonancia, o correlación artificiosa exprimida, es la sutileza objetiva."

32 Ibid., p. 27: "Hállase simetria intelectual entre los terminos del

pensamiento, tanto más primorosa, que la material entre columnas y acroteras, cuánto va del objeto del ingenio, al de un sentido."

33 See Góngora's defense of the obscurity of the *Soledades* in *Obras poéticas,* Bibliotheca Hispanica Edition (New York, 1921), III, p. 272.

34 *On the Copia of Words and Ideas,* trans. Donald B. King and H. David Rix (Milwaukee, 1963), pp. 38–42.

35 "The Problem of Meaning in Primitive Languages," in C. K. Ogden and I. A. Richards, *The Meaning of Meaning,* 8th ed. (New York, 1946), pp. 321–322.

36 See Harold C. Conklin, "Linguistic Play in Its Cultural Context," *Language,* 32 (1956), 136–139.

37 See Alf Sommerfelt, *La Langue et la société: Charactères sociaux d'une langue de type archaïque* (Oslo, 1938).

38 *Aranda Traditions* (Melbourne, 1947), pp. xx–xxi.

39 *Language: Its Nature, Development, and Origin* (New York, 1921), p. 429.

40 See Edward Sapir, *Language* (New York, 1921), p. 128; and Joseph Greenberg, *Essays in Linguistics* (Chicago, 1963), pp. 60–61.

41 *Ancient and Medieval Grammatical Theory in Europe* (London, 1951), p. 12. See also Robins's superb *A Short History of Linguistics* (Bloomington, Ind., and London, 1967), pp. 138–139: "The western tradition tended to concentrate on words as individual minimal meaning bearers and to regard the sentence as the product of word combinations in specific types of logical proposition. Plato and Aristotle mostly discussed meaning in relation to words as isolates, and Aristotle stressed the semantic minimality (in his view) and independence of the word as such. . . . The Stoics appear to have pointed to the further limitation of the word's field of reference or its disambiguation as the result of specific collocations . . . , and this doctrine was developed in the course of the distinction between *significatio and suppositio* in the Middle Ages. . . . Indian linguists debated the whole question of the word as against that of the sentence. One set of thinkers maintained a view very like the general western attitude that the sentence is built up of words each contributing its meaning to the total meaning of the sentence. But an opposite view, particularly associated with Bhartrhari,

author of *Vākyapadīya* (ca. seventh century A.D.), regarded the sentence as a single undivided utterance conveying its meaning 'in a flash,' just as a picture is first perceived as a unity notwithstanding subsequent analysis into its component coloured shapes. Given the conception of the word unit, sentences can be identified as one-word sentences or as many-word sentences, but for the speaker and hearer they are primarily single sentence unities, words and word meanings being largely the creation of linguists and self-conscious speakers trying to analyse and classify sentence meanings in terms of smaller components."

42 *Language,* pp. 32–37.

43 In the *Categories,* 1a, 20–29, for example, Aristotle speaks of "uncombined words" as pieces of "grammatical knowledge"; in *De Interpretatione,* 16a–16b, he speaks of subjects and predicates not as concepts (as they are in Plato) but as words in a proposition. Quotations and subsequent references are to the Loeb Classical Library edition of these works, trans. Harold P. Cooke (Cambridge, Mass., 1938).

44 *Categories,* 2a, 4–10. Cf. Plato's *Sophist,* 262a–262c.

45 *Poetics,* 1456b–1457a.

46 "The Grammar of Dionysus Thrax," trans. Thomas Davidson, *Journal of Speculative Philosophy,* 8 (1874), 338.

47 *Categories,* 6b, 33; *De Interpretatione,* 16b, 1; *Rhetoric,* 1364b, 33.

48 Robins, *Ancient and Medieval Grammatical Theory,* p. 26.

49 Varro, *On the Latin Language,* trans. Roland G. Kent (Cambridge, Mass.: Loeb Classical Library, 1938), II, p. 370n.

50 Ibid., VIII, 1, 1.

51 See F. H. Colson, "The Analogist and Anomalist Controversy," *Classical Quarterly,* 13 (1919), 24–36.

52 *Ancient and Medieval Grammatical Theory,* p. 25.

53 *Sophist,* 264b.

54 (Oxford, 1948), pp. 187–188.

55 "The Epicurean Analysis of Language," *American Journal of Philosophy,* 60 (1939), 85–86.

56 II, 104–135.

57 *The Ars Minor of Donatus,* ed. Wayland Johnson Chase, University of Wisconsin Studies in the Social Sciences and History, no. 11 (Madison, 1926), p. 34.

58 Trans. Daniel D. McGarry (Berkeley and Los Angeles, 1959), p. 39.

59 *Philosophical Writings,* ed. Philotheus Boehner, O.F.M. (New York, 1957), p. 23.

60 A. C. Howell has observed this shift in the meaning of the term *res* and identified it as a seventeenth-century phenomenon in "*Res et Verba:* Words and Things," *ELH,* 13 (1946), 131–142.

61 Thomas Sprat, *History of the Royal Society,* ed. Jackson I. Cope and Harold Whitmore Jones (St. Louis, 1958), p. 113.

62 *The Urquhart-Le Motteux Translation of the Works of Francis Rabelais,* ed. Albert Jay Nock (New York, 1931), I, p. 344.

63 See A. J. Krailsheimer, *Rabelais and the Franciscans* (Oxford, 1963), pp. 80–81.

64 *Linguistics and Literary History: Essays in Stylistics* (Princeton, N.J., 1948), p. 21.

65 *Essays Towards a Real Character and a Philosophical Language* (London, 1668). According to Wilkins, the term *father* may be "represented by the character ⎣—Ʒ—⏌, which consists of the basic sign ——Ʒ——, for the genus 'economical' (interpersonal) relation, to which are added a right oblique line on the left, indicating the first subdivision, in the case of economical relations that of consanguinity, an upright line on the right indicating the second subdivision, in the marking the relation of direct ascending, and a semi-circle above the middle of the character, indicating male. Should the character be used metaphorically, this can be specified by the addition of a short vertical line over the left end of the character: ⎣—Ʒ—⏌ " (p. 452).

Chapter 2

1 *An Essay Concerning Human Understanding* (Chicago, 1956), p. 171.

2 See Cassirer, *The Philosophy of Symbolic Forms,* I, p. 129.

3 *Selected Writings,* ed. R. T. Davies (Evanston, Ill., 1965), pp. 154–155.

4 *Collected Letters of Samuel Taylor Coleridge,* ed. Earl Leslie Griggs (Oxford, 1956–1959), I, pp. 625–626.

5 *Institutio Oratoria,* VIII, 89.

6 III, 25, 27, pp. 113, 116–119.
7 *Arte of English Poesie,* p. 119.
8 *Reflections on the Nature and Property of Languages in General, And on the Advantages, Defects, and Manner of Improving the English Tongue in Particular* (London, 1731), p. 99. See Cassirer on the origin of the "energetic" theory of language, *The Philosophy of Symbolic Forms,* I, pp. 145–146.
9 *History of the Royal Society,* p. 113.
10 Cf. John Williams, *Thoughts on Language* (London, 1783), pp. 10–13: We should, Williams says, "consider language as a widespreading oak, having many branches, and these bearing many others. If I were desirous of examining any of these branches, in order to see their composition, and texture, I should not lay hold of any one branch to get to the top of the tree. Common sense would direct me first to examine the trunk, to observe its construction and appearance; then, as I advanced, I should more easily perceive the connection of every branch with and upon the others; and of the whole with and upon the trunk and roots."
11 *The Works of James Harris* (London, 1801), I, p. 23.
12 *Laocoön: An Essay on the Limits of Painting and Poetry,* trans. Edward Allen McCormick (New York, 1962), p. 78: "Objects or parts of objects which exist in space are called bodies. Accordingly, bodies with their visible properties are the true subjects of painting. Objects or parts of objects which follow one another are called actions. Accordingly, actions are the true subjects of poetry."
13 *The Philosophy of Symbolic Forms,* I, p. 150.
14 *The New Science of Giambattista Vico,* trans. Thomas Goddard Bergin and Max Harold Fisch (Ithaca, N.Y., 1968), p. 150. [Revised translation of the third edition (1744)].
15 "Essay on the Origin of Languages," *On the Origin of Language,* trans. John H. Moran and Alexander Gode (New York, 1966), p. 11.
16 "Essay on the Origin of Language," ibid., pp. 97–98.
17 *Wordsworth's Literary Criticism,* ed. Nowell C. Smith (London, 1905), p. 14.
18 *Prelude,* VI, 110–114, ed. Ernest de Selincourt (Oxford, 1926), p. 177.
19 *The Art of Poetry, 1750–1820: Theories of Poetic Composition*

and Style in the Neo-Classic and Early Romantic Period (New York, 1967), p. 161.

20 *The Philosophical Lectures of Samuel Taylor Coleridge,* ed. Kathleen Coburn (New York, 1949), p. 201.

21 *The Notebooks of Samuel Taylor Coleridge,* ed. Kathleen Coburn, (New York, 1961), II, 2245 17.19.

22 *The Complete Works of Samuel Taylor Coleridge,* ed. W. G. T. Shedd (New York, 1854), IV, p. 45.

23 *Inquiring Spirit: A Coleridge Reader,* ed. Kathleen Coburn (New York, 1968), p. 101. The passage is from MS Egerton 2801, f. 145.

24 *Philosophical Lectures,* p. 441.

25 *The Friend,* ed. Barbara E. Rooke (London, 1969), I, p. 20.

26 *Coleridge on Logic and Learning,* ed. A. D. Snyder (New Haven, 1929), p. 57.

27 *Structural Anthropology,* trans. Claire Jacobson and Brooke Grundfest Schoepf (New York, 1967), pp. 92–93. For a discussion of Saussure's conception of language, see below, pp. 97–98.

28 *Notebooks,* II, 2629 17.187.

29 Ibid., I, 383 27.37.

30 *The Friend,* II, pp. 241–242n* [2]

31 *Shelley's Prose: or, The Trumpet of Prophecy,* ed. David Lee Clark (Albuquerque, 1954), p. 172.

32 I, 135–151. *Shelley's "Prometheus Unbound": A Variorum Edition,* ed. Lawrence John Zillman (Seattle, 1959), pp. 139–140.

33 *Humanist Without Portfolio: An Anthology of the Writings of Wilhelm von Humboldt,* trans. Marianne Cowan (Detroit, 1963), pp. 235–236.

Chapter 3

1 See above, pp. 21–22. See also Thomas Wilson, *The Arte of Rhetorique* (London, 1553), fol. 90: "A figure is a certain kinde, either of sentence, oration, or worde, used after some new yor straunge wise, muche unlike to that, which men communely use to speake."

2 *Sidney's Apologie for Poetrie,* ed. J. Curton Collins (Oxford, 1907), pp. 59–60.

3 *The Works of Francis Bacon,* ed. James Spedding et al. (London, 1857), I, p. 653: "Grammaticum etiam bipartitam ponemus:

ut alia sit Literaria, alia Philosophica. Altar adhibetur simpliciter ad linguas, nempe ut quis aut celerius perdiscat, aut emendatius et purius loquatur. Altera vers aliquatenus Philosophiae
ministrat." Interestingly, "Literaria" is sometimes translated as
"popular."

4   Boris Eichenbaum, "The Theory of the Formalist Method"
    (1926), in *Russian Formalist Criticism: Four Essays,* trans. Lee
    T. Lemon and Merion J. Reis (Lincoln, Nebr., 1965), pp. 99–
    139. See Frederic Jameson, *The Prison-House of Language: A
    Critical Account of Structuralism and Russian Formalism*
    (Princeton, N.J., 1972), pp. 43–98. The reader should also
    consult the essays in *Readings in Russian Poetics: Formalist and
    Structuralist Views,* ed. Ladislav Matejka and Krystyna Pomorska (Cambridge, Mass., 1971).

5   See Vladimir Markov, *Russian Futurism: A History* (Berkeley
    and Los Angeles, 1968), pp. 140–141; and Victor Erlich, *Russian
    Formalism: History—Doctrine,* 2d ed. (The Hague, 1965), pp.
    70–86.

6   *Russian Formalist Criticism,* p. 11.

7   (Paris, 1965), p. 83.

8   Reference should be made here to a number of essays which
    appeared in the formalist periodical *Sborniki* during 1916–
    1917: Leo Jakubinsky's "O zvukakh poeticheskovo yazyka [On
    the Sounds of Poetic Language]" and "Skopleniye odinakovykh
    plavnykh v prakticheskom i poeticheskom yazykakh [The Accumulation of Identical Liquids in Practical and Poetic Language]" and Shklovský's "O poezii i zaumnon yazke [On Poetry
    and Nonsense Language]." See also Erlich, *Russian Formalism,*
    pp. 43–50, for a discussion of the Russian Futurist conception
    of the "self-valuable word" and its influence upon Russian Formalist thought.

9   "The Functional Differentiation of the Standard Language,"
    trans. Paul L. Garvin, *A Prague School Reader on Esthetics,
    Literary Structure, and Style* (Washington, D.C., 1964), p. 10.
    Subsequent references to Mukařovský's essay "Standard Language and Poetic Language" will also be to Garvin's translation.

10 *Syntactic Structures,* p. 15.

11 *The Art of Poetry,* pp. 170–171.

12 See Brian Lee, "The New Criticism and the Language of
    Poetry," in *Essays on Style and Language,* ed. Roger Fowler

(London, 1966), pp. 29–52; I. A. Richards, *The Philosophy of Rhetoric* (New York, 1936), passim; Eliseo Vivas, *Creation and Discovery* (New York, 1955), esp. pp. 133–139; and Murray Krieger, *The New Apologists for Poetry* (Minneapolis, 1956), pp. 167–201. See also T. E. Hulme's "Notes on Language and Style" (1909–1914), in *Further Speculations*, ed. Sam Hynes (Lincoln, Nebr., 1962), pp. 77–100.

13 *Style in Language*, ed. Thomas A. Sebeok (New York and London, 1960), p. 358.

14 *The Collected Poems of Wallace Stevens*, pp. 75–76.

15 *The Necessary Angel* (New York, 1951), p. 32.

16 *Opus Posthumous*, p. 171.

17 *Philosophy in a New Key* (New York, 1951), p. 204.

18 See E. D. Hirsch, Jr., *Validity in Interpretation* (New Haven, 1967), pp. 44–46.

19 *Œuvres*, ed. Jean Hytier (Paris, 1957), I, p. 96.

20 *Prisms: Studies in Modern Literature* (Bloomington, Ind., 1967), p. 7.

21 Noam Chomsky, *Cartesian Linguistics* (New York, 1966), pp. 31–51.

22 *Biographia Literaria*, ed. John Shawcross (Oxford, 1907), II, p. 9.

23 See Boris Tomashevsky, "Thematics," in *Russian Formalist Criticism*, pp. 78–87; and Eichenbaum, "The Theory of the Formalist Method," pp. 119–122.

24 *Fiction and the Unconscious* (New York, 1962), p. 153. See David Lodge's discussion of this matter in *Language of Fiction* (New York, 1966), pp. 6–18 ff.

25 "To Write: Intransitive Verb?" in *The Languages of Criticism and Sciences of Man: The Structuralist Controversy*, ed. Richard Macksey and Eugenio Donato (Baltimore, 1970), p. 142. Barthes first elaborated the concept of *writing* as a special category of discourse in *Le Degré zéro de l'écriture* (Paris, 1953), the "zero degree" being that neutral or "amodal" writing that, in contrast to political modes of writing, for example, can be described as "intransitive" or (in the manner of Camus's *L'Étranger*) uninvolved. A more lucid formulation of this notion is to be found in a later essay, "Écrivains et écrivants" (1960): "Language is neither an instrument nor a vehicle: it is a structure, as we increasingly suspect, but the author [*écrivain*] is the only man, by definition, to lose his own structure and that of the world

in the structure of language. Yet this language is an (infinitely) labored substance; it is a little like a superlanguage—reality is never anything but a pretext for it (for the author, *to write* is an intransitive verb); hence it can never explain the world, or at least, when it claims to explain the world, it does so only the better to conceal its ambiguity: once the explanation is fixed in a work, it immediately becomes an ambiguous product of the real, to which it is linked by perspective; in short, literature is always unrealistic [*irréaliste*], but its very unreality permits it to question the world—though these questions can never be very direct. . . . The *writer* [*écrivant*], on the other hand, is a 'transitive' man, he posits a goal (to give evidence, to explain, to instruct), of which language is merely a means; for him language supports a *praxis*, it does not constitute one. Thus language is restored to the nature of an instrument of communication, a vehicle of 'thought' " (*Critical Essays*, trans. Richard Howard [Evanston, Ill., 1972], pp. 145–147).

26 See especially the discussion of "poetic writing" in *Le Degré zéro de l'écriture*, which is discussed on pp. 194–196.

27 *The Languages of Criticism*, p. 143.

28 Ibid., p. 144.

29 See Jacques Derrida, "Structure, Sign, and Play in the Discourse of the Human Sciences," in *The Languages of Criticism*, pp. 247–265. Derrida's theme is that moment of "rupture" in the history of the idea of structure, "in which language invaded the universal problematic [*le champ problematique universel*]; that in which, in the absence of a center or origin, everything became discourse—provided we can agree on this word—that is to say, when everything became a system where the central signified, the original or transcendental signified, is never absolutely present outside a system of differences" (p. 249). For a discussion of Derrida in relation to the structuralist thought of Barthes and Michel Foucault, see Edward W. Said, "*Abecedarium culturae:* Structuralism, Absence, Writing," *TriQuarterly*, no. 20 (Winter 1971), 33–71.

30 *Cours de linguistique générale* (Paris, 1949), p. 162; "Quand on dit qu'elles correspondent à des concepts, on sous-entend que ceux-ci sont purement différentiels, définis non pas positivement par leur contenu, mais négativement par leurs rapports avec les autres terms du système." See Derrida, "Differance,"

Speech and Phenomena, trans. David B. Allison (Evanston, Ill., 1973), pp. 129–160.

31 *Cours de linguistique générale,* p. 159; "Puisque la langue est un système dont tous les termes sont solidaires et ou la valeur de l'un ne resulte que de la presence simultanée des autres."

32 *Signs* (Evanston, Ill., 1964), p. 46.

33 *The Languages of Criticism,* p. 250.

34 "Science versus Literature," in *Structuralism: A Reader,* ed. Michael Lane (London, 1970), p. 411.

35 *The Order of Things: An Archeology of the Human Sciences* (New York, 1970), p. 300.

36 *Labyrinths: Selected Stories and Other Writings,* ed. Donald A. Yates and James E. Irby (New York, 1964), p. 52.

37 Ibid., p. 57.

Chapter 4

1 *Mallarmé: Selected Prose Poems, Essays, and Letters,* trans. Bradford Cook (Baltimore, 1956), p. 24. Because I have emended occasionally Cook's translations, I have referred both to the translation and to the French text, *Œuvres complètes* (Pléiade Edition), ed. Henri Mondor and G. Jean-Aubrey (Paris, 1945). See *Œuvres,* p. 378, for the above quotation. References to the letters will be to Stéphane Mallarmé, *Correspondance,* I (Paris, 1959), ed. Henri Mondor; II (Paris, 1965), ed. Henri Mondor and Lloyd James Austin.

2 Cazalis was the author of a book on Buddhism entitled *Le Livre du néant* (1872).

3 Trans. Gustave Emil Meuller (New York, 1959), p. 103.

4 *Richard Wagner's Prose Works,* trans. William Ashton Ellis (London, 1893), III, p. 319.

5 *The Structure of Poetry* (London, 1951), p. 152.

6 (New Haven, 1950), pp. 35–38, 118–122.

7 "Music and Silence," in *Reflections on Art,* ed. Susanne K. Langer (Baltimore, 1958), p. 103. The essay was first published in *La Revue musicale,* 22 (1946), 169–181.

8 *Le "Livre" de Mallarmé* (Paris, 1957), 2 *(suite):*
L'armature intellectuelle du
poeme, se dissimule et—in lieu—tient dans l'espace qui
isole les strophes et

parmi le blanc du papier; significatif silence qu'il
n'est pas moins beau de composer que les
vers.

9 Ibid., 191 (A):

> pureté lumière électr—
> —le volume, malgré l'im-
> pression fixe, devient par ce jeu, mobi-
> le—de mort il devient vie

10 A facsimile of the 1914 Gallimard edition of *Un Coup de dés
jamais n'abolira le hasard* appears at the end of chap. 4.

Chapter 5

1 Roman Jakobson and Morris Halle, *Fundamentals of Language*
(The Hague, 1956), p. 76.

2 Ibid., p. 78.

3 *The Collected Poems of Dylan Thomas* (New York, 1957), p. 80.

4 *Novelists on the Novel,* trans. Miriam Allott (New York, 1959),
pp. 312–313. For the French text, see Flaubert, *Correspondance,*
revised and enlarged edition (Paris, 1926), II, p. 399. Subsequent
references to Flaubert's correspondence will be to Steegmuller's
translations in *The Selected Letters of Gustave Flaubert,* as
well as to the French text.

5 *Fundamentals of Language,* p. 80.

6 *Œuvres* (Pléiade Edition), ed. Albert Thibaudet and René
Dumesnil (Paris, 1936), p. 385.

7 *Mimesis: The Representation of Reality in Western Literature*
(Garden City, N.Y., 1953), p. 427.

8 *Madame Bovary: Ébauches et fragments inédits,* ed. Gabrielle
Leleu (Paris, 1936), I, p. 276.

9 "En relisant *Madame Bovary,*" *La Table Ronde* (March 27,
1950), p. 164; trans. Paul de Man, *Madame Bovary: Backgrounds
and Sources, Essays in Criticism* (New York, 1965), p. 296.

10 *The Art of Poetry,* p. 146.

11 *La Part du feu* (Paris, 1949), p. 83.

12 See Blanchot's discussion of Flaubert in "Le Probleme de
Wittgenstein," in *L'Entretien infini* (Paris, 1969), pp. 487–493.

13 See, for example, Harry Levin, *James Joyce: A Critical Intro-
duction* (New York, 1960), p. 172; and Hugh Kenner, *The*

Stoic Comedians: Flaubert, Joyce, and Beckett (Boston, 1962), passim.

14 *Dubliners* (New York, 1971), p. 105; *Finnegans Wake* (New York, 1959), p. 21.

15 *A Portrait of the Artist as a Young Man* (New York, 1964), p. 170.

16 *The Art of James Joyce* (London, 1961), p. 44.

17 *Ulysses: The Mechanics of Meaning* (Englewood Cliffs, N.J., 1970), p. 85.

18 *Ulysses* (New York, 1961), p. 699.

19 *Mechanics of Meaning*, p. 70.

20 *Fundamentals of Language*, p. 60.

21 "The Language of *Finnegans Wake*," *Sewanee Review*, 72 (1964), 83–84. "The normal word," Thompson says, "is like a Lucretian atom: it is hard and discrete; Joyce's word is like a Bohr atom: there is still the old word as the nucleus, but about it there are new electrons of meanings. The atom is a convenient model, for the word had an independent reality for Joyce, so that he hoped to achieve a chain reaction of meaning through polymorphemic fusion" (p. 83).

22 (Evanston, Ill., 1962), pp. 166–167.

23 See Claude Lévi-Strauss, "Introduction à l'œuvre de Marcel Mauss," in Marcel Mauss, *Sociologie et anthropologie* (Paris, 1950), pp. xlviii–xlx.

24 *A Second Census of "Finnegans Wake"* (Evanston, Ill., 1963), pp. lx–lxvi.

25 *James Joyce Today: Essays on the Major Works* (Bloomington, Ind., and London, 1966), pp. 152–153.

26 *A Second Census of "Finnegans Wake,"* p. 2.

27 See Clive Hart, "*Finnegans Wake* in Perspective," pp. 157–165.

28 *The Structure of Poetry*, p. 131.

29 "*Finnegans Wake* in Perspective," p. 157.

30 *The Structure of Poetry*, p. 102.

31 Ibid., p. 104.

Chapter 6

1 *Murphy* (New York, 1957), p. 107.

2 *The Unnamable*, in *Three Novels* (New York, 1959), p. 418.

Quotations from *Molloy* and *Malone Dies* will also be from this edition.

3 *Transition,* no. 5 (1949), 98.

4 See especially Hugh Kenner, *Samuel Beckett: A Critical Study* (New York, 1961), pp. 28–32.

5 *Creative Intuition in Art and Poetry* (New York, 1955), pp. 194–195.

6 *Watt* (New York, 1959), p. 126.

7 Kenner, *Samuel Beckett,* pp. 96–112.

8 *Philosophical Investigations,* p. 20ᵉ. Wittgenstein is invoked here simply as an analogy. The possibility that Beckett might have been acquainted with Wittgenstein's *Tractatus Logico-Philosophicus* was raised by Jacqueline Hoefer in her excellent essay, "*Watt,*" *Perspective,* 11 (1959), 166–182. But John Fletcher, *The Novels of Samuel Beckett* (London, 1964), p. 88, reports that Beckett, by his own admission, had not read Wittgenstein until at least 1959 (*Watt* was composed during 1942–1944). It is clear, nevertheless, that the problem of language posed in *Watt* is precisely that with which Wittgenstein was most deeply concerned: Watt's experience may be said to dramatize the very breakdown of the "classical" theory of language (that is, that words are names for things) which moved Wittgenstein to abandon his "picture-theory" of language and to argue in its place that speech involves the playing of a diversity of language games.

9 Cf. William Carlos Williams, *The Great American Novel* (1923): "Progress is to get. But how can words get. —Let them get drunk. Bah. Words are words. Fog of words. The car runs through it. The words take up the smell of the car. Petrol. Face powder, arm pits, food-grease in the hair, foul breath, clean musk. Words. Words cannot progress. There cannot be a novel. Break the words. Words are indivisible crystals. One cannot break them —Awu tsst grang slith gra pragh og bm— Yes, one can break them. One can make words. Progress? If I make a word I make myself into a word. Such is progress. I shall make myself into a word. One big word. One big union. Such is progress. It is a novel. I begin small and make myself into a big splurging word: I take life and make it into one big blurb. I begin at my childhood. I begin at the beginning and make one big—Bah" (*Imaginations,* ed. Webster Scott

[New York, 1970], pp. 159–160). The writer's problem in *The Great American Novel* is strikingly similar to that faced by Beckett's storytellers: he is driven by a need to write, but this need is countered by the impossibility of writing—an impossibility which fixes the writer's attention on words, moving him to regard them as so many objects. Language in *The Great American Novel* asserts its intransitivity: it will not "progress" toward an end, but turns back upon itself and establishes a resistance, if not to speech, at least to a use of words that will generate plot, character, and so on.

10 *Stories and Texts for Nothing* (New York, 1967), p. 111.

11 *How It Is* (New York, 1964), p. 7.

12 "Samuel Beckett's *How It Is*," *James Joyce Quarterly*, 8 (1971), 318–331.

13 (London, 1969), pp. 7–8.

Chapter 7

1 *The Order of Things*, p. 36.

2 *Jenenser Realphilosophie*, ed. Georg Lasson (Leipzig, 1932), I, p. 211: "Die erste Akt, wodurch Adam seine Herschaft über die Tiere konstitutiert hat, ist, dass er ihnen Namen gab, d.h. sie als Seinde vernichtete."

3 Trans. James H. Nichols, Jr., ed. Allan Bloom (New York and London, 1969), p. 201. The quotation is from "The Dialectic of the Real and the Phenomenological Method in Hegel" (1934–1935), a lecture given by Kojève at the École des Hautes Études. The text was originally compiled from notes and transcripts by Raymond Queneau.

4 *Mallarmé: Selected Prose Poems, Essays, and Letters*, p. 95; *Correspondance*, I, pp. 245–246.

5 Trans. Janina Makota and Shia Moser, in *Readings in Existential Phenomenology*, ed. Nathaniel Lawrence and Daniel O'Connor (Englewood Cliffs, N.J., 1967), pp. 310–311. Ingarden describes the essay as "a little part of my book in Polish about the cognition of a literary work (Lwow, 1937). It is a complementary study to the book, *Das literarische Kunstwerk* (Halle, 1931)." The essay first appeared in this translation in *Philosophy and Phenomenological Research*, 21 (1961), 289–313.

6 *The Collected Works of Paul Valéry,* trans. Stuart Gilbert (New York, 1970), xiv, pp. 562–563.

7 *The Philosophy of Hegel,* ed. Carl J. Friedrich, trans. B. Bosanqet and W. M. Bryant (New York, 1954), p. 335. For the German text, see Hegel, *Werke,* ed. Eva Moldenhauer and Karl Markus Michel (Frankfurt am Main, 1970), xiii, p. 392.

8 *Anthology,* ed. Jack Hirschman, trans. David Rattray (San Francisco, 1965), p. 86.

9 *Nausea,* trans. Lloyd Alexander (New York, 1959), p. 169.

10 *Writing Degree Zero,* pp. 44, 46–47.

11 *Creative Intuition in Art and Poetry,* p. 137. See also William Carlos Williams, "A Note on the Recent Work of James Joyce": "Style is the substance of writing which gives it its worth as literature." But he goes on to observe that this "worth" cannot be defined in terms of beauty: "Styles can no longer be described as beautiful" (*Imaginations,* p. 333).

12 *ELH,* 23 (1956), 280. For the French poet Francis Ponge, however, the "corporeality" of words incorporates meaning, although Ponge clearly regards meaning itself as a kind of substance, as he once indicated in an interview with Serge Gavronsky: "As for their definitions, the ultimate would be in finding the propriety of the term, as it used to be said in the seventeenth century, and as it is still being said, finding in each sentence, in each paragraph, in the whole text, all the semantic levels, all the successive definitions, beginning with its roots, simultaneously respected. Naturally that is an impossible expectation, but to consider it does allow one to arrive at a certain thickness, at a degree of certitude of the propriety of the terms involved. One has to ask the most in order to obtain the least. It is an impossible absolute that all words, that the texts, be written in such a way as to allow the words their complete semantic thickness. This is impossible. But if one has that sensitivity to the thickness of words, to the fact that they do have a history, that they have provoked associations of different ideas in each language and in each of the periods of the evolution of language, then this provides a much thicker material, graver, much graver in the sense of weight, a material that is not superficial, which is a thing that one can mold precisely because it has the quality, the thickness, of potter's clay. It is a physical

object with many dimensions" (see *Poems and Texts,* ed. and trans. Serge Gavronsky [New York, 1969], p. 41).

13 *The Papers and Journals of Gerard Manley Hopkins,* ed. Humphrey House and Graham Storey (London, 1959), p. 269.

14 To be precise, one should refer here to the act of writing rather than of speech, for the concept of negative discourse really takes on significance only within the context of written language. See William Butler Yeats, "Literature and the Living Voice," in *Explorations* (New York, 1962), p. 206: "Irish poetry and Irish stories were made to be spoken or sung, while English literature, alone of great literatures, because of the newest of them all, has all but completely shaped itself in the printing-press. In Ireland today the old world that sang and listened is, it may be for the last time in Europe, face to face with the world that reads and writes, and their antagonism is always present under some name or other in Irish imagination and intellect."

15 *Finnegans Wake,* p. 83.

16 *Dublin's Joyce* (Bloomington, Ind., 1956), p. 303.

17 *Writing Degree Zero,* p. 48.

18 *La Part du feu,* pp. 325–326: "Je dis: cette femme, et immé-diatement je dispose d'elle. . . . Sans doute, mon langage ne tue personne. Cependant: quand je dis 'cette femme,' la mort réelle est annoncée et déjà présente dans mon langage; mon langage veut dire que cette personne-ci, qui est là, maintenant, peut être détachée d'elle-même, soustraite à son existence et à sa présence et plongée soudain dans un néant d'existence et de présence; mon langage signifie essentiellement la possibilité de cette destruction; il est, à tout moment, une allusion résolue à un tel événement. Mon langage ne tue personne. Mais, si cette femme n'était pas réellement capable de mourir, si elle n'était pas à chaque moment de sa vie menacée de la mort, liée et unie à elle par un lien d'essence, je ne pourrais pas accomplir cette negation idéale, cet assassinat différé qu'est mon langage."

19 Ibid., p. 327; "Le langage ne commence qu'avec le vide; nulle plénitude, nulle certitude ne parle."

20 Ibid.: "L'idéal de la littérature à pu être celui-ci: ne rien dire, parler pour ne rien dire."

21 Ibid.: "Le langage aperçoit qu'il doit son sens, non à ce qui

existe, mais à son recul devant l'existence. . . . Si des choses on
ne parle qu'en disant d'elles ce par quoi elles ne sont rien, eh
bien, ne rien dire, voilà le seul espoir d'en tout dire."

22   Ibid., p. 329: "Le langage de la littérature est la recherche de ce
moment qui la précède."

23   Ibid., p. 330: "Tout ce qui est physique joue le premier rôle:
le rhythme, le poids, la masse, la figure, et puis le papier sur
lequel on écrit, la trace de l'encre, le livre."

24   Ibid.: "Dans la matérialité du langage, dans ce fait que les mots
aussi sont est choses, une nature, ce qui m'est donné et me
donné plus que je n'en comprends."

25   *On the Way to Language,* p. 80.

26   Ibid., p. 136. The quotation is from Humboldt's *Über die Ver-
schiedenheiten des menschlichen Sprachbaues* (1827–1829).

27   *Was Heisst Denken* (Tübingen, 1954), p. 119: "Jedes anfängliche
und eigentliche Nennen sagt Ungesprochenes und zwar so, dass
es ungesprochen bleibt."

28   *On the Way to Language,* pp. 161, 192.

Chapter 8

1   *Truth and Art* (New York and London, 1965), p. 38.

2   Trans. Frank Justus Miller (London and New York: Loeb
Classical Library, 1916), II, 71. The Orpheus myth falls into
three parts: Orpheus as the poet who holds the natural world
in his power; Orpheus and Eurydice and the descent into the
underworld; and the dismemberment of Orpheus by the Mae-
nads and the affirmation of his immortality. Here we will be
concerned with the first part—with Orpheus as the poet of the
earth.

3   See Elizabeth Sewell, *The Orphic Voice: Poetry and Natural
History* (New Haven, 1960), pp. 57–58; and Joseph Bidez and
Franz Cumont, *Les Mages hellénisés* (Paris, 1939), II, pp. 17,
139–140. See also Walter Rehm, *Orpheus: der Dichter und die
Toten* (Düsseldorf, 1950); Eva Kushner, *Le Mythe d'Orphée
dans la littérature français contemporaine* (Paris, 1961); and
especially Walter A. Strauss, *Descent and Return: The Orphic
Theme in Modern Literature* (Cambridge, Mass., 1971).

4 *The Philosophy of Symbolic Forms,* I, p. 118; see also II, pp. 51–53, 181–182; and Toshihiko Izutsu, *Language and Magic: Studies in the Magical Function of Speech* (Tokyo, 1956), pp. 15–26.

5 *Sämtliche Werke* (Wiesbaden, 1955), I, p. 732.

6 In the Neoplatonic tradition, to be sure, the world of things is knowable only insofar as the mind casts its light upon it. Even so, *mimesis* remains the fundamental principle of the poet's activity. Thus Plotinus: "The arts are not to be slighted on the ground that they create by imitation of natural objects; . . . they give no bare reproduction of things but go back to the Ideas from which Nature itself derives" (*Enneads,* trans. Stephen McKenna [London, 1926], v, viii, 1).

7 *Time and the Modes of Being,* trans. Helen Michejda (Springfield, Ill., 1964), p. 7. See also pp. 8–16, 24–26. The translation is from Ingarden's *Spor o istnienie swiata* (Warsaw, 1960).

8 *Immanuel Kant's Critique of Pure Reason,* trans. Norman Kemp Smith (London, 1950), p. 272.

9 See M. H. Abrams, *The Mirror and the Lamp: Romantic Theory and the Critical Tradition* (New York, 1953), p. 58: "The Copernican revolution in epistemology—if we do not restrict this to Kant's specific doctrine that the mind imposes the forms of time, space, and the categories on the 'sensuous manifold,' but apply it to the general concept that the perceiving mind discovers what it itself has partly made—was effected in England by poets and critics long before it manifested itself in academic philosophy."

10 (Hamburg, 1957): "Die idealische welt der Kunst, und die reelle der Objekte sind also Produkte einer und der derselben Tätigkeit."

11 Ibid.: "Die Objektive Welt ist nur die ursprüngliche, noch bewusstlose Poesie des Geistes." See also pp. 281–293.

12 *Werke, Briefe, Dokumente,* ed. Ewald Wasmuth (Heidelberg, 1953), III, p. 23: "Die Poesie ist das echt absolut Reelle" (Fr. 1853).

13 Ibid., II, p. 53: "Wir wissen etwas nur—insofern wir es ausdrükken—id est machen können" (Fr. 161). See also III, p. 131: "Die Welt ist ein Universaltropus des Geistes, ein symbolisches Bild desselben" (Fr. 2257).

14 Ibid., III, p. 50: "Durch Poesie entsteht die höchste Sympathie und Koaktivität, die innigste Gemeinschaft des Endlichen und Unendlichen" (Fr. 1915).

15 Ibid., I, p. 317: "Wir sind auf einer Mission: zur Bildung der Erde wir berufen" (Fr. 35).

16 III, 143–145. *The Prelude,* p. 77.

17 III, iii. 49–55. *Shelley's "Prometheus Unbound": A Variorum Edition,* p. 238.

18 *Shelley's "Prometheus Unbound": A Critical Reading* (Baltimore, 1965), p. 20.

19 *The Complete Works of Edgar Allan Poe,* ed. James A. Harrison (New York, 1965), IV, p. 140.

20 *Aesthetic: A Science of Expression and General Linguistic,* trans. Douglas Ainslie (New York, 1964), p. 327.

21 *Truth and Art,* p. 41.

22 "Character and Meaning of the New Philosophy of the Spirit," in *Philosophy, Poetry, and History: An Anthology of Essays by Benedetto Croce,* trans. Cecil Sprigge (London, New York, and Tronto, 1966), pp. 14–15.

23 "Philosophy as Absolute Historicism," ibid., p. 83.

24 Heidegger's career falls roughly into three parts: the early period, which includes the publication of *Sein und Zeit* (1927); the middle period, which extends from "Was ist Metaphysik?" (1929) to *Über den Humanismus* (1949), and which includes the major essays on poetry; and the later period, which includes *Was heisst Denken?* (1954) and the essays on language gathered in *Unterwegs zur Sprache* (1959). The character of Heidegger's thought remains remarkably consistent, yet for our purposes we may notice this shift in emphasis: in the essays of the thirties, Heidegger's concern is with the speech of the poet; in the later essays (as we saw in chapter 7) his concern is with the speech of language itself, which becomes now a being in its own right, appropriating the speech of the poet and disclosing its essence as the "language of being."

25 *Über den Humanismus* (Frankfurt, 1949), p. 5.

26 See Else Buddeberg, *Denken und Dichtung Seins: Heidegger, Rilke* (Stuttgart, 1956), pp. 134–147.

27 *Holzwege* (Frankfurt, 1950), p. 286: "Wenn wir zum Brunnen, wenn wir durch den Wald gehen, gehen wir schon immer durch das Wort 'Brunnen,' durch das Wort 'Wald' hindurch, auch

wenn wir diese Worte nicht aussprechen und nicht an Sprachliches denken."

28 "Hölderlin and the Essence of Poetry," in *Existence and Being*, trans. Douglas Scott (Chicago, 1949), p. 276.

29 *On the Way to Language*, p. 73. I have modified this translation slightly. See *Unterwegs zur Sprache* (Tübingen, 1959), p. 177: "Ohne das also verhatende Wort sinkt das Ganze der Dinge, di 'Welt,' ins Dunkel weg, samt dem 'Ich'."

30 Trans. Ralph Manheim (New Haven, 1959), pp. 124–125.

31 Trans. Albert Hofstadter, in *Philosophies of Art and Beauty*, ed. Albert Hofstadter and Richard Kuhns (New York, 1964), p. 673. The German text appears in *Holzwege*.

32 "Another Weeping Woman," *Collected Poems*, p. 25.

33 Helen Hennessy Vendler makes good sense when she argues that Stevens repeatedly casts his poems into the form of hypotheses, and that accordingly his conception of imagination and its relation to the world takes on a problematical character as a possibility to be entertained, not as a dogma. See Mrs. Vendler's essay, "The Qualified Assertions of Wallace Stevens," in *The Act of the Mind: Essays on the Poetry of Wallace Stevens*, ed. Roy Harvey Pearce and J. Hillis Miller (Baltimore, 1965), pp. 163–178.

34 *The Necessary Angel*, p. 118.

35 Ibid., p. 27: "I am interested in the nature of poetry and I have stated its nature from one of the many points of view from which it is possible to state it. It is an interdependence of the imagination and reality as equals."

36 See, for example, Aron Gurwitsch, "A Non-egological Conception of Consciousness," in *Studies in Phenomenology and Psychology* (Evanston, Ill., 1966), pp. 287–300.

37 Richard Macksey has done as much in his essay, "The Climates of Wallace Stevens," in *The Act of the Mind*, pp. 192–193: "For Stevens as for Husserl 'the world' is an irreducible component of the given; consciousness is relational and not substantial, not so much mental as '*weltlich.*' Moods suffuse and penetrate the moving chaos of the world around one, an enormous field of intentional relations."

38 On the question of time in Stevens, see Frank Doggett, *Stevens' Poetry of Thought* (Baltimore, 1966), pp. 55–74.

39 See Pearce, *The Continuity of American Poetry* (Princeton, N.J.,

1961), pp. 410–411; and "The Last Lesson of the Master," in *The Act of the Mind,* pp. 123–126.

40 *Stevens' Poetry of Thought,* p. 198.

41 *The Clairvoyant Eye* (Baton Rouge, 1965), p. 245.

42 Trans. Peter Koestenbaum (The Hague, 1964), p. 8.

43 Pearce, *The Act of the Mind,* p. 138.

44 *Opus Posthumous,* p. 165.

45 Ibid., pp. 95–96. From the poem, "A Discovery of Thought."

Conclusion

1 Heidegger, *Being and Time,* trans. John Macquarrie and Edward Robinson (New York and Evanston, Ill., 1962), pp. 61–62; and "A Dialogue on Language," in *On the Way to Language,* pp. 9–12. See Heinrich Ott, "Hermeneutics and the Personal Structure of Language," in *On Heidegger and Language,* ed. and trans. Joseph L. Kockelmans (Evanston, Ill., 1972), pp. 160–193; and Richard E. Palmer, *Hermeneutics: Interpretation Theory in Schliermacher, Dilthey, Heidegger, and Gadamer* (Evanston, Ill., 1969), pp. 124–161.

2 Roland Barthes, "The Structuralist Activity," in *Critical Essays,* pp. 213–220.

3 Heidegger, "Words," in *On the Way to Language,* pp. 155–156; and Barthes, "The Imagination of the Sign," in *Critical Essays,* pp. 205–211. See also Louis Hjelmslev, *Prolegomena to a Theory of Language,* trans. Francis J. Whitfield (Madison, Wisc., 1961), pp. 41–47; and Emile Benveniste, "The Nature of the Linguistic Sign," in *Problems in General Linguistics,* trans. Mary Elizabeth Meek (Coral Gables, Fla., 1971), pp. 43–48.

4 *Warheit und Methode* (Tübingen, 1965), p. 394; "Das sprachliche Wort ist kein Zeichen, zu dem man greift, es ist aber auch kein Zeichen, das man macht oder einem anderen gibt, kein seiendes Ding, das man aufnimmt und mit der Idealität des Bedeutens belädt, um dadurch anderes seiendes sichtbar zu machen . . . Veilmehr liegt die Idealität der Bedeutung im Worte selbst. Es its immer schon Bedeutung."

5 *Critical Essays,* p. 218.

6 *Being and Time,* p. 209.

7 *The Crisis of the European Sciences and Transcendental Phe-*

nomenology, trans. David Carr (Evanston, Ill., 1970), p. 359. See Jacques Derrida, *Speech and Phenomena,* pp. 3–104.

8   Ibid., p. 358.

9   Trans. Dorion Cairns (The Hague, 1969), p. 21.

10   *Logical Investigations* (1900–1901), trans. J. N. Findlay (New York, 1970), II, p. 526.

11   Ibid., p. 525, pp. 552–596 ("Consciousness as Intentional Experience") and pp. 675–706 ("Meaning Intention and Meaning-Fulfillment").

12   *Formal and Transcendental Logic,* p. 22.

13   *The Philosophy of Symbolic Forms,* I, pp. 110–111.

14   *On Bentham and Coleridge* (New York, 1962), pp. 99–100.

15   *Freud and Philosophy: An Essay on Interpretation,* trans. Denis Savage (New Haven and London, 1970), p. 384. See also "New Developments in Phenomenology in France: The Phenomenology of Language," *Social Research,* 34 (1967), 1–30.

16   "Structure, Word, Event," *Philosophy Today,* 12 (1968), 118.

17   "Husserl and Wittgenstein," in *Phenomenology and Existentialism,* ed. Edward N. Lee and Maurice Mandelbaum (Baltimore, 1967), p. 216.

18   Ibid., p. 216.

19   *Language and Mind* (New York, 1968), p. 27.

20   Ibid., pp. 49–50.

21   *Cartesian Linguistics: A Chapter in the History of Rationalist Thought* (New York and London, 1966), p. 42.

22   *Syntactic Structures,* pp. 92–105 ("Syntax and Semantics"); and *Aspects of a Theory of Syntax* (Cambridge, Mass., 1965), pp. 148–163 ("The Boundaries of Syntax and Semantics").

23   Among a welter of studies in this area, see the following: Willard V. Quine, "The Problem of Meaning in Linguistics," in *The Structure of Language: Readings in the Philosophy of Language,* ed. Jerry A. Fodor and Jerrold J. Katz (Englewood Cliffs, N.J., 1965), pp. 21–32; Uriel Weinreich, "Explorations in Semantic Theory," in *Current Trends in Linguistics,* ed. Thomas Sebeok (The Hague, 1966), III, pp. 395–477; J. D. McCawley, "The Role of Semantics in Grammar, " in *Universals in Linguistic Theory,* ed. E. Bach and R. T. Harms (New York, 1968), pp. 124–169; Jerrold J. Katz, *Semantic Theory* (New York, 1972), esp. pp. 363–452.

24 "Levels of Linguistic Analysis," in *Problems in General Linguistics,* p. 109.

25 *Aspects of a Theory of Syntax,* p. 68; and Chomsky, "Topics in the Theory of Generative Grammar," in *Current Trends in Linguistics,* III, pp. 42–47.

26 *Aspects of a Theory of Syntax,* pp. 111–127; and "Topics in the Theory of Generative Grammar," p. 46: "Deviation from selectional rules gives such examples as 'colorless green ideas sleep furiously,' 'sincerity admires John,' etc.; deviation from strict subcategorization rules gives such examples as 'John persuaded to leave,' 'John found sad,' etc. Sentences of the former type are often interpreted as [not logical but] somehow metaphorical." See text, pp. 248–249.

27 *Logical Investigations,* II, p. 510.

28 Ibid., p. 515. See James Edie, "Husserl's Conception of 'the Grammatical' and Contemporary Linguistics," in *Life-World and Consciousness: Essays for Aron Gurwitsch,* ed. Lester E. Embree (Evanston, Ill., 1972), pp. 263–286.

29 It should be pointed out that Ricoeur seeks in Chomsky's theory of grammar a confirmation, not an explanation, of this linguistic process. He is concerned less with the rules than with the effects of this process.

30 See Theodore Drange, *Type-Crossings: Sentential Meaninglessness in the Border Area of Linguistics and Philosophy* (The Hague, 1966), esp. pp. 37–57.

31 See Susanne K. Langer, *Introduction to Symbolic Logic* (New York, 1953), pp. 64–81 ("Context"); and Chomsky, *Aspects of a Theory of Syntax,* p. 149: "Sentences that break selectional rules can often be interpreted metaphorically (particularly as personification) . . . or allusively in one way or another, if an appropriate context of greater or less complexity is supplied." But semantic interpretation for Chomsky almost always resolves itself into interpretation of form: hence by "context" he finally means a "context of rules" whereby "deviant" sentences "are apparently interpreted by a direct analogy to well-formed sentences that observe the selectional rule in question." See also Chomsky, "Degrees of Grammaticalness," in *The Structure of Language,* pp. 384–389, in which he proposes that the generative grammar be supplemented by a "hierarchy of categories" of grammaticalness that would account for the ability of speak-

ers to produce deliberately a deviant sentence. My argument would be that, even so, all sentences, whether deviant or well-formed, need to be accounted for ontologically as well as formally. There must, as Heidegger might say, be "a call for" any human utterance, a reason for speaking which fulfills the meaning of the utterance. See Jerrold Katz, "Semi-Sentences," in *The Structure of Language,* pp. 400–416; and Roman Jakobson, "Boas' View of Grammatical Meaning," *American Anthropologist,* 61 (1959), 139–145.

32 See Henry Hiz, "Disambiguation," in *Sign, Language, Culture,* ed. A. J. Greimas *et al.* (The Hague, 1970), p. 125: "How does it happen that an ambiguous sentence ceases to be ambiguous when placed in the context of other sentences?"

33 There is currently considerable controversy over this issue. See MacCawley, n. 23 above; George Lakoff, "Generative Semantics," in *Semantics: An Interdisciplinary Reader in Philosophy, Linguistics, and Psychology,* ed. Danny Steinberg and Leon Jakobovits (London, 1971), pp. 183–216; and Lakoff, "Presupposition and Relative Well-formedness," ibid., p. 329: "It is often assumed that one can speak of a well- or ill-formedness of a sentence in isolation, removed from all presuppositions about the nature of the world. I think it has become clear over the past several years that such a position cannot be maintained." See Chomsky's replies to the alternatives proposed by Mac-Cawley and Lakoff, *Studies on Semantics in Generative Grammar* (The Hague, 1972), pp. 62–119 ("Deep Structure, Surface Structure, and Semantic Interpretation") and pp. 120–202 ("Some Empirical Issues in the Theory of Transformational Grammar").

34 "What is a Text? Explanation and Interpretation," in David Rasmussen, *Mythico-Symbolic Language and Philosophic Anthropology* (The Hague, 1971), p. 138.

35 "Levels of Linguistic Analysis," in *Problems in General Linguistics,* pp. 109–110.

36 *The Structure of Language,* pp. 490–491: "Discourse can be treated as a single sentence in isolation by regarding sentence boundaries as sentential connectives. . . . Hence, for every discourse, there is a single sentence which consists of the sequence of *n*-sentences that comprises the discourse connected by the appropriate sentential connectives and which exhibits the same

semantic relations exhibited in the discourse." My argument is that discourse is not linear but hierarchical.

37 *Morphology of the Folktale,* trans. Laurence Scott, 2d ed. (Austin, Tex., 1968).
38 *Grundzüge der Phonologie* (Prague, 1939).
39 *Structural Anthropology,* pp. 206–215.
40 See A. J. Greimas, "Éléments pour une theorie de l'interpretation du récit mythique," *Communications,* 8 (1966), 1–27; and Roland Barthes, "Linguistique de discours," in *Sign, Language, Culture,* pp. 580–584.
41 (The Hague, 1970).
42 *Du Sens: Essais sémiotiques* (Paris, 1970), pp. 165–167.
43 "Language Structure and Language Function," in *New Horizons in Linguistics,* ed. John Lyons (Harmondsworth, Middlesex, and Baltimore, 1970), p. 143.
44 Ibid., pp. 160–161.
45 See *Papers in Textual Linguistics* (Hamburg, forthcoming).
46 See K. E. Heidolf, "Kontextbezeihungen zwischen Sätzen in einer generativen Grammatik," *Kybernetika Cislo,* 3 (1966), 273–281; William O. Hendricks, "Linguistic Models and the Study of Narration: A Critique of Todorov's *Grammaire du Décaméron,*" *Semiotica,* 5 (1972), 263–289; Julia Kristeva, *Le Texte roman: Approche semiologique d'une structure discursive transformationelle* (The Hague, 1971); and János S. Petöfi, "The Syntactico-Semantic Organization of Text-Structures," *Poetics,* 3 (1972), 56–99.
47 *Poetics,* 3 (1972), 29–55.
48 See Teun A. van Dijk, "Some Problems of Generative Poetics," *Poetics,* 2 (1971), 5–31; J. Levy, "Generative Poetics," in *Sign, Language, Culture,* pp. 548–557. The concept of a "generative narrativics" is discussed by Jens Ihwe, "On the Foundation of a General Theory of Narrative Structure," *Poetics,* 3 (1972), 5–14.
49 "The Textual Function of the French Article," in *Literary Style: A Symposium,* ed. and trans. Seymour Chatman (New York and London, 1971), p. 221.
50 For example, J. L. Austin, *How to Do Things with Words* (London, 1962), and his "A Plea for Excuses," *Proceedings of the Aristotelian Society,* 57 (1956–57). 1–30.
51 *Studies in Functional Logical Semiotics of Natural Language* (The Hague, 1971), p. 42.

52 "Chocorua to Its Neighbor," *Collected Poems,* p. 300. See Thomas Whitaker, "On Speaking Humanly," in *The Philosopher Critic,* ed. Robert Scholes (Tulsa, Okla., 1970), pp. 67–88.

53 "Style and Its Image," in *Literary Style: A Symposium,* p. 7. Barthes says that "we lack, clearly, a grammar of the written language," but it seems obvious that the contrary is true, that our understanding of what constitutes linguistic competence, and indeed our very concept of grammar, derives from written speech. Grammar has its origin in the art of the scribe; the word itself derives from the Greek, *gramma,* letter, and ultimately from *graphein,* to write. One is reminded of Yeats's astonishment upon meeting Oscar Wilde for the first time: "I never before heard a man talking with perfect sentences, as if he had written them all overnight with labour and yet all spontaneous" (*The Autobiography of William Butler Yeats* [New York, 1965], p. 87).

54 "Style and Its Image," p. 8.

55 *The Presence of the Word* (New Haven, 1967), pp. 111–112.

56 Julia Kristeva, "Le Texte clos," *Langages,* 12 (1968), 103–125.

57 *Language and Philosophy,* p. 73.

Index

PIERRE ALBERT-BIROT, *Grabinoulor.*
YUZ ALESHKOVSKY, *Kangaroo.*
FELIPE ALFAU, *Chromos.*
   Locos.
   Sentimental Songs.
ALAN ANSEN,
   Contact Highs: Selected Poems 1957-1987.
DAVID ANTIN, *Talking.*
DJUNA BARNES, *Ladies Almanack.*
   Ryder.
JOHN BARTH, *LETTERS.*
   Sabbatical.
AUGUSTO ROA BASTOS, *I the Supreme.*
ANDREI BITOV, *Pushkin House.*
ROGER BOYLAN, *Killoyle.*
CHRISTINE BROOKE-ROSE, *Amalgamemnon.*
GERALD L. BRUNS,
   Modern Poetry and the Idea of Language.
GERALD BURNS, *Shorter Poems.*
GABRIELLE BURTON, *Heartbreak Hotel.*
MICHEL BUTOR,
   Portrait of the Artist as a Young Ape.
JULIETA CAMPOS,
   The Fear of Losing Eurydice.
ANNE CARSON, *Eros the Bittersweet.*
CAMILO JOSÉ CELA, *The Hive.*
LOUIS-FERDINAND CÉLINE, *Castle to Castle.*
   London Bridge.
   North.
   Rigadoon.
HUGO CHARTERIS, *The Tide Is Right.*
JEROME CHARYN, *The Tar Baby.*
MARC CHOLODENKO, *Mordechai Schamz.*
EMILY HOLMES COLEMAN,
   The Shutter of Snow.
ROBERT COOVER, *A Night at the Movies.*
STANLEY CRAWFORD,
   Some Instructions to My Wife.
RENÉ CREVEL, *Putting My Foot in It.*
RALPH CUSACK, *Cadenza.*
SUSAN DAITCH, *Storytown.*
PETER DIMOCK,
   A Short Rhetoric for Leaving the Family.
COLEMAN DOWELL, *The Houses of Children.*
   Island People.
   Too Much Flesh and Jabez.
RIKKI DUCORNET, *The Complete Butcher's Tales.*
   The Fountains of Neptune.
   The Jade Cabinet.
   Phosphor in Dreamland.
   The Stain.
WILLIAM EASTLAKE, *The Bamboo Bed.*
   Castle Keep.
   Lyric of the Circle Heart.

STANLEY ELKIN, *Boswell: A Modern Comedy.*
   Criers and Kibitzers, Kibitzers and Criers.
   The Dick Gibson Show.
   The MacGuffin.
   The Magic Kingdom.
   The Rabbi of Lud.
ANNIE ERNAUX, *Cleaned Out.*
LAUREN FAIRBANKS, *Muzzle Thyself.*
   Sister Carrie.
LESLIE A. FIEDLER,
   Love and Death in the American Novel.
FORD MADOX FORD, *The March of Literature.*
JANICE GALLOWAY, *Foreign Parts.*
   The Trick Is to Keep Breathing.
WILLIAM H. GASS, *The Tunnel.*
   Willie Masters' Lonesome Wife.
ETIENNE GILSON, *The Arts of the Beautiful.*
   Forms and Substances in the Arts.
C. S. GISCOMBE, *Giscome Road.*
   Here.
KAREN ELIZABETH GORDON, *The Red Shoes.*
PATRICK GRAINVILLE, *The Cave of Heaven.*
HENRY GREEN, *Blindness.*
   Concluding.
   Doting.
   Nothing.
JIŘÍ GRUŠA, *The Questionnaire.*
JOHN HAWKES, *Whistlejacket.*
ALDOUS HUXLEY, *Antic Hay.*
   Point Counter Point.
   Those Barren Leaves.
   Time Must Have a Stop.
GERT JONKE, *Geometric Regional Novel.*
DANILO KIŠ, *A Tomb for Boris Davidovich.*
TADEUSZ KONWICKI, *A Minor Apocalypse.*
   The Polish Complex.
ELAINE KRAF, *The Princess of 72nd Street.*
EWA KURYLUK, *Century 21.*
DEBORAH LEVY, *Billy and Girl.*
JOSÉ LEZAMA LIMA, *Paradiso.*
OSMAN LINS, *The Queen of the Prisons of Greece.*
ALF MAC LOCHLAINN,
   The Corpus in the Library.
   Out of Focus.
D. KEITH MANO, *Take Five.*
BEN MARCUS, *The Age of Wire and String.*
WALLACE MARKFIELD, *Teitlebaum's Window.*
   To an Early Grave.
DAVID MARKSON, *Collected Poems.*
   Reader's Block.
   Springer's Progress.
   Wittgenstein's Mistress.
CARL R. MARTIN, *Genii Over Salzburg.*
CAROLE MASO, *AVA.*

Visit our website: www.dalkeyarchive.com

Visit our website: www.dalkeyarchive.com